Disorganization Theory

Organizational analysis has moved in a number of directions since its origins in mainstream theories of positivism and functionalism. This challenging new book sets out an alternative agenda for the field, discussing existing critical discourses, whilst exploring a selection of emerging ideas and arguments.

Addressing a series of key epistemological, conceptual and methodological issues, *Disorganization Theory* is designed to encourage reflexive thinking on the part of the reader. Influenced by critical philosophies of deconstruction and discourse, the book not only offers insight into established debates surrounding, for example, postmodernism and actor-network theory, but also brings forth new insights in the field: mimesis, consumption, retrospection, decoration, governmentality, and fluidity theories are all discussed.

Written by an international team of leading organizational theorists, this book is an important and contentious addition to the literature. It is an ideal companion for students and researchers working in the fields of advanced organization and management theory, and critical management studies.

John Hassard is Professor of Organizational Analysis at the Manchester Business School and Senior Professorial Research Associate at the Judge Business School, University of Cambridge.
Mihaela Kelemen is Professor of Management Studies in the School of Economic and Management Studies, Keele University.
Julie Wolfram Cox is Professor of Management in the Bowater School of Management and Marketing at Deakin University, Victoria, Australia.

Disorganization Theory

Explorations in alternative organizational analysis

John Hassard, Mihaela Kelemen and Julie Wolfram Cox

LONDON AND NEW YORK

First published 2008 by Routledge
2 Park Square, Milton Park, Abingdon, Oxon OX14 4RN

Simultaneously published in the USA and Canada
by Routledge
270 Madison Avenue, New York, NY 10016

Routledge is an imprint of the Taylor & Francis Group, an informa business

Typeset in Times New Roman by Keyword Group Ltd.
Printed and bound in Great Britain by Antony Rowe Ltd, Chippenham, Wiltshire

British Library Cataloguing in Publication Data
A catalogue record for this book is available from the British Library

Library of Congress Cataloging in Publication Data

A catalog record for this book has been requested

ISBN10: 0-415-41728-7 (hbk)
ISBN10: 0-415-41729-5 (pbk)
ISBN10: 0-203-08951-0 (ebk)

ISBN13: 978-0-415-41728-0 (hbk)
ISBN13: 978-0-415-41729-7 (pbk)
ISBN13: 978-0-203-08951-4 (ebk)

Contents

Illustrations

Figures

Tables

Authors

John Hassard is Professor of Organizational Analysis at the Manchester Business School and Senior Professorial Research Associate at the Judge Business School, University of Cambridge. He has published a large number of books on organizational analysis and social theory, including *Sociology and Organization Theory* (Cambridge, 1991), *Postmodernism and Organizations* (Sage, 1993), *The Theory and Philosophy of Organization* (Routledge, 1993), *Actor Network Theory and After* (Blackwell, 1999) and *Body and Organization* (Sage, 2000). Professor Hassard co-organized the 2001 and 2007 Critical Management Studies conferences and in recent years has been a board member of the Critical Management Division of the Academy of Management. He is currently a council member of the Society for the Advancement of Management Studies.

Mihaela Kelemen is Professor of Management Studies in the School of Economic and Management Studies, University of Keele. Professor Kelemen's doctoral research, completed at Oxford University in 1995, examined the management of quality from a multiparadigm perspective. She has published numerous chapters in edited collections as well as articles in journals such as: *Human Relations; Journal of Management Studies; Organization; British Journal of Management; Gender, Work, Organisation;* and the *Scandinavian Journal of Management*. Professor Kelemen's books include *Managing Quality: Managerial and Critical Perspectives* (Sage, 2003), *Cross-cultural Management* (Dartmouth, 1995) and *Critical Eastern European Management Research* (Palgrave, 2002). Her new book, *Critical Management Research*, will be published by Sage in 2008.

Julie Wolfram Cox is Professor of Management at Deakin University, Victoria, Australia. She received BA (Honours) and MA (Research) degrees in psychology from the University of Melbourne and holds a PhD in organizational behaviour from Case Western Reserve University, Cleveland, USA. Her publications include articles in the journals *Organization; Journal of Applied Behavioural Science; Organization Studies; Journal of Management Studies;*

Culture and Organization; Journal of Management and Organization; Journal of Material Culture; International Journal of Management Reviews; and *Journal of Organizational Change Management*; she recently co-edited a four-volume book series on *Fundamentals of Action Research* (Sage, 2005). Professor Cox is a member of the editorial boards of the journals *Organization Studies*; *Group and Organization Management; Journal of Applied Behavioural Science;* and *Tamara*. She is also an associate editor for *Qualitative Research in Organizations and Management*.

Acknowledgements

A number of chapters are the result of joint research between the authors and colleagues in Britain and Australia. In this respect we would like to thank Ian Atkin (Manchester Metropolitan University), Christine McLean (Manchester University), Nick Lee (Warwick University), Beverly Metcalfe (Hull University) and Stella Minahan (Deakin University) for their collaboration in the *Disorganization Theory* project. In addition we would like to thank Sue Haffner (Manchester University) for her assistance in preparing the bibliography and finalizing the manuscript for delivery. Although no previous work by the authors has been reproduced exclusively, some chapters extend arguments made earlier in the journals: *Organization* (Sage), *Organization Studies* (Sage) and the *Journal of Management Studies* (Blackwell). Also Chapters 1 and 3 reflect upon, respectively, some arguments made previously in the books: *Debating Organization* by Robert Westwood and Stewart Clegg (Sage) and *Postmodern Management and Organization Theory* by David Boje, Robert Gephart and Tojo Thatchenkery (Sage). Finally, at Routledge, we would like to thank our proposal reviewers for their suggestions on the structure and contents of the book, and above all our commissioning editors, Francesca Heslop and Simon Whitmore, for nurturing the project from conception to completion. We are grateful to Georgina Caillard for her assistance in compiling the index for this volume.

About the Cover

The cover is abstracted from the painting *Green Secret* by Alaskan artist Sonya Kelliher-Combs. This work formed part of her 'Unraveled Secrets' exhibition at the Institute of American Indian Arts, Sante Fe, New Mexico, December 2006 to March 2007, an exhibition that comprised a range of paintings, drawings and mixed media needlework. In her description and endorsement of the exhibition, art analyst Asia Freeman described Kelliher-Combs' work in terms of exploring the relationship of 'art to skin', or the 'surface by which a person is culturally mediated'. Freeman suggests that through the introduction of pigments, thread, beads and hair, Kelliher-Combs produces a 'fleshy body' resembling epidermis or organs, a tattooed or scarred body, or a wound. In the process, complex overlays draw one to examine and experience content 'beneath the surface' as the locus of identity or meaning within the work. As such, the artist both 'reveals and resists the possibilities of defining identity only through the surface'. For Freeman, the mix of synthetic, organic, traditional and modern materials challenges oppositional cultural thought patterns such as Western/Native, self/other, man/nature, pure/impure. Freeman concludes that, permeated by delicate lines, Kelliher-Combs' 'secret drawings' express rich connections between 'line, lineage and thread' in works that both build and unravel the threads of identity.

Introduction

The aim of the book is to present a series of epistemological, conceptual and methodological explorations appropriate to the development of critical organizational analysis. On the one hand, we explore a series of recent or emerging issues for the field (e.g. mimesis, consumption, retrospection, decoration, governmentality, fluidity) while on the other, we offer fresh insights into existing concerns (e.g. postmodernism, actor-networks, feminism, paradigms, identity). These explorations are the product of what we call an *alternative* agenda for organization theory and analysis, one influenced by critical philosophies of deconstruction and discourse rather than mainstream ones of positivism and functionalism.

The target audiences for the book are: *undergraduate and postgraduate students*, *doctoral and postdoctoral researchers*, and *university and college teachers*. Respectively, for undergraduate and postgraduate students the book provides a critical text for use on modules in advanced organization theory and critical management studies; for doctoral and postdoctoral researchers it offers a guide to contemporary issues in critical methodology and philosophy; and for university and college teachers it presents a guide to current debates in alternative organizational analysis and tools for developing a critically informed curriculum in management and organization studies. The book will appeal, therefore, to those studying, researching or teaching alternative/critical perspectives on management and organization. Above all, it adopts a style of theory, method and analysis that emphasizes plurality and reflexivity when establishing its main approaches to studying, researching and teaching.

In terms of relevant associated literature, well-known early contributions to this field have included David Silverman's *Theory of Organizations* (1970), Gibson Burrell and Gareth Morgan's *Sociological Paradigms and Organizational Analysis* (1979) and Stewart Clegg and David Dunkerley's *Organizations, Class and Control* (1980). Other notable contributions over the years have been Stewart Clegg's *Modern Organizations* (1990), Gareth Morgan's *Images of Organization* (1986), Mike Reed's *Redirections in Organizational Analysis* (1985) and Gibson Burrell's *Pandemonium* (1997). In addition, books published in the area since 2000 include Mats Alvesson and Stanley Deetz' *Doing Critical Management Research* (2000), Phil Hancock and Melissa Tyler's *Work, Postmodernism and*

Organization (2001), Catherine Casey's *Critical Analysis of Organizations* (2002), Martin Parker's *Against Management* (2004) and Mats Alvesson's *Studying Management Critically* (2003). All of these books reflect how a *critical theory* approach has emerged as a major research and teaching field within management and organization studies since the early 1970s. In the UK this growth of interest in developing an *alternative* management and organization studies has been witnessed by participants of the Critical Management Studies conference regularly out-numbering those of the more mainstream management conferences, notably the British Academy of Management conference. And in the USA it is witnessed similarly by the Critical Management Studies Division becoming the fastest growing of the Academy of Management. We note also how in recent years interest in developing alternative perspectives has seen critical management-based research extend beyond its original home in organization studies to fields such as human resource management, business strategy and marketing, and even to more far flung, technical disciplines such as accounting, finance and operations.

Finally, the principal title of the book, *Disorganization Theory*, as many readers will have guessed, is derived predominantly from Robert Cooper's work on the relationship between organization and disorganization (for examples of Cooper's theoretical work on organization and organizing, see Cooper, 1983, 1986, 1989, 1990, 2005; Cooper and Burrell, 1988, Cooper and Law, 1995; also the feschrift by Chia, 1998, for a collection of essays in honour of Cooper). In his 1986 article 'Organization/disorganization', published in the journal *Social Science Information*, Cooper developed the thesis that, in its fundamental sense, the concept of organization is the 'appropriation of order out of disorder'. As Cooper (1986: 305) famously argued, from the position of an emerging poststructuralist philosophy of organization, the work of organizing is directed towards 'transforming an intrinsically ambiguous condition into one that is ordered so that organization, as a process, is constantly bound up with its contrary state of disorganization' (see Chapters 3 and 7 of our book for detailed analyses of this argument). Drawing, over the years, on the philosophy of Derrida, Deleuze, Lyotard and Bateson, Cooper's work has brought to organizational analysis writing, *inter alia*, a reluctance to ground discourse in any theory of metaphysical origins, a general distrust of systematic scientificity, and above all an insistence on the inevitable plurality and instability of meaning. In the spirit of Cooper's theorizing on (dis)organization, our book represents a series of complementary deconstructionist investigations into 'alternative' concepts and methods in organizational analysis, ones based predominantly on poststructuralist philosophical positions.

Structure and contents

The structure of the book sees 11 substantive chapters divided into three parts addressing issues of alternative *knowledge*, *concepts* and *methodology* in organizational theory and analysis. While the parts relate logically to one another, the objective is not to impart a new 'grand narrative' of alternative organizational analysis, but rather to offer the reader a series of theoretical and analytical explorations into issues relevant to the field. As such, the pedagogical philosophy is more 'smorgasbord than recipe'. Overall, the arguments for research and theorizing are based on relationist assumptions of 'situated knowledges' (Haraway, 1989) and 'partial connections' (Strathern, 1991; see also Jensen and Lauritsen, 2005) rather than positivist-inspired ideas of neutral observation and empirical objectivity.

Part I: Alternative knowledge

Part One, *Alternative knowledge*, explores issues affecting the nature of epistemological practice in both mainstream and alternative organizational analysis, and discusses *inter alia*: the prospects of paradigm plurality in organization studies (Chapter 1); relations between knowledge production and consumption in the area (Chapter 2); and how mainstream organization theory can be emancipated by use of poststructuralist concepts (Chapter 3).

To expand, in the first substantive chapter, *Paradigm plurality and its prospects*, we argue that the merits of paradigm proliferation far outweigh the shortcomings and that it is important for organizational researchers to preserve and encourage theories and methods emanating from a range of intellectual viewpoints. This is desirable we feel on both practical and theoretical grounds in order to understand the complex changes taking place in contemporary organizational realities. We argue that our responsibility as organizational researchers is to promote *local* narratives and ensure that a range of analytical voices are heard. The proliferation of multiple discourses will serve to counteract any tendency for a dominant paradigm to suppress others in the practice of management and organizational research.

Chapter 2, *Organizational knowledge: production and consumption*, focuses on knowledge production as analyzed from a largely postmodernist, sociology-of-consumption perspective. Drawing upon the works of Jean-François Lyotard, Michel de Certeau and Stanley Deetz in particular, our analysis rejects both positivist and conventionalist theses on knowledge production in favour of a deconstructionist approach that embraces acts of production and consumption in a reflexive way. Through an assessment of scientific status and institutional control — centrally in relation to the paradigm incommensurability debate — we develop a taxonomy of critical styles of knowledge production and consumption. Ultimately, we outline the basic knowledge philosophies identified by this taxonomy and subject each to evaluation and critique.

Our third chapter, *Escaping the confines of organization theory* (with Ian Atkin), explores the argument that the textual representation of mainstream organization theory reflects a system of self-imprisonment. Initially we suggest that within organizational analysis, attempts by the early critical theorists of radical separatism to release themselves from such imprisonment resulted only in their conceptual recapture. Given this situation, we offer a theoretical strategy for deconstructing organizational orthodoxy, yet one that operates unusually from *within* the conventions of systems-based analysis. This analysis sees Jacques Derrida's work on undecidability and Luce Irigaray's analysis of residue, from her thesis on mimesis, deployed to recover the *extra* of organizational life, that which is situated outside, the space beyond, otherness. In so doing, we outline how poststructural concepts can be used to deconstruct particular forms of textual representation.

Part II: Alternative concepts

Part Two, *Alternative concepts*, considers a series of conceptual issues for an alternative organizational analysis to explore and develop. Specifically, Chapter 4 explores issues of sociological symmetry in relation to the production of actor-network accounts; Chapter 5 discusses the theoretical and poetical writings of Irigaray to illustrate how organization theory can be 're-imagined'; Chapter 6 analyzes concepts of organizational time and social temporality in relation to modernism and postmodernism; Chapter 7 unpacks the relationship between decoration and disorganization within an analysis of contested aesthetic positions; and Chapter 8 explores the Foucauldian concept of governmentality in relation to inter-organizational networks.

To expand, Chapter 4, *Actor-networks and sociological symmetry* (with Christine McLean), explores one of the major alternative methodologies for organizational analysis — actor-network theory (ANT). Our aim is to present critical notes on core issues related to the production of ANT accounts, for example, the inclusion and exclusion of actors; the treatment of humans and non-humans; the handling of agency and structure; and the nature of politics and power. We discuss in particular the relationships between these issues and the key ANT goal of achieving a sense of general symmetry in the accounting process. In so doing we note how ANT authors are frequently chastised for either failing to take sufficient account of, or promoting too strong a sense of, analytical symmetry in their writings. We argue that the primary challenge facing researchers wishing to undertake organizational research in ANT is to produce accounts that are robust enough to negate the twin charges of symmetrical absence and symmetrical absurdity.

In Chapter 5, *Fluidity and identity* (with Beverly Metcalfe), to advance a feminist poststructuralist organization theory, we again draw on the theoretical and poetical writings of Luce Irigaray. We focus here on three aspects of her work — the fluidity of identity construction as an ongoing change process; mimetic strategies for unveiling sexuate language structures; and the dialogic mode of reading/writing texts. Emphasizing the transformational possibilities arising from exploring 'inter-subjectivities within shifting textualities', we suggest that organizational modes of inquiry can benefit from applying an Irigarayan lens, that is, by inviting in the feminine 'other' we can begin to open up new knowledge territories and unveil the writing of the fluidity of gender in process.

Chapter 6, *Time and temporality*, explores various concepts of time in relation to alternative metaphors of social and organizational analysis. Initially we explore images of time and temporality emerging from critical philosophy and social theory. In so doing, we discuss representations of temporality as reflected in two key metaphors, the line and the cycle. Subsequently, we examine the predominant images of time to emerge under modern capitalist organization. Here we analyze modernist linear notions stemming from the commodification of the labour process and ideographic images that reflect the social construction of organizational culture and identity. Finally, we discuss the postmodernist debate in the sociology of time, and particularly the notion of instantaneous time, whereby organizational practices are based on time-frames that lie beyond conscious human experience. This concept is associated concretely with the complex shifts from Fordism to the flexible accumulation of post-Fordism. We extend this analysis theoretically to consider the notion of the time-space compression of physical processes and human experiences.

In Chapter 7, *Decoration and disorganization* (with Stella Minahan), we examine another emergent concept for alternative organizational analysis. While decoration has been of interest to those who study, for example, workplace artefacts, we consider the conceptual ways in which it is worthy of attention in critical organization studies. We argue, first, that decoration, ornament and embellishment are not only what we *see* but also what we *do* as managers, consultants, writers and designers of both physical and organizational spaces. Second, and drawing on the art/craft debate, we note that decoration occupies a contested and even liminal aesthetic position and that decorative art lies betwixt and between fine art and craft. Neither fully accepted nor fully marginalized, decoration is only *applied* and embodies shifting tensions between form and function. Third, we review the particular negotiations of these tensions at the Bauhaus, a controversial and highly influential aesthetic organization in early twentieth-century Germany. Finally, we describe how decoration, like disorganization, provides a source of complication and confusion for mainstream organization studies.

In Chapter 8, *Governmentality and networks*, we examine these concepts in relation to intertextual analyses of organization. Specifically we consider Foucault's use of governmentality — and his emphasis on population, security and self-government — in relation to a study of neo-liberal politics and inter-organizational alliances. The formation and later disaggregation of networks is presented as an example of such alliances, with intertextual discourse analysis being used to study the changing representation of organizational networks in public reports and accounts. Inter-organizational networks are presented not only as organizational forms but also as changing intertextual constructions that are formed and reformed through processes of elaboration, condensation, simplification and omission within and between the texts of such reports. We discuss finally some implications of this study for further intertextual analyses of organizational change.

Part III: Alternative methodology

Our final section, *Alternative methodology*, discusses some methodological and applied issues for an alternative organization theory to consider. In Chapter 9 we consider issues of research strategy in relation to our earlier discussion of actor-network theory; in Chapter 10 we extend our discussion of paradigm plurality to examine the status of methodological choice through reworking the concept of triangulation; and in Chapter 11 we explore the possibilities for retrospective research in critical/alternative organizational analysis.

To expand, in Chapter 9, *Actor-networks, research strategy and organization* (with Nick Lee), we extend our analysis of Chapter 4 to develop two related actor-network theory arguments for organizational analysis. The first concerns *research strategy* and draws upon Latour's (1999) notion of definitional 'sliding' to describe how ANT overcomes its analytical limitations by removing conditions that exclude the 'other'. Through this discussion, we argue that, research-wise, ANT appears to be ontologically relativist, in permitting the world to be organized differentially, yet empirically realist in providing theory-laden descriptions of organization. Our second argument concerns *institutional boundedness and flexibility*, and suggests that ANT's ontological slipperiness may actually be of value for critical studies of organization. Contrasting the critical theory contention that rational organization has become progressively reified and disembodied, with the 'new flexibility' mantra that there is 'nothing but life' (i.e. boundaryless development), we take recourse to ANT's well-known treatment of human and non-human actors to elide this ontological discrimination of 'live' and 'dead'. We outline how, under ANT, the analytical focus shifts from structural prescription to processual deconstruction, the associated political dimension concerning where and for whom boundaries are produced/consumed. Overall the chapter argues for organizational research that avoids any obligation to impose and defend its own theoretical discriminations.

In Chapter 10, *Rethinking triangulation*, we extend our earlier discussion of paradigm plurality through a discussion of methodological choice. In particular the chapter offers a re-presentation of the notion of triangulation in organizational research from a critical deconstructionist perspective. Initially triangulation is defined through the contrasting lenses of positivism and postmodernism and analyzed as a metaphor for fixing and capturing the research subject. Subsequently, triangulation is re-presented as *metaphorization*, in terms of process and movement between researcher-subject positions. Rethinking the lines and angles of inquiry in triangulation, we suggest a methodological shift from the traditional 'triangulation of distance' notion to a more critical and reflexive consideration of 'researcher stance'. This movement is represented across three perspectives: the researcher as a follower of nomothetic lines; the researcher as the taker of an ideographic overview; and the researcher as the finder of a critical angle. Implications of this re-presentation are then discussed in terms of perspective, reflexivity and metatriangulation.

In Chapter 11 we explore another emerging perspective within critical organizational analysis — *Critical retrospective research*. We identify, describe and analyze four positions relevant to the development of this approach: controlling the Past, in which attempts are made to reveal potential sources of bias; interpreting the Past, in which understanding of the present is informed by the social construction of past reality; co-opting the Past, in which causal explanations link the past and the present; and representing the Past, which involves the problematization of time and research on time. These positions are compared in terms of method, ontology, epistemology, exemplars and variants. Their potential contribution to a deconstructionist organizational analysis is discussed, and from this analysis methodological implications are drawn for the practice of retrospective research in alternative organization studies.

Our concluding chapter presents a summary of the ontological, epistemological and methodological tenets of our version of alternative organizational analysis. The chapter also examines the issue of 'thinking reflexively' and argues that reflexive methodology is a key process in the development of an alternative management and organization studies. Finally, we discuss a potential agenda for alternative/critical organizational studies in the years to come.

Part I

Alternative knowledge

1 Paradigm plurality and its prospects

This initial chapter maps out the development of paradigm plurality in a number of management and organizational disciplines. In so doing, it argues that the benefits of paradigm plurality far outweigh the shortcomings and that it is important for researchers to encourage perspectives emerging from multiple paradigmatic viewpoints. We argue that not only is this scenario desirable from a theoretical point of view, but it is also welcome in light of the complex changes taking place in contemporary organizational realities. Despite the historical controversy over its meaning and definition, we suggest that the concept of paradigm has increased in significance for the contemporary analysis of organizational phenomena, continuing to shape in a direct or indirect way the thinking and approach of organizational researchers. The most common understanding of the concept of 'paradigm' derives from Kuhn's work (1962, 1970): a paradigm is considered to be a set of shared beliefs and assumptions about the world. Consensus around such beliefs within a particular scientific community is regarded by some as a mark of maturity, while for others the existence of multiple paradigms bears the mantra of pre- or non-science (Lakatos and Musgrave, 1970). For the purpose of this chapter we define paradigm in a rather loose manner, as a shared set of views, values, and writing conventions around which research communities are being formed. Also, despite arguments that paradigm purity is a sign of scientific maturity within a particular field of study (Pfeffer, 1993, 1997), we argue that what is happening in reality is a shift towards paradigm plurality in numerous management and organizational disciplines; for example, organization theory (Hassard, 1993b; Schultz and Hatch, 1996; Casey, 2002; Jones and Munro, 2005), international business (Parkhe, 1993; Earley and Singh, 1995), strategic management (McKinley, 1995; Scherer, 1998), operational research (Mingers, 1992, 1997) and technology studies (Lewis and Grimes, 1999). In what follows, then, we explore the conditions under which multiple paradigms have emerged in these fields, highlight the advantages and disadvantages of the multiparadigm approach, present specific strategies of multiparadigm research within organizational analysis, and finally conclude with a plea for a discursive postmodern approach to paradigm plurality.

A rationale for paradigm plurality

The emergence of paradigm plurality within the fields mentioned above can be explained in a number of ways: first, by the argument that positivist epistemology has severe shortcomings in explaining contemporary organizational action; second, by the view that organizational realities are becoming ever more complex and diverse, and thus that representation in one dimension is no longer appropriate; third, through the suggestion that there is an increasing moral crisis facing contemporary society and our ability to attach meaning to it takes many forms; and fourth, by the prosaic argument that the quest for scientific uniqueness and personal prominence in academia, linked to notions of accelerated career advancement, is a key determinant of theoretical and empirical development.

Positivist epistemology and its problems

At the outset, positivism provided the theoretical foundations and the language for studying organizational phenomena. Chief among positivist assumptions are the beliefs that organizational reality is objective and scientifically apprehensible and that good scientists must abide and commit to the methods and aims of 'natural' science, which are perceived to be superior to other approaches for acquiring knowledge. This is not to say that positivist social science is considered monolithic, for those who adhere to positivism's mission of applying social science to improve social conditions often differ markedly in their values and approaches, as much as they share a commitment to disseminating knowledge that will facilitate positive action. However despite positivism's 'positive' agenda, its explanations, particularly in management studies, are seen by some to have already reached their highpoint in terms of theoretical refinement, making it seemingly difficult to offer many genuinely fresh insights into the management of organizations (Jackson and Carter, 1991: 112).

The discipline of organizational analysis is not the only one in which new paradigms have been seen to emerge. A significant number of other disciplines have seemingly grown dissatisfied with the prevailing positivist orthodoxy and turned towards exploring alternatives. For example, a number of authors (McKinley, 1995; Scherer and Dowling, 1995; Scherer, 1998) discuss the emergence of alternative approaches in strategic management in response to the inability of positivist research methods to capture and account for the social and contingent nature of strategy. While most scholars in strategic management perhaps still hold to the primary explanatory power of positivism and its underlying research methodologies (cf. Shrivastava, 1987), one can witness 'a growing "mess" of models, approaches and schools of strategy-making' (Scherer and Dowling, 1995: 201). Scherer and Dowling advocate the need to bracket such schools, models, or paradigms with the view of arriving at a more comprehensive understanding of the processes through which strategy is enacted and the consequences it may have upon stakeholders and the overall environment.

Similarly international business, a discipline whose roots are deeply embedded in positivist science, has witnessed the emergence of interpretive approaches, which, it is argued, complement well the more established deductive methodologies (Parkhe, 1993; Earley and Singh, 1995). Technology studies have also benefited from research derived from a number of paradigms (Grint, 1991), with Lewis and Grimes (1999) proposing 'metatriangulation' as a method for building theory from plural paradigms within the area of advanced manufacturing technology. And in operational research, the dominance of positivism began to be questioned during the 1990s (see Mingers, 1997), with the debate on the status of the discipline considering various forms of pluralism in both methodological and philosophical terms. Here Mingers (1992) argued that three paradigms coexisted in operational research: namely, the 'hard' paradigm, whose roots lie in positivism; the 'soft' paradigm, which bears close similarities with social constructivism; and a 'critical' paradigm, which emphasizes the oppressing and inequitable nature of the social world. Again, a multiparadigm understanding of operational research is advocated on the grounds of achieving deeper, more complex insights into organizational realities.

Shifts in organizational realities

It is almost commonplace to suggest that organizations populate a universe qualitatively different from that of the past, a universe which is far from closed and settled, and which is in many respects indeterminate and in the making. In such a plural universe it is regularly argued that no single point of view can ever account for such multifaceted, contentious and continuously changing organizational realities. Reed (1997), for example, suggests that this stratified, multidimensional ontology calls for multiple epistemological and methodological lenses to be deployed to explore the plurality of organizational realities. Indeed, as researchers have attempted to keep pace with and comprehend organizational changes they have called upon various epistemologies, producing an explosion of diverse, often contentious perspectives (Lewis and Grimes, 1999; Casey, 2002; Jones and Munro, 2005). Organizations are now seen to inhabit a so-called postindustrial (White and Jaques, 1995) space where new forms of production and distribution have come into being. For example, the network, the process-driven, and the virtual organization coexist alongside bureaucratic organizations. Fordist technologies of mass production and distribution coexist alongside post-Fordist technologies that allow flexible specialization and niche distribution (Piore and Sabel, 1984; Jaffee, 2001). These dramatic transformations are seen to have called for new ways of theorizing and researching (Burrell, 1996, 2003; Casey, 2002).

The moral crisis

It is recognized similarly that such organizational uncertainty is reflected in an inability to secure final meanings located in an objective reality (MacIntyre, 1985; Parker, 1998). The challenge of theorizing such uncertainty has given rise to numerous debates as to how best to account for the problematic nature of the individual, the organization, and society at large. According to Bauman (1993, 1995) one of the most important goals of modernity was to construct a world free of moral ambiguity by transferring individual responsibilities to impersonal, scientific methods and procedures. While such transfer took place via the rise of bureaucracy, the inherent morality of scientific procedures itself became questioned, as this was characterized seemingly as much by human catastrophe as improving the human condition. With few robust prescriptive frameworks to guide our actions, it becomes increasingly difficult to justify our research position simply on ontological or epistemological grounds. It follows that our personal ethical stance should guide our engagement with the social world and more specifically our research of organizational practices (Parker, 1999). Given the existence of a plurality of personal moral values it is inevitable that we will end up with a proliferation of theories, models and paradigms which reflect our various ideological positions.

The quest for uniqueness and career advancement in academia

The quest for uniqueness and career advancement in the academic world has led to a situation where social scientists appear keener than ever to generate new models, theories and approaches in order to carve a space for themselves and ensure academic prominence and rapid career advancement (McKinley and Mone, 1998). This can be witnessed in the proliferation of new, apparently discrete fields such as entrepreneurship, e-commerce and knowledge management. McKinley and Mone argue that there is nothing inherently wrong in the apparent fragmentation of organizational analysis; what is worrying, they suggest, are the wars fought between disciplines and schools, with each trying to secure legitimacy in the eyes of the scientific community and recruit followers at the expense of the rest. Such wars, they suggest, are fought around the view that various schools, models and paradigms are incommensurable — in other words, they share little or no ontological, epistemological or methodological grounds. As such, communication between them is difficult if not impossible. Such a state of affairs, however, is seen as attractive by some theorists, largely because of the reputational advantages associated with safeguarding the distinctiveness and survival of one's own theory (McKinley and Mone, 1998). This as has been argued may have emancipatory value in that the overarching positivist paradigm can be challenged head-on by other voices (Jackson and Carter, 1991; Jones and O'Doherty, 2005). It has also been argued, however, that this may lead to the stagnation of the entire field (Gioia and Pitre, 1989; Willmott, 1993).

Paradigm plurality

A map of advantages

The advantages of paradigm plurality have been widely acknowledged in the literature. For example, it is argued that the use of a single paradigm produces too narrow a view to reflect the multifaceted nature of organizational reality

(Gioia and Pitre, 1990). Consequently, the use of multiple paradigms is 'a better way of fostering more comprehensive portraits of complex organizational phenomena' (ibid.: 587).

Furthermore, knowledge about more than one paradigm can raise awareness of alternative research styles and agendas and, in so doing, foster innovation and creativity in research (Morgan, 1983; Brocklesby, 1997; Jones and O'Doherty, 2005). Knowledge of other paradigms allows an academic to become detached from a preferred view of the world and engage in exploring new research avenues. While some of these avenues may lead to contradictory findings, researchers could build upon such contradictions to produce accounts which are richer and more illuminating and question the interests reflected by and re-enacted in such accounts. Paradox and contradiction, it has been argued, are in fact drivers of scientific innovation (Lewis, 2000).

By becoming literate in multiple paradigms, researchers can also engage more effectively in conversation with other colleagues and with practitioners. Only through an open and democratic dialogue, involving all stakeholders, can organizational disciplines decide what is most important to study, what are the most appropriate methodologies, and what will be the effects that emerging theories will have upon surrounding social realities. Cooperation rather than competition could prove much more valuable in the enterprise of knowledge production.

Paradigm plurality also allows reconciliation between the various agendas pursued by researchers. We can identify four main agendas in this respect: (1) some researchers aim to create theories that control and predict the social world; (2) others are driven by an interest in understanding how meaning is constructed, negotiated and enacted; (3) still others pursue some form of critical science which aims to emancipate various groups of people; and (4) there are researchers whose main agenda consists of providing practical solutions to short-term organizational practices. While there are substantial tensions between these cross-cutting agendas, it can be argued that some areas of research may benefit if pursued at their intersection. Whereas most organizational researchers readily embrace the first two positions, they perhaps rarely consider the effects their work has upon the objects of inquiry. Put another way, gaining understanding is what drives their research; what happens afterwards is no longer the concern of the theorist. However, such findings could perhaps be put usefully to the service of improving organizational efficiency or emancipating organizational members (i.e. agendas 3 and 4).

Finally, the pursuit of multiparadigm research ensures the preservation and legitimization of points of view that might otherwise be perceived as marginal or indeed be suppressed by the dominant orthodoxy. Thus, those theories that speak 'in the name of the silent and the unheard' (Lyotard, 1997: 64) (cf. labour process theory, critical theory, feminism, poststructuralism) construct a place from which to voice their concerns. If management and organization studies are to be indeed 'ethical' they have to encourage a plurality of diverse voices, some of which will stand in total opposition to the interests promulgated by positivist social science.

A map of disadvantages

There are indeed numerous hurdles and disadvantages to doing multiparadigm research. One's socialization in a particular paradigm and its reinforcement through existing institutions make it difficult for researchers to question their preconceived ideas about the world, binding them to a particular vision of the world. Furthermore, a researcher's acceptance of and engagement with a plurality of paradigms does not come easily. It requires far more training and effort than that for researching out of a single paradigm. In instances where this does occur, it is perhaps more common for positivists to explore 'alternative' paradigms than for interpretive/critical researchers to go 'back to basics' (and study positivism) (Kelemen and Hassard, 1997). Committing to more than one paradigm brings with it cognitive and emotional costs. Leaving a particular paradigm in order to engage with a new one can be a painful operation. Indeed, for some individuals it may be impossible to move across paradigms, either because they consider it their moral duty to defend a particular set of scientific interests, or because they do not possess the emotional or technical repertoire necessary for venturing into new domains.

Knowing and acting effectively in a new paradigm makes substantial demands upon the individual, demands which can be satisfied only through active bodily involvement, experience and practice (Brocklesby, 1997; Hassard *et al.*, 2000). Assuming that the researcher can actually become socialized within the language and practice of a new paradigm, problems may arise if there are significant and substantive conflicts (or dissonances) between the metatheoretical assumptions of the new paradigm and the old. The researcher must search for strategies to reconcile such conflicts or dissonances, a process that may require a great deal of cognitive resourcefulness and determination.

Operating across paradigms undoubtedly makes it more difficult to engage in acts of scientific certification. Researchers pursue certification of their knowledge as much as they pursue knowledge itself, because knowledge without an audience is redundant (McCloskey, 1994). In so doing, researchers rely on multiple rhetorical devices as instruments of persuasion. Thus a positivist account would make use of statistical data in order to convey a particular point of view, while a social constructivist analysis would ground the argument in rich ethnographic data. A multiparadigm study would have recourse to both types of evidence, but in so doing may ultimately upset both scientific camps for not taking seriously enough the conventions and rigours embraced by them, respectively. Career choices may also be more limited given the general lack of institutional legitimacy attached to such pluralist research approaches. Traditionally, in social science you are either a qualitative or quantitative researcher, but rarely both.

Finally, the use of multiple lenses comes with a theoretical caveat. Scherer and Steinmann (1999) warn that mixing several positions may not necessarily lead to more comprehensive explanations of the organizational world. If the various paradigm positions adopted in a research investigation each have theoretical or empirical deficiencies, then research based on a combination of these may actually lead to sub-optimal analysis.

The pursuit of multiparadigm research: the case of organizational studies

An increasing number of organization researchers, however, have advocated the need to engage in multiparadigm forms of enquiry. Such researchers argue that this is not only theoretically feasible but also empirically crucial if we are to comprehend better the complex nature of contemporary organizations and their environments.

Gioia and Pitre (1990) are among the writers who argue for the theoretical feasibility of multiparadigm research. They suggest that one must accept that paradigms share certain common concepts, entities or 'transition zones', otherwise new theories would have no basis from which to refute or amend previous theories. With reference to Kuhn's (1970, 1974) later works, Gioia and Pitre argue that, in order for a paradigm to gain credibility and achieve a position of dominance, it would have to question continually an existing paradigm in terms of its favoured assumptions and procedures. Therefore, in order to question an existing paradigm, proponents of the new paradigm have to be able to converse in terms that can be understood by the 'old guard', their prospective audience. According to Gioia and Pitre's interpretation, Kuhn's later works suggest that even though there might not be a common language in which the contents of a rival theory can be *fully* expressed or evaluated, there is always a degree of commensurability, for otherwise a new theory could never develop.

In support of the theoretical feasibility of multiparadigm research, Weaver and Gioia (1994) build on Giddens's (1984) theory of structuration. They do so to argue that the typical divisions between determinism and voluntarism, object and subject, description and prescription, and holism and individualism, can be resolved via a dialogue between paradigms. They argue that paradigms reflect various facets of one social phenomenon, and the denial of this principle would mean we have different phenomena rather than multifaceted ones. According to Weaver and Gioia, the use of any single research paradigm would produce a view which is too narrow to reflect the multifaceted nature of organizational reality. As each paradigm constitutes a legitimate part of a larger scheme, it is important to pursue multiparadigm research from the position that paradigms are distinctive but at the same time permeable.

Schultz and Hatch (1996: 55) also advocate the need for multiparadigm research: 'multiparadigm thinking is both likely and desirable, in light of predictions about diversity in postindustrial society'. They propose a strategy of 'paradigm crossing', named 'interplay', which is defined as the simultaneous recognition of both 'contrasts and connections' between paradigms. In interplay, the researcher is seen to move back and forth between paradigms, allowing multiple views to be held in tension. This approach has sympathy with the work of Lewis and Grimes (1999) who provide a step-by-step guide to building theory from multiple paradigms, a process they term 'metatriangulation'.

In the United Kingdom multiparadigm thinking and research has been advocated by Hassard (1988, 1991, 1993b), who is concerned not only with the theoretical underpinnings of paradigm commensurability but also with producing empirical accounts of a multiparadigmatic nature. Hassard argues that although the 'later' Kuhn (1970, 1974) talks about tentative communication between paradigms, this position is still not satisfactory. As Hassard (1988: 253) notes, 'for the goal of paradigm mediation, Kuhn fails to go far enough toward a form of analysis which would retain paradigm identity while offering an alternative to hermeticism'. Hassard suggests instead that we turn to the later works of Wittgenstein (esp. 1953), which provide a more acceptable solution to overcoming theoretical hermeticism in organization theory. Wittgenstein (1953) considers that our metalanguage, or everyday language game (our basic language, the first language that we accommodate), underlies all technical and special language games. As a result, the rules and conventions of our metalanguage-in-use 'allow us to deal not only with a present language game but also with a new language game into which we may be trained' (Hassard, 1988: 257). Since the metalanguage-in-use is the basis for training into other technical languages, it appears clear that understanding and using two or more technical language games at the same time is achievable. Hassard's (1991, 1993b) fourfold account of work behaviour in the British Fire Service is an illustration of how researchers could muster more than one language game and write multifaceted accounts of the same organizational phenomenon.

While the above authors attempt to preserve the identity of paradigms, others suggest that boundaries might need to dissolve at least on a temporary basis in order to ensure the creation of common reference systems, or dictionaries which are democratically accepted by all. McKinley (1995), for example, suggests that the adoption of a 'reasonable realism' may be the key to overcoming hermeticism. Reasonable realism, in its quest for a truth that can be known only with uncertainty, could help to create a common reference system by which paradigms can be reconciled and evaluated. The aim is to disconfirm all paradigms that do not conform to that reality as defined by standard constructs. This argument is refined further by McKinley and Mone (1998). Here the ambiguity of the key constructs that form the building blocks of organization studies is identified as the major reason for persistent interschool incommensurability. The authors recommend the creation of a dictionary that would include democratically produced definitions of key organization studies constructs.

Contrary to this idea, Scherer and Dowling (1995) suggest that there is little point in searching for the 'right' criteria to evaluate systems of orientation from an observer's perspective. Instead, researchers should seek methods for how to interact and communicate with each other in order to improve practice. Instead of acting as passive observers, researchers should engage in the resolution of the paradigm debate as active participants. Given that the ultimate goal of science is to improve practice, a dialogue among the participants will have a significant impact on improving managerial and organizational practice.

Wicks and Freeman (1998) have also discussed this appeal to pragmatism. They urge researchers to move beyond epistemological distinctions between paradigms by making room for ethics and thus increasing the relevance of research. Pragmatism is highlighted as a useful tool in that it sheds light on the moral dimension of organizing. Wicks and Freeman (1998) do not think it is possible simply to combine various paradigms or split the difference between them in order to create a compelling alternative to the current situation. They advocate instead a different approach to organization studies, one which they term 'pragmatic experimentation'. Building on Richard Rorty's (1985) work, Wicks and Freeman construct an alternative vision of organization theory, one that subscribes to usefulness as a central organizational value. The pragmatic value of usefulness requires those engaged in research to scrutinize the practical relevance of a set of ideas as defined by their purposes and those shared by the community. Researchers doing this type of work would see organization studies as a vehicle to help people lead 'better' lives and would promote novel and innovative approaches aimed at precisely the same objective (Wicks and Freeman, 1998).

The discursive approach in multiparadigm research

Organizational analysis is a discursive domain. Researchers rely on language to convey, construct, and enact meaning as well as to persuade their audience of a particular argument. Thus, when researchers adhere to certain paradigmatic assumptions they embrace the language of a particular scientific community which, in their view, is superior to others. The language conventions, techniques and representational practices that are recognized as legitimate, and are mustered by the members of a particular scientific community, establish their paradigm (Kaghan and Phillips, 1998). A paradigm, then, can be seen as a heterogeneous collection of language conventions embedded in the practice of a particular context.

It has been argued that the dominant positivist language game of organizational analysis no longer offers robust explanations of the increasingly complex and elusive structures and processes of organizational phenomena and that localized technical language games may offer more realistic alternatives and insights. Various writers talk of a 'postmodern condition' having emerged in philosophy, social science and the humanities (see Harvey, 1989; Hassard and Parker, 1993; Casey, 2002; Jones and Munro, 2005). For many, this represents an alternative explanatory medium for social theory and affairs, one founded on the recognition and importance of 'local' rather than 'grand' genres of intellectual discourse.

One of the main exponents of this form of analysis has been Jean-François Lyotard, especially in his book *The Postmodern Condition* (1997). In a key passage, Lyotard discusses the role of *petit récit* (or small narratives) as the 'quintessential form of imaginative invention, particularly in science' (1997: 60). For Lyotard *petit récit*, like Wittgenstein's (1953) 'technical language games' (see Phillips, 1977), thrive in linguistic life worlds that are altogether different from those of 'grand narratives', whose habitats, it is claimed, are now under threat. As each 'small narrative' possesses its own specific way of representing the world, conflicts between them are bound to arise. The notion of *differand* is advocated to account for the existence of a state of 'continuous difference' between small narratives and the difficulty in making judgements about linguistic conflicts. Consequently, the researcher has to be an active player in the conversation of research by taking on the job of the philosopher. In so doing, the researcher will, among others, attempt to seek out new idioms which can 'speak for the silent' and, by and large, write about the world 'in the service of the unknown' (Lyotard, 1997). Writing from this position locates the moral responsibility of the researcher who cannot claim innocence from the representational force that he or she brings to the theory (Calás and Smircich, 1999).

Deetz (1996) was among the first theorists to advocate this line of thought in organization studies. This position views research differences as arising not so much from the ontological and epistemological assumptions of the individual researcher (and the procedures or methodologies used) but from the relation of research practices to the language games prevailing in the society at large and the ways in which research concepts emerge. Consequently, whereas some discursive positions embraced by researchers will seek consensus by reinforcing prevailing language, others will attempt to destabilize and challenge the *status quo*. Consensus research is defined and demarked by its search for hegemonic order, integration and harmony. Such research focuses on representing organizational reality through a 'neutral' language that is seen to be able to capture the social world 'objectively'. Research validity is a major concern for the consensus scientist. Organizational science is viewed as neutral and organizational theories as abstractions of researchers. On the other hand, dissensus research presents order as historicized and politicized and attempts to deconstruct its pillars in as much as they suppress conflict and struggle. Language is seen to be not so much a neutral instrument at the disposal of researchers but a means of reconstructing reality, a means of active engagement with the world. The ability to challenge assumptions and social practices is valued more highly than the representational validity of the research. Researchers engage in the exercise of science — seen as political — for they are also deemed part of networks that are not value-free.

We advocate, therefore, the importance of reflecting upon both our discursive position and the consequences this might have for the prevailing social order. Only by fostering multiple perspectives that seek to address the limitations of consensual positions can researchers speak in the name of the 'unheard', the 'liminal', and the 'marginalized' (Lyotard, 1997). Such multilensical research ensures that the boundaries between the core and the periphery are constantly challenged and that organizational analysis plays a significant role in constructing a more democratic reality. However, adopting such a position not only entails the disadvantages discussed earlier, but also, and crucially, places considerable moral strain on the researcher, who must ensure that his/her intentions and the consequences of his/her efforts are seriously reflected upon.

Conclusion

This chapter has mapped the development of paradigm plurality in a number of organizational disciplines, such as organization theory, strategic management, international business, operational research and technology studies. In so doing, it has reviewed some of the advantages and disadvantages of multiparadigm research, arguing that the overall benefits from paradigm plurality outweigh the shortcomings. The position adopted here is that it is crucial for researchers to preserve and encourage theories emerging from multiple paradigms, a scenario that is not only possible from a substantive and theoretical point of view, but is also highly desirable in light of the changes taking place in contemporary organizational realities. We have also argued that the discursive turn that organizational analysis has taken in recent times infuses the researcher with a moral responsibility for his/her representations and theories. In this respect it is important to ask ourselves why certain voices and positions are absent from the conversation of research and what values and interests are being suppressed as a result of our theorizing. These are questions which organizational theorists can no longer avoid asking (Calás and Smircich, 1999; Casey, 2002; Jones and Munro, 2005). Our moral responsibility is to challenge and change some of the deeply entrenched research practices that continue to be hailed as 'best practice' by the research community. In order to realize this responsibility, we must accommodate local voices and ensure that a multitude of stories are told and heard. The proliferation of multiple local discourses will ensure that one dominant paradigm cannot replace all others.

2 Organizational knowledge

Production and consumption

We now move from the generic political analysis of paradigm plurality and proliferation within management and organization studies to more localized issues of knowledge creation and use. In so doing, we interpret debates on the production of knowledge from a largely postmodernist, 'sociology of consumption' perspective. Drawing theoretically upon the work of Jean-François Lyotard, Michel de Certeau and Stanley Deetz in particular, our analysis rejects both positivist and conventionalist theses on knowledge production in favour of a deconstructionist approach that embraces acts of production and consumption in a reflexive way. The argument is developed by way of a case study of production and consumption in the specific field of organizational analysis. Through an assessment of scientific status and institutional control — centrally in relation to the 'paradigm incommensurability' debate (see Chapter 1) — a taxonomy of styles of knowledge production and consumption is proposed. Five main 'camps' comprise this taxonomy — non-consumers, integrationists, protectionists, pluralists and postmodernists. We describe the basic knowledge philosophies of the camps and subject each to evaluation and critique. This analysis sees, *inter alia*, Jeffrey Pfeffer's proposals for producing a unified and integrated knowledge paradigm for organizational analysis — the so-called 'Pfefferdigm' thesis — confounded by the indeterminate rationalities and networks of signification of postmodern analysis. We argue that at this predominantly intra-disciplinary level of analysis the concept of discourse is as useful as paradigm for explaining processes of knowledge production and consumption.

The nature of knowledge in organization theory

This chapter concerns debates surrounding the nature of knowledge within academic social science in general and organization theory in particular. As we discussed in Chapter 1, since the mid-1960s one of the key debates within this field has centred upon whether organizational knowledge is best accrued from the theories and empirical practices of a single research paradigm or a number of competing ones. During the 1970s and 1980s a crude interpretation of this debate pictured an ongoing struggle between mono-paradigm absolutism, largely favouring coherence around the axioms of traditional social systems theory, and pluri-paradigm relativism, under whose auspices a number of theory communities proliferates within a volatile, contested terrain of 'anything goes' (Feyerabend, 1970). In organizational analysis a popular shorthand phrase for this debate has been the dispute between 'contingency theory and the critics' (see Donaldson, 1985, 1996a).

From the mid-1990s the debate has been vitalized by views expressed by the influential American administrative scientist Jeffrey Pfeffer (1993, 1997). Notable here is his suggestion that in order to achieve academic respectability organizational analysis should concern itself with producing a discrete paradigm of clearly articulated practices and standards. Pfeffer offers the example of political science as a sub-discipline of social science that has achieved this aim. The 'Pfefferdigm debate', as it has become known, is predicated on the view that the theoretical variety and epistemological relativism advocated by 'the critics' will lead ultimately to the nascent discipline of organizational analysis committing professional suicide. It is Pfeffer's belief that paradigm plurality will ultimately ring the death knell for organizational analysis, because the type of knowledge it offers is insufficient to enlist the support of influential institutions, especially research funding agencies.

The present chapter questions the logic of much of Pfeffer's (1993) thesis. We take issue with his largely 'integrationist' view, one that apparently wishes to 'settle' the paradigm incommensurability debate, for we doubt that the production of such community consensus is achievable given the current status of knowledge practices. Such practices are not stable and coherent, but continuously in the making; they shape and are shaped by power relations and competing discourses (Foucault, 1980); they infer a process in which knowledge is at the same time produced and consumed. Typically referred to as 'the postmodern condition of knowledge' (Lyotard, 1997), this scenario views knowledge as a set of cultural practices situated in and inextricably linked to the material and social circumstances in which it is produced and consumed. As socio-material practice, knowledge is processual and provisional; its production relies on resources disembodied from their original content and made available through their transformation, legitimization and institutionalization (Gherardi and Nicolini, 2000). Knowledge consumption is ensured through processes of social participation in a community of practice — a means of 'being in the world', not simply 'knowing the world' (Bourdieu, 1990).

Our argument, therefore, is that even *de facto* codification of community standards is something that is beyond our analytical grasp. Our reason is simply that the largely unbridled nature of knowledge production and consumption in contemporary organizational analysis (see, for example, the contributions in Jones and Munro, 2005) serves to make such integrationism mere wishful thinking. In short, we believe that consumption practices will continue to confound any firm bounding of organizational knowledge in the foreseeable future.

Our argument is developed in three main phases. First, we review, briefly, the relationship between theory communities and the production of knowledge in organization theory. This analysis, which takes recourse to debates on the nature of scientific status and institutional control, rejects linear explanations of research practice in favour of a politically infused perspective in which knowledge production takes place and reflects a highly contested terrain (Reed, 1992). We note how the fashion, since the mid-1960s, for establishing clear community demarcations has reflected the development of a strong 'productivist' (Casey, 2002) orientation in organizational analysis. We argue, however, that this perspective should be employed with caution. At best it should be used as a heuristic device to allow researchers to identify and subsequently question their own intellectual practices and those of hypothetical academic 'others' (Cooper, 1983).

The second phase of the argument begins by confirming this emphasis on the production of knowledge in traditional commentaries on scientific progress. We argue that any analysis of knowledge production must engender an appreciation of acts of consumption. The consumption of knowledge fuels the creation of new knowledge while new knowledge acquires its status as knowledge only when selected for consumption by those who find it meaningful. We believe that all producers of knowledge are also consumers, although one does not have to produce knowledge simply because of the act of consumption. In debating such processes we take recourse to the work of de Certeau (1984) and Lyotard (1997) to explore the various 'forms of manoeuvre' available to consumers of organizational knowledge. Such consumers range from academic peers to students, managers, workers, government administrators and the public at large. We focus mainly on academic peers who by, for example, sitting on research panels and journal boards, acting as conference organizers, journal and book reviewers or as mere readers of published and unpublished work, have the institutional power to decide what forms of organizational information are to be accorded the status of 'knowledge'. This section discusses how the consumption of knowledge is a process characterized by instability, fragmentation and heterogeneity; above all, it is a process that is difficult to control 'at a distance' (Law, 1987). Our argument ultimately revolves around a postmodern position under which attempts at the codification of scientific practice are subverted by researchers' 'tactics of consumption' (de Certeau, 1984). This sees the knowledge space of social science characterized as a heterogeneous network of shifting research identities, with knowledge being constructed at the intersection of processes of production and consumption.

The third phase of the chapter then attempts to place some (temporary) structure on this shifting space by offering a modernist interpretation of current styles of knowledge production and consumption in organizational analysis. In so doing, we offer a taxonomy of characteristic responses to the paradigm incommensurability debate — a debate that has become central to understanding the state of knowledge practices in the field (see e.g. Jackson and Carter, 1991; Hassard, 1993b; Pfeffer, 1993; Schultz and Hatch, 1996; Scherer, 1998; Burrell, 1996, 2003; Casey, 2002). This taxonomy classifies responses to the debate in terms of five main styles or 'camps' of production and consumption — non-consumers, integrationists, protectionists, pluralists and postmodernists — and literature representative of each is reviewed and discussed. We suggest that such multifaceted, and sometimes contradictory, responses are not only natural but actually desirable in light of a sociology-of-consumption that reflects the fragmented nature of social science and society. Given the substantive content and epistemological stance of the chapter, our analysis emphasizes the explanatory power of postmodernism, and in particular the role of research *discourses*, in making sense of production and consumption processes.

Finally, in conclusion, we offer some implications for future research and analysis. We argue that in the light of new empirical realities (especially the rise of consumerism in postindustrial society) discussions of community practice in organizational analysis should embrace acts of consumption as well as production. In so doing, we promote the explanatory power of discourse in the analysis of the disciplinary matrices of social science in general and organizational analysis in particular.

Knowledge production

The traditional emphasis in analyses of the nature of scientific knowledge is on a phenomenon that is relentlessly *produced* through either inductive or deductive means. In this view, the products of scientific enterprise are frequently consumed through cause-and-effect type relationships. Knowledge is produced in order to be consumed at a later stage, commonly following dissemination through appropriate academic and/or professional channels. A strong sense of linearity and positivist logic underpins the process.

Often associated with this essentially positivist and unilinear view is the metaphor of the so-called 'hierarchy of sciences' (Cole, 1983). The dominant image is of natural science, through its success in adopting cold and factual methodologies, being located at the top of the scientific hierarchy, with other, less 'pure' sciences — commonly the human and social — situated at the bottom. One implication is that the modern, Western natural science model can or should provide a methodological exemplar for the social sciences, given that the latter struggles to achieve academic and social legitimacy. Natural science, underpinned by experimental methods and positivist philosophies, is deemed to be scientifically superior to social science in that it appears to offer an *objective* way of looking at the world. Scientific progress, as a 'rational' enterprise, is equated with the 'cumulative growth in knowledge' (Reed, 1985: 201) whereby 'knowledge grows linearly as new data are added to the existing stock of research findings' (Astley, 1985: 479). The natural sciences are deemed successful in that they progressively add more dust to the dust pile of knowledge.

In contrast, conventionalist philosophy, and in particular the writings of Thomas Kuhn (1962, 1970) and his followers (see Lakatos and Musgrave, 1970) take exception to such rationalist historicism. Under conventionalism the process of knowledge production and accumulation is not such a linear, incremental accomplishment. Instead it is the result of scientific wars in which 'Old Guards' are recurrently overthrown by bands of 'Young Turks' (Shapere, 1971). Here, rather than take recourse to the dictates of rational or formal logic, science practice reflects the irrational forces of consensus, dogma and belief, essentially mirroring the culture of the political community. The production of knowledge concerns the (re)solving of 'puzzles' rather than problems, for answers already reside within the dominant scientific 'exemplar' (Kuhn, 1970). This process involves sociological consensus as much as scientific experimentation. Knowledge progresses through recurrent phases of 'normal' and 'revolutionary' activity, rather than by (scientific) giants standing on one another's shoulders (Kuhn, 1970).

We wish to question the efficacy of both of these 'progress' narratives — positivism and conventionalism — as frameworks for defining the status of knowledge in organizational analysis. Instead we will turn to postmodernism and consider the notion of *discourse* as a metaphor for conceptualizing knowledge production and consumption in the field. In so doing, we attempt to depart from a linguistically naïve version of postmodernism and discourse theory — one which privileges language as constitutive of social phenomena at the expense of non-linguistic, material practices. Instead we emphasize the material and heterogeneous nature of discourse. We are concerned, in Foucauldian fashion, to highlight the institutional bases of discourse, the positions from which people speak and the power relations that make this possible or restrain it. In particular, we see scientific discourse as a practice (or rather a set of practices) that allows institutions to privilege particular forms of knowledge and the conditions that make them possible.

Paradigms and production

Of the two progress narratives outlined above, it can be argued that an adapted version of Kuhnian conventionalism has become normative in explanations of knowledge development and community practice in organizational analysis. This version sees the theoretical and empirical cake sliced into various sociological paradigms, the number and composition of which varies according to the metatheoretical recipe being used. From a production of knowledge perspective, such paradigms represent sets of assumptions and convictions that are held in common by communities of researchers.[1]

In organizational analysis, the debate on paradigms and their role in the research process was given momentum by the publication of Burrell and Morgan's (1979) *Sociological Paradigms and Organizational Analysis*. This book outlined a number of key debates concerning the production of knowledge in the field. One of their main arguments was that in order to place knowledge production in context we must first possess a structuralist understanding of the scientific and political assumptions that underpin major intellectual traditions. Burrell and Morgan *produce* this context through specifying the philosophical and methodological (meta)theories that serve to define the intellectual character of well-known research approaches. Both mainstream and alternative schools and movements are situated in terms of their relative position on a map of intellectual terrain produced through relating 'theories of social science' to 'theories of society'. A two-by-two matrix provides the technology for this map, whereby four sociological paradigms are produced to represent the major belief systems of academics and others who practise organizational analysis.

One of the more contentious aspects of this thesis, however, was the suggestion that instead of such paradigms being arenas for open, scholarly debate, they represent, instead, hermetically sealed intellectual compartments. In Burrell and Morgan's analysis, an extremely strong version of the conventionalist notion of paradigm incommensurability is applied. Here such incommensurability presupposes that:

> synthesis [between paradigms] is not possible, since in their pure form [paradigms] are contradictory, being based on at least one set of meta-theoretical assumptions. They represent alternatives, in the sense that one can operate in different paradigms sequentially over time, but mutually exclusive, in the sense that one cannot operate in more than one paradigm at any given point in time, since in accepting the assumptions of one, we defy the assumptions of all the others.
>
> (Burrell and Morgan, 1979: 25)

As these four incommensurable sociological paradigms — functionalism, interpretivism, radical humanism and radical structuralism — are found to coexist at one time, it is argued that benchmarking between paradigms is impossible, for proponents live in different life-worlds and speak different technical languages. Scientific communication is not so much difficult as logically impossible (Burrell and Morgan, 1979).[2] It is to this form of 'hyper-relativism' that Pfeffer (1993) so strongly objects in his much cited article 'Barriers to the advance of organizational science'. Although Pfeffer's meta-narrative, like that of Burrell and Morgan, is largely 'productivist' (Casey, 2002), it is one directed at entirely different ends.

We wish to argue, however, that such ends are impossible to achieve due to the heterogeneity, fragmentation and dynamic nature of knowledge practices brought about by the so-called 'postmodern condition' (Lyotard, 1997). For Lyotard, the postmodern condition is one characterized by increased cultural fragmentation, new modes of experience, subjectivity and culture triggered by the development of new types of information, knowledge and technology. These new modes of experience and subjectivity foreground the power of consumption acts in constructing difference, playfulness, inclusion and exclusion.

Knowledge consumption

While it can be argued that knowledge is produced through the interaction of institutional materials and symbolic conditions, it can be argued also that it is reproduced only when singled-out for attention by those who find it meaningful (Knights, 1997). According to Munro (1998), for example, knowledge is never meaningful in its own right: to become meaningful, it has to 'exteriorize' itself. Knowledge is usually mediated/exteriorized through linguistic and non-linguistic practices in which actions and interactions are made accountable to oneself and to the other (Gherardi and Nicolini, 2000). Such practices are in fact acts of consumption, serving purposes as diverse as expressing one's identity, marking attachment to social groups, exhibiting social distinction or ensuring social participation in various activities (Edgell *et al.*, 1996).

The consumption of knowledge, however, has generally played a secondary role in the (grand) narrative explanations of scientific progress, for in terms of the use of material and symbolic resources the focus has been placed primarily on the strategic and operational actions of producers and the attributes of their theories. McKinley *et al.* (1999), for example, argue that evolving schools of thought must display a combination of novelty, continuity and scope to achieve legitimacy and therefore 'paradigm' status. The consumption of knowledge is seen to be directly correlated with and resulting from such attributes, in that 'the more that both novelty and continuity are displayed by a developing organization theory school of thought, the more likely detection and assimilation of the school's intellectual products by organizational scholars will be' (McKinley *et al.*, 1999: 639) and 'the greater the scope of a developing school and its intellectual products, the greater the detection and assimilation of those products will be' (McKinley *et al.*, 1999: 641).

According to de Certeau (1984), however, the consumption of knowledge should not be limited to such a secondary role, for its social and intellectual significance is profound. It can be argued that a more thoroughgoing understanding of processes of paradigm proliferation and regulation would involve exploration of those forms of manoeuvre available to the consumers of knowledge in the simultaneous spaces created by the producers. The propagation and consumption of knowledge depends, to a large extent, on what individuals or communities do with it. Individuals and communities may behave in different ways: they may ignore it, alter it, traduce it, supplement it, or appropriate it (Gherardi and Nicolini, 2000). Thus, the consumption of knowledge is a process characterized by instability, fragmentation and heterogeneity (de Certeau, 1984). To repeat, it is a process that is difficult to 'control at a distance' (see Law, 1987). From this point of view, the project of producing a universalistic, ubiquitous and centralized paradigm for any social science discipline or field appears akin to the proverbial search for the holy grail; given, for example, the analytical elusiveness of social reality, the political character of the social scientific enterprise, and the heterogeneous nature of acts of consumption.[3] Put simply, de Certeau feels that responses to the strategy of knowledge production cannot be predicted, anticipated or indeed managed according to any grand plan. Such responses, which he terms 'tactics of consumption', cannot be articulated by producers of knowledge, individually or collectively, nor can they be fixed by the system in which they are found to proliferate.[4]

It can be argued, therefore, that in the sphere of organizational analysis, the concept or project of producing a dominant analytical paradigm is one that is likely to trigger a set of heterogeneous and shifting responses from researchers. Some may reject it, others internalize it and still others subvert it. While some authors suggest ways in which a dominant paradigm *could* or even *should* be 'produced' — notably Pfeffer (1993) who as we know illustrates the apparently comparable and commendable case of political science — we will argue that the nature and logic of such heterogeneous 'acts of consumption' serve to confound such an enterprise.

Further, it is our view that consumption is a far more elusive concept analytically, given that there are few mechanisms for boundary setting, or for ensuring 'control at a distance'. From a predominantly consumption-of-knowledge perspective, the dynamic of paradigms is not one exclusive to documenting static sets of structuralist assumptions about science and the determined role of scientists. Instead, after Lyotard (1997) it is our view that dependence on such presuppositions as the basis for sociological explanation may lead ultimately to an internal erosion of the 'legitimacy principle'. In processes of deconstruction, there are simply no ways to justify situating science and scientists metatheoretically within such spatial and temporal concrete.[5]

Our view is that, primarily, it is the *language* conventions, techniques and representational practices — recognized as scientifically legitimate and which are regularly mustered by members of a particular scientific community — that serve in practice to establish paradigm identity. Allegiance to a paradigm is allegiance to a heterogeneous and shifting collection of language conventions embedded in the practice of a particular context — in other words, allegiance primarily to a set of *discourses*.

***Consumption, discourse and the* petit récit**

Since the early 1970s much attention has focused on the view that social science (and in particular that branch concerned with the study of organizations) is in the midst of a knowledge 'crisis' (see Grint, 1991; Hassard, 1993b; Reed, 1996). From Gouldner (1970) and Friedrichs (1970) onwards, writers have claimed that the traditional grand narratives of social science no longer offer robust explanations of the increasingly complex and elusive structures and processes of social and cultural phenomena.

Similar arguments have been advanced by writers who talk of a 'postmodern condition' in philosophy, social science and the humanities (see Harvey, 1989; Lyotard, 1997). For many, postmodernism represents an alternative explanatory medium for social theory and affairs, one founded on the recognition and importance of 'local' rather than 'grand' *genres* of intellectual discourse. As noted, one of the main exponents of this form of analysis has been Jean-François Lyotard, especially in his book *The Postmodern Condition: A Report on Knowledge* (1997, first edition 1984). In a key passage, Lyotard discusses the role of *petit récit* (or 'little narratives') as the 'quintessential form of imaginative invention, particularly in science' (1997: 60). For Lyotard, *petit récit*, like Wittgenstein's (1953) 'technical language-games' (see Phillips, 1977), thrive in linguistic life-worlds that are altogether different to those of 'grand' narratives, whose habitats, it is claimed, are now under threat.

For Lyotard, each 'little narrative' possesses its own specific way of representing the world. As such, conflicts between them are difficult if not impossible to resolve, given the lack of a 'judgement rule' applicable to both. Lyotard, in fact introduces the notion of *differand* to account for such processes, a term he employs to reflect the maintenance of a state of 'continuous difference', and to account for the difficulty in making judgements about linguistic conflicts. For Lyotard, there is no way in which a scientific discourse can dominate all others through invoking a source of meta-narrative authority to ensure legitimacy.

Lyotard (1997) suggests that the 'postmodern condition' is also one of conflict. In order to understand scientific relations, Lyotard insists we require not only a theory of linguistic communication but also a theory of language 'games' — which accepts conflict, or 'agonistics', as a fundamental principle.[6] Most theories of scientific communication, however, appear wedded to a production of knowledge perspective, which claims to have access to what is right or wrong by upholding the 'scientific method' as the supreme arbiter. Lyotard's stance is different. He argues that although the *appearance* of communication between 'little narratives' is a necessary function of scientific action, it is also a contingent one.[7] As there are no meta-narratives to regulate such linkages; this is an area where a researcher has to be 'active', i.e. by taking on the job of the 'philosopher', not just that of the 'scientist'. In so doing, the researcher will, among other things, attempt to seek out new idioms which can 'speak for the silent', guarantee the conditions for 'participating in idioms', 'witness *differands*', and by-in-large write about the world 'in the service of the unknown' (Lyotard, 1997). Writing from this position, we locate the moral responsibility of the researcher who cannot claim innocence from the representational force that he or she brings to theory (Calás and Smircich, 1999).

Lyotard develops this argument further to suggest that a theory of games, based on agonistics, represents a case of move-and-countermove on the part of researchers and their narratives. This is accomplished to the extent that the research game remains continuously open and heterogeneous. New moves provide opportunities for establishing new *petit récit*, which remain outside of the narrative domain of those in positions of institutional authority. Agonistics, therefore, emphasize processes of knowledge consumption, with the 'new moves' representing 'tactics of consumption' which function actively in response to strategies of knowledge production.

In Lyotard's philosophy, therefore, explanations of community and institution in social science take recourse not to the absolutism of positivism or the relativism of conventionalism but to the deconstructive reflexivity of postmodernism. Lyotard offers a critique of the production perspective on knowledge, which is predicated on the existence of paradigms and their aspiration to be based on *inherent* emancipatory qualities. The postmodern notion of discourse, on the other hand, reflects a process of scientific interaction that includes not only the production of knowledge and the products of knowledge, but more importantly the act of consumption.

From a postmodernist perspective on knowledge, therefore, what one should fear is the 'naturalisation' of discourse(s), that is, the closure of potential meanings when a particular discourse is elevated into a 'standard' language and heralded as the key to knowledge and scientific progress (Lyotard, 1997). Naturalization does not affect only the meanings of words used by researchers, but also their interactional routines and identities (Fairclough, 1996). Naturalization, however, is a process that is constantly resisted and subverted through tactics of consumption — the points of resistance which attempt to manipulate, subvert, oppose or delegitimize the standard language. As we have stressed, these points of resistance are irregularly distributed across the knowledge space. They form a heterogeneous network of shifting and decentred identities which researchers may take on at various points in time. In what follows, we offer a tangible expression of our argument through discussing some of these 'tactics' in relation to the Pfefferdigm debate on paradigm commensurability and incommensurability.

Responses to the 'paradigms debate': a case analysis

Based on this reading of the sociology of consumption, and in particular the view of the knowledge space as consisting of a heterogeneous network of shifting research identities, we now wish — for the purpose of case explanation — to place some (temporary) structure on this space through identifying contemporary responses to knowledge production. In so doing, we offer an essentially modernist 'taxonomy' of the forms or styles of knowledge production and consumption witnessed in relation to the paradigm incommensurability debate in organizational analysis. Although elements of this taxonomy may possibly be deemed to be employed largely as productivist straw men, innocently awaiting postmodern deconstruction, and whilst indeed a postmodern position is favoured in the analysis, our intention primarily is to develop such a classification for pedagogical reasons of case explanation. The aim is for the taxonomy to be of explanatory value to students/researchers/teachers seeking to make sense of the 'paradigms debate' in terms of the distinctive discourses of production and consumption at work. In the event, this taxonomic assessment forms the basis of a discourse-analytic case study of the debate, and *inter alia* a critique of Pfeffer's (1993) proposals for paradigm integration. Finally it should be noted that this taxonomy is essentially the personal or social construction of the authors, who are themselves seeking to consume the debate in a particular way (although it is hoped that the substance of the argument may have wider resonance).

Paradigms and Pfefferdigms: a taxonomy of responses

For explanatory purposes, it is our view that responses to the 'paradigms debate' in organizational analysis can usefully be typified, classified and clustered into five main 'camps'. First, those researchers who may not be aware of the debate on paradigms, and/or do not make it explicit in their writings, we call 'non-consumers'. Second, to Pfeffer (1993) and his followers, who advocate the production of an overarching integrated paradigm, we give the appellation 'integrationists'. Third, those who support a strong version of the relativist thesis of paradigm incommensurability we name 'protectionists'. Fourth, those who would jettison the paradigm incommensurability thesis by urging us to engage in multi-paradigm research we term 'pluralists. And finally, those who advocate the need to challenge the essentially productionist discourse of the paradigms debate we call the 'postmodernists'.

We now offer a description and analysis of each camp. Although this analysis is offered primarily as a case study of tactics of consumption, in keeping with our desire to remain reflexive, we seek to acknowledge openly — by way of critique and deconstruction — the 'camp' in which the analysis for this chapter resides, that of postmodernism. As such, our case explanation is developed at two levels — one taxonomic and descriptive, the other critical and partisan.

Non-consumers

The *non-consumers* form a vast camp and fall, we feel, into three main categories. First, there are those who are simply unaware of debates relating to paradigm assumptions, proliferation and incommensurability. These researchers are oblivious to arguments that suggest the power of paradigmatic assumptions to shape perceptual orientation in their professional activities.[8] Second, there are those who are perhaps cognisant of the debate but find its level of abstraction less than useful in the pursuit of their everyday research duties. Such researchers may not be convinced of the practical value of the debate for empirical or experimental purposes and thus choose not to engage with it. Third, there are those who, although possibly at ease with the terminology of the debate, may simply refuse to engage with its arguments in order to strengthen the position of mainstream management studies, as portrayed in so-called 'functionalist' paradigms.

This non-consumers taxonomy is, of course, largely hypothetical and impressionistic. It is also probably by no means exhaustive or definitive and should at best be regarded as heuristic. The boundaries between these groupings are in any case not clearly definable and it would be indeed very difficult to judge if someone does not engage with the debate due to its level of abstraction or because of a wish to propagate mainstream practice. Although an empirical study may shed some light on the makings and motivations of this camp, the non-consumers group is one we need spend relatively little time on in our analysis of production and consumption practices.

Integrationists

The second camp, the *integrationist*, we feel subscribes to the view that organizational analysis is in a 'pre-paradigmatic' state, meaning that it has yet to achieve scientific maturity (at which time one paradigm dominates for a considerable period). While we accept that 'organization studies is a subject area that, since its development as a discrete academic specialism has suffered considerably from a crisis of identity' (Knights, 1997: 7), we do not believe that the crisis can be resolved via an integrationist project. Although the integrationist project posits a need to combine paradigms into a newly integrated field, it often appears to suggest (somewhat unreflexively perhaps) that a version of a positivist paradigm will provide most of the necessary foundations for this integration (see Donaldson, 1985, 1998; Pfeffer, 1993).

As noted, Pfeffer (1993) basically argues that there is no future for organizational analysis (strictly speaking 'organizational science') unless the academic community reaches consensus over the nature of a dominant paradigm. He states that:

> consensus itself, however achieved, is a vital component for the advancement of knowledge in a field. Without some minimal level of consensus about research questions and methods, fields can scarcely expect to produce knowledge in a cumulative, developmental process.
>
> (Pfeffer, 1993: 611)

Pfeffer's views thus appear deeply rooted in productionist assumptions. In particular he appears to support a 'hierarchy of the sciences' thesis. The field of organizational science is apparently characterized by a considerably low level of paradigm development, particularly when compared with adjacent sciences such as psychology, economics and (especially) political science. Pfeffer contends that at present there is not only disagreement over which of the nascent paradigms available to organizational analysis is more 'useful', but also crucially over the process by which this can be decided.[9]

Pfeffer's analysis, therefore, appears grounded primarily in a production of knowledge perspective, one which takes organizational analysis's 'anything goes' (Feyerabend, 1970) attitude to be a reflection of the pre-paradigmatic state in which the field finds itself. On a pessimistic note, Pfeffer contends that this current state of affairs will lead to disastrous consequences as academic disciplines compete for less and less resources from key institutions, for disciplines in a more developed state paradigmatically will be favoured. Consequently, his advice is to produce a strong, unified discipline of organization studies, one which is to be consumed by researchers in ways dictated and directed by a professional intellectual academy.

We have argued that a more reflexive production/consumption perspective on knowledge may challenge such proposals on several counts. First of all, it can be argued that it is not only difficult but in fact impossible to manage acts of consumption 'at a distance'. This argument would suggest that it is beyond the power of institutions to appropriate intellectual co-ordinates and fix them according to some grand plan. Furthermore, heterogeneous acts of consumption challenge the so-called objectivity of the knowledge practices espoused by social scientific institutions. Such institutions are viewed merely as self-validating gatherings that attempt politically to decide upon criteria that will permit access to a 'profession', one controlled predominantly by themselves!

Pfeffer's suggestion, whilst perhaps well intended in its pragmatism, can thus be viewed as hegemonic, or even elitist. He basically suggests that organizational analysis should become more institutional, and that consensus should be enforced by professional bodies whose legitimacy is derived from 'expert' knowledge and whose main task is to decide on sets of methodological standards to be followed by the community. Diversity is welcome only to the extent that it is inscribed in an institutional way of seeing the world. To quote Pfeffer (1993: 617) 'disagreement in theoretical approaches and even in methodology will not prove detrimental . . . as long as there are some agreed upon ways of resolving theoretical and methodological disputes'. Such resolution, however, is not so much a by-product of democracy, where both producers *and* consumers determine standards, but rather that of producers of knowledge expecting consumers to respond passively and in ways that are strategically anticipated. The integrationist meta-narrative thus largely ignores human agency and the political nature of acts of consumption.

Protectionists

For us, the *protectionists* suggest that paradigms, as discrete intellectual lenses, are not so much complementary as competing, each enshrining a particular worldview. Silverman (1969), for example, suggested that the attempt to blur the boundaries between paradigms is a major obstacle to the growth of organizational analysis. Rather than promote 'pseudo-linkages' between paradigms, we should, according to Silverman, instead address questions concerning their fundamental differences. According to the protectionist camp, there can be no linguistic or analytical bridges between paradigms, as each takes recourse to particular ontological, epistemological and methodological presuppositions. These advocates of paradigm incommensurability, therefore, reject any form of communication that suggests the inter-paradigmatic or dialectical synthesis of ideas.

Jackson and Carter (1991) are typical of writers who argue strongly for the logic and practice of paradigm incommensurability. They suggest that incommensurability, as a concept, has emancipatory value, for it serves to protect 'alternative' modes of organizational inquiry from the imperialistic tentacles of 'functionalist orthodoxy'. They vehemently criticize those who would oppose or decry paradigm incommensurability by suggesting that such writers have misunderstood the conventionalist message, especially of the Burrell and Morgan kind, which invites difference not synthesis. Jackson and Carter argue that abandoning paradigm incommensurability can lead us 'inexorably' towards 'epistemological authoritarianism'. They advocate that paradigms should be developed on their own terms, for each presupposes a unique perspective from which concepts are defined and theories emerge. As each paradigm serves to preserve and re-enforce its academic practices and cultural characteristics: 'competing paradigms constitute for each other an otherness which gives each paradigm its specific identity' (Jackson and Carter, 1991: 123). In their view, denial of paradigm incommensurability is symptomatic of fears for epistemological heterogeneity and will eventually lead to sterility and the failure to produce any significant new perspectives for the field.

It can be argued, however, that Jackson and Carter's position is also rooted primarily in a production of knowledge meta-narrative. Whereas they suggest that the process of knowledge production is characterized by incommensurability and diversity, and indeed by incommensurable products, they avoid discussion of the diversity and heterogeneity present similarly in processes of knowledge consumption. In other words, they overlook the fact that their response to the paradigm crisis is but one of the many 'tactics of consumption' deployed in the space of knowledge production. For Jackson and Carter, like Burrell and Morgan before, it is metatheory that determines identity. 'Otherness' is essentially the otherness of alternative paradigms, whose practices and discourses are to all intents and purposes located in other intellectual worlds.

Pluralists

As we outlined at length in Chapter 1, an increasing number of researchers have questioned the paradigm incommensurability thesis by advocating degrees of commensurability between paradigms, communication across paradigms, the need to engage in multiparadigm research, or by suggesting the need to move beyond paradigms by adopting a 'pragmatic' perspective. These researchers we call the *pluralists*. Whilst we do not wish to rehearse the arguments made in Chapter 1, suffice it to say that a core proposition of this group is that scientific paradigms can hold a range of concepts, constructs and practices in common. The pluralists, therefore, present us with various approaches to attaining a sense of paradigm commensurability in organizational theory and research. Their views, however, again subscribe primarily to a productionist meta-narrative in that they variously champion the development of a field of studies that is consensually multiparadigmatic. Consumption issues are rarely discussed in their work, as is any reflexive philosophy that would include simultaneous assessments of production and consumption. Instead, a strategy of multiple paradigm research is thrown onto the world as a demonstrably 'good thing' methodologically.

Postmodernists

Finally, the camp we term the *postmodernists*, adopts a reflexive perspective on knowledge production and consumption. Although, the label 'postmodernism' makes room for a wide pallet of competing positions, postmodernists usually champion and call for new types of knowledge, modes of writing, values and politics to overcome the deficiencies of modern discourses and practices (Best and Kellner, 1991). Although it is beyond the purpose of this chapter to chart the murky territory of postmodern thought, suffice to say that postmodernists typically rebuke the notion of paradigm as being fundamentally rooted in a production perspective on knowledge. In so doing, they call attention to acts of consumption in two major ways: first by inquiring into the ways in which researchers consume existing knowledge in order to construct new knowledge and second, by questioning the nature of research practices and their relation to prevailing organisational and societal discourses.

Deetz (1996) was among the first organization theorists to advocate this line of analysis. By shifting attention away from paradigmatic assumptions, he located research differences not in the ontological and epistemological assumptions of the individual researcher and the procedures or methodologies used, but in the modalities by which research concepts emerge, and the relation of research practices to the dominant discourses prevailing in organizations, the research community and the wider community. In pursuing this case, it can be argued that researchers promote a move from meta-narrative to *petit récit*, or in other words from 'grand' strategies of knowledge production to 'local' tactics of consumption.

Deetz (1996) argues that there are in fact four discourses available to organizational researchers, namely the normative, interpretive, critical and dialogic. Put briefly, the *normative* discourse relies on *a priori* research concepts and emphasizes consensus; the *interpretive* discourse, while stressing consensus, adopts an emergent perspective on the origin of concepts and problems; the *critical* discourse adheres to dissensus and *a priori* modes of conceptualisation; and the *dialogic* discourse embraces an emergent and dissentive logic of research (see Figure 2.1).

Deetz's classification calls attention to acts of consumption in two distinct ways. First, by questioning the processes by which research concepts emerge, Deetz calls into question the sort of knowledge researchers consume in order to produce their new categories. For Deetz, research concepts may be developed in relation to organizational members' day-to-day practices, as local and *emergent* concepts, or they may exist *a priori*, being brought to the research setting by researchers themselves. While in the first case concept development is the result of numerous and heterogeneous acts of consumption that act as bridges between the researcher and his/her subjects, in the later case, the researcher takes on board (consumes) the definition embraced by the scientific community.

Emergent research thrives on a multiplicity of language games. Theoretical vocabulary as established by the scientific community is considered only a starting point, and is constantly challenged and redefined by ulterior acts of consumption which involve the interplay between the researchers' and the field members' language-games. Knowledge is equated with insight rather than truth; with the temporal and contextual — with that which cannot be generalized.

A priori research, on the other hand, privileges the language game of the scientific community and tends to be theory-driven, with careful attention being

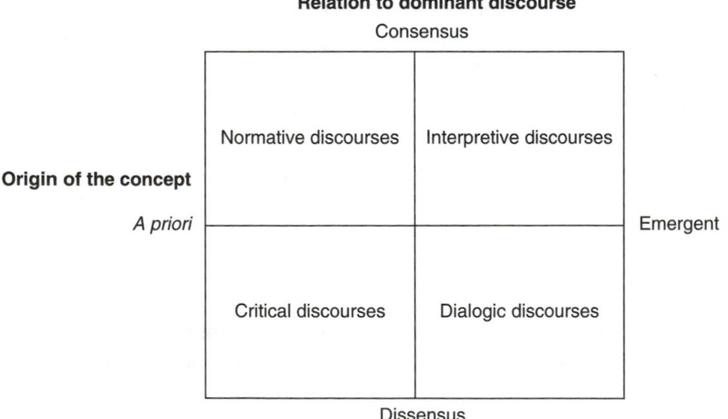

Figure 2.1 Postmodernist discourses
Source: Adapted from Deetz (1996)

paid to consuming definitions prior to the research process. There is a tendency to universalize while decoding the experiences of the objects of research into the language-game of the researcher. The knowledge produced is considered politically free and thus not bound by prevailing power relations and discourses.

Deetz's second point regarding acts of consumption concerns the relation between the knowledge produced and the prevailing social and scientific orders. If knowledge is consumed in such a way that it supports and reinforces an existing order, it is held to be of a *consensus* type. If the opposite is the case, i.e. consumption helps to problematize an existing order, it is held to be of a *dissensus* type.

Consensual knowledge is typically characterized by a search for order, integration and harmony. It focuses on representing existing order through a neutral language that allows the researcher to mirror the present and the consumer of knowledge to grasp its reality.[10] On the other hand, dissensus knowledge views order as historicized and politicized, attempting to deconstruct its pillars in as much as it suppresses conflict and struggle. Language is not seen to be a neutral instrument at the disposal of researchers but a means of reconstructing reality. The consumption of such knowledge is aimed at challenging taken-for-granted assumptions and social practices.[11]

While the normative and interpretive discourses may appeal to the dominant logic for purposes of legitimization, the remaining discourses 'witness *differands*' and thus (in Lyotard's 1997 sense) speak in the name of the 'unknown, unheard and absent'. As *petit récit*, such discourses are concerned with moves and countermoves which serve to limit processes of naturalization. They may be regarded as tactics of consumption, calculated actions determined by the absence of a 'proper' locus (de Certeau, 1984). Thus, from a postmodern perspective, consensus has become an outmoded and suspect value (Lyotard, 1997) and there is no reason to limit enquiry to a few paths marked by a particular elite (Kilduff and Mehra, 1997).

Conclusions

The chapter has considered the need to move away from a primarily productionist perspective on knowledge to one which embraces acts of production and consumption in a more reflexive way. In its strongest sense, the former emphasizes a hierarchy of sciences and bemoans the pre-paradigmatic state in which organizational studies finds itself. The latter, in contrast, points to the language-game character of science, the heterogeneous and slippery nature of knowledge and rejects any hypothetical science hierarchy.

We have discussed the need for a more reflexive approach on ontological and epistemological grounds. From an ontological point of view, it can be argued that the explanadum of organizational analysis has changed dramatically in the last few decades (Burrell, 1996, 2003; Casey, 2002; Jones and Munro, 2005). Organizations are now seen to inhabit a so-called postindustrial world where new forms of production and consumption have come into being. The bureaucratic organization, for example, is undermined by the network organization, the process-driven organization or the virtual organization. Fordist mass production has given way to post-Fordist technologies that allow for flexible specialization and niche marketing (Clegg, 1990; Casey, 1995; Jaffee, 2001). These new organizational realities point to the importance of the consumer in organizing both production and distribution (Bauman, 1998).

But it is not just the nature of organizational reality that has shifted, for new forms of knowing, or new 'explanans' (Lyotard, 1997) have accompanied the move from the industrial to postindustrial. The move from modernist to postmodernist epistemologies has allowed researchers to question not only the efficacy of *strong* productive forms, but also the conditions that make them possible and the role they have in (re)producing social and economic relations (Hassard and Parker, 1993; White and Jaques, 1995; Casey, 2002). In this view, knowledge and power are seen as intertwined. Knowledge cannot escape the regime of power that made it visible in the first place (Foucault, 1980). Rather than ultimate and objective, knowledge is tentative and slippery, located in a space populated by both its producers and consumers.

The chapter argues, therefore, that most responses to the paradigm 'crisis' are grounded primarily in a productionist meta-narrative on knowledge. For example, the non-consumers produce accounts of the organizational world without paying explicit attention to paradigmatic inclinations or language conventions in use. The protectionists insist that boundaries around paradigms must be protected and respected as they serve as mechanisms for protecting paradigm identity and legitimacy. In so doing, they vehemently oppose the dominant positivist discourse without acknowledging that their own response is a 'tactic of consumption' aimed at undermining the mainstream. The pluralists praise communication between paradigms and the importance of undertaking multiparadigm research. They do not believe in an inherent paradigmatic hierarchy but view each paradigm as a collection of shared, static assumptions rather than as a collection of dynamic language conventions. And the much-vaunted integrationist camp suggests that the scientific community needs to agree on a consensus paradigm in order to rescue the field from the pre-paradigmatic state in which it finds itself. In so doing, it elevates the process of knowledge production to a supreme status and downplays the role of researchers as consumers of knowledge. The present chapter, however, not only questions the aims served by this latter scenario but also engages in a postmodern project to undermine it. We agree with Burrell's (1996: 645) argument that:

> the idea that one voice could drown out the rest is an attractive one . . . but it is a dream which can never be realised fully. There will, thank goodness, always be the voices of dissent and the clamour of alternatives vying for aural space.

Furthermore, we suggest that the production of a unique organizational paradigm is improbable given the existence of heterogeneous 'tactics of consumption', i.e. *petit récit* which speak about 'the silent' and 'the invisible'. The consumption of knowledge cannot be systematically managed and regulated by institutions irrespective of the community motives and agendas that prevail.

3 Escaping the confines of organization theory (with Ian Atkin)

In this chapter we argue that the conceptual/textual representation of organization theory and analysis reflects a system of intellectual self-imprisonment. In a further case analysis, we claim that attempts by the early proponents of 'radical separatism' to release themselves from this confinement resulted only in their recapture. We contend that this was largely inevitable, given that radical separatism — predominantly in the guise of the original agenda for Radical Organization Theory (see Benson, 1977a; Burrell and Morgan, 1979; Clegg and Dunkerley, 1980) — failed to break with the conventions of representation within orthodox, systems-based or functionalist theories of organization. We argue further that this assessment can be applied similarly to recent attempts to specify an agenda for Critical Management Studies (see Alvesson and Willmott, 1992; Fournier and Grey, 2000; Casey, 2002; Grey, 2004).

Given this contention, we speculate upon a different approach for the liberation of radical/critical theories of organization from the hegemony of what has traditionally been termed the 'functionalist orthodoxy', one based theoretically on the fluid process of 'undecidability'. Unusually this form of liberation is realized through disruption from *within* the conventions of orthodox organizational analysis. Our approach sees Luce Irigaray's (1985b, 1991a, 1991b) notion of the enactment of textual mimicry adopted to open what we call the 'extra' of organizational life — that which is situated outside, excess, otherness, the space beyond. We wish to explore theoretically that which is predominantly excluded as 'excess' by an empowered and hegemonic functionalist community. To liberate the feminine, Irigaray mimics the symbolic representation of the female body to excess so as to expose the contradictions of phallocentric discourse. When applied to organization theory, this sees a deliberate mimicking of critiques of radical separatism so as to make explicit the latter's imprisonment within functionalism. Through excessive mimicking of the functionalists' critique, the radical/critical organization theorist may become cognizant of, but perhaps not so subjugated by, the hegemony of functionalist discourse.

In sum, through a retrospective case analysis we suggest that the mimicry of functionalism's representation of the original attempt to establish a Radical

Organization Theory agenda may provide the conditions, if not the solution, to effect the radical/critical theorist's escape; this is an escape, via what Irigaray (1985b) calls the 'residue', to the discourse of the 'other' (Cooper, 1983, 1990) in organizational analysis.

Escaping the confines of organization theory?

It is difficult to escape the authoritative discourse of organization theory. This is the outcome of the theorist-author being confined within a chain of statements that represent the organization. The predominant definition of the organization is 'a circumscribed administrative-economic function' (Cooper and Burrell, 1988: 92). As such, the textual topography of organization theory is a confined 'inside', a boundary of exclusion. As Pugh writes: 'organization theory can be defined as the study of the structure, function and performance of organizations, and the behaviour of groups and individuals *within* them' (Pugh, 1990: ix — emphasis added).

As intellectual capital, the orthodox concept of organization was described in Morgan's (1986) well-known book on metaphor as a fundamental construct of the 'psychic prison' of management thought. It can be argued that increasingly this prison is guarded and managed by officers of the academy of administrative sciences, and specifically of the (USA-based) Academy of Management. The prison metaphor suggests that the 'formal' organization is a disciplined space, with the term 'formal' being an imperative that privileges order. For those sympathetic to radical/critical approaches to management studies, this order is reproduced *inter alia* through the theories and methods of functionalist organizational analysis (Cooper and Burrell, 1988; Casey, 2002; Grey, 2004).

Cognizant of the hegemonic discourse of mainstream organization theory, the early proponents of radical separatism (e.g. Benson, 1977a, 1977b; Goldman and Van Houten, 1977; Burrell and Morgan, 1979; Burrell, 1980; Clegg and Dunkerley, 1980) sought emancipation through developing distinct intellectual gestures from those of functionalism. In their work, emancipation was the outcome of an escape from the powerful institutional consensus of systems theory. Thus: 'the immediate need is for "paradigmatic closure" — a clear-cut separation of radical organization theory from its orthodox functionalist counterpoint' (Burrell, 1980: 92).

The motivation to establish a separate voice arose from the apparent under-development of radical theories of organization (Burrell, 1980). This lack of a self-sustaining capacity was based upon the tendency for radical theorists to become ensnared by the very concepts they sought to reject. As the metaphors of orthodox theory remained the agency of mediation, the radical theorist became influenced by the writings of 'a community of scholars to whom [s/he] is in many ways fundamentally opposed' (Burrell, 1980: 91). Although these metaphors were not directly identified by Burrell, they were indicative of modes of thought which enabled the conventions of 'the orthodoxy' to 'govern the terms of all debate' (Burrell, 1980: 91).

The primary task, therefore, of what was to become the main tangible product of radical separatism, Radical Organization Theory, was to create a self-sustaining discourse built on independent philosophical traditions. To realize a truly emancipatory analysis of organization, organizations and organizing, radical theorists advocated a policy of intellectual separatism. Without such sectarianism, it was felt that the metaphoric conventions of conservative systems thinking would continue to govern the radical theorist's self-concepts.

Analytical openings: undecidability, intertexuality and the index

It can be argued, however, that the attempts by the early radical separatists to develop a distinct theoretical position inevitably ran up against the 'theorizing power' (Clegg, 1979) of organizational science's conceptual/textual representations and institutions. This made the development of an emancipatory discourse difficult, if not impossible, because radical critiques were themselves defined as institutionally 'orderly'. This orderliness was perhaps inevitable, given the power of the academy over the professional life-world of the theorist.[1]

Although this may appear a mischievous claim — for during the past 30 years or so the hegemony of functionalist theory has been challenged, decade-on-decade, by 'alternative agendas' (from Silverman, 1970; through Burrell, 1980; to Alvesson and Willmott, 1992; and recently Fournier and Grey, 2000; Casey, 2002; Grey, 2004, etc.) — we feel it can be justified through reference to analysis that takes recourse to the postmodern metaphor of 'undecidability'. To identify logical problems with attempts to escape from the confines of conceptual/textual representation, we can draw upon conceptions of undecidability in, for example, Cooper's (1986, 1990) analysis of 'organization/disorganization', Derrida's (1981a) work on inter-textual mime, and the Art & Language movement's construction of the 'Index' of intellectual capital (Harrison, 1991).

To open up the undecidability of organizational analysis, Cooper (1990) argues that texts on that discourse called 'organization theory' represent the supplementary 'organization of organization'. He notes that often texts on organization are themselves organized according to a set of normalized scientific and/or academic criteria. As the content of a study of organization — and the theoretical or methodological context that frames the text — are indistinguishable, it follows that a text does not strictly add information on the study of organization, for it also produces statements on that which it designates to *be* organization. In this way, the text, as supplementary, 'includes itself in the structure it seeks to analyse and understand, therefore creating undecidability' (Cooper, 1990: 197).

Textual undecidability, however, is not restricted to a single text. Derrida (1981a) for instance offers the example of a reading of Mallarme's *Mimique* to illustrate the point. This story revolves around a mime whose gestures imitate no tradition of mime, and whose performance of a *pierrot* who murders his unfaithful wife appears to be unscripted. In sum an original mime. Derrida's reading, however, reveals the self-deceptions that have been hidden within the text of this unscripted mime. This reading finds that at the moment Mallarme begins his story it is, already, caught up within a chain of supplementary inscriptions.

To expand, Mallarme bases his story on a 'second edition of a pamphlet'. The author of the pamphlet, Beissier, had been a witness to the mime of the murder five years previously. The reader of Mallarme's text is, therefore, confronted by a story that is already composed of multiple writings and readings. Mallarme's mime artist is not inventing the script, but is rather a phase in a chain of textual representation and transmission. While Mallarme's story concerns an original mime, it must admit to the lack of an original foundation or logos. Derrida's reading of *Mimique* thus invokes the notion of an infinite chain of representations.

To prevent representations taking on the form of an infinite set of readings, it can be argued by implication that the academies of administrative science (e.g. the annual meeting and journals of the Academy of Management) control meaning by defining the limits of intellectual authority. In everyday academic discourse, this is achieved through specifying what shall count as the bounded networks of intertextuality.[2]

The control by the academy of both the textual representation of the concept 'organization' and the network of intertextual mimes through which it is expressed can be encapsulated, we feel, in the notion of the 'Index' of intellectual capital (Harrison, 1991). We have appropriated this metaphor from the notion of 'indexes' designed and constructed by the members of the Art & Language movement. For Art & Language, it is the theorizing power of the Index which enables the various textual statements made by its members about art to be connected (Harrison, 1991). By extension to organization theory, the Index of intellectual capital represents a repository for the textual materials of the academy of administrative science. The Index is the ordering technology for referencing representations of a concept, and thus the means by which the reproduction of a discourse is controlled. It brings together written materials in a way compatible with its intentional object.

The Index, however, is not a passive technology, for while circumscribed it still allows readers to add ('within reason') representations through the cross-referencing of conceptual chains. Through its ability to define what shall count as authentic or reasonable knowledge, the Index plays a role similar to Eco's (1984) librarian in *The Name of the Rose*, who informs the monks in the scriptorium of partial chains of reference in order that mysteries remain unsolved.

In seeking to develop an emancipatory alternative for organization analysis, therefore, the aim of our analysis is largely to disrupt the hegemony of the index of organization theory. It can be argued that the way to disclose the conventions of orthodoxy in organization theory is through a breaching of its boundary characteristics. This is important for it makes known the undecidable moment between what a text permits in meaning and what it constrains.

To explore the possibilities for an alternative emancipatory analysis, our method is to invert the original incommensurability thesis of radical separatism and instead work from *within* the conventions of orthodox organization theory. As the discourses and institutions of orthodox organization theory largely inhibit the realization of a separatist analysis, we argue that the liberation of the radical/critical theorist's selfhood — the perceptible self-images of what we might call an 'extra-radical' position — may arise from within its mirror image, as represented by systems/functionalist analysis.[3] These self-images will be articulated through a reading of Luce Irigaray's (1985b, 1991a) enactment of mimicry.

Prior to this, however, it is necessary to consider that part of Irigaray's work from which the thesis on mimicry arises. Two objectives inform this consideration. The first is to introduce, albeit partially, the writing of Irigaray to organization theory, an academic specialization in which her work is little known. The second is to identify the mimetic gestures which Irigaray deploys in her use of mimicry in order that we may mime the 'excess' of organization theory.[4]

Irigaray and mimicry

Irigaray's work is concerned in part with the liberation of the feminine from phallocentric structures of discourse. To achieve this Irigaray deliberately mimics the oppressive symbolic representation of the female body to excess, so as to make explicit, by playful repetition, woman's exploitation through the representation of the feminine by masculine discourse.

The function of Irigaray's mimetic gesturing, however, is not to overthrow the phallocentric order, nor to elaborate a new theory of which 'woman' would be the subject or the object. Less ambitiously, it is to emphasize the theoretical self-disruptions of 'suspending its [the phallocentric discourse's] pretension to the production of a truth and of a meaning that are excessively univocal' (Irigaray, 1991a: 126). Through thus disrupting the phallocentric discourse, it can be argued that Irigaray potentially opens up a set of conditions for altering the status of woman in society (Whitford, 1988).

The intellectual location from which mimetic analysis emerges is the sexualization of discourse. For Irigaray, it is primarily Freud's work which portrays 'the sexual indifference that underlies the truth of any science, the logic of every discourse' (Irigaray, 1991a: 118). While in this sense sexual indifference has a long history, Irigaray maintains that its effects are hidden. In Irigaray's reading of Freud, this covert indifference becomes apparent in the way female sexuality is defined in masculine terms. The feminine is always described in terms of 'lack' or 'deficiency', for instance in the theory of penis envy.

The statements of Freud that describe feminine sexuality, therefore, fail to note that the female might have its own specificity. Freud does not identify two sexes whose differences are articulated in the act of intercourse, or more generally speaking in the imaginary and symbolic processes that regulate the workings of society and culture. Rather, the feminine is defined as either a complement to the operation of male sexuality or, more commonly, as a negative image that provides male sexuality with an unfailing phallic self-representation.

Irigaray suggests, however, that Freud, rather than making original statements about male or female sexuality, is merely describing an actual state of affairs. As a 'man of science', Freud accounts for sexuality without examining the contextualizing historical factors (Irigaray, 1991a: 119). He takes female sexuality as he sees it, and accepts this as normative. Women's dissatisfactions — epitomized perhaps in the case of 'hysterical Dora' — are artefacts of individual histories whose resolution is achieved through women's submission to a rapport with the father-figure. The pathology of these cases is not questioned in relation to differing styles of society or culture. The specific demands of women are thus silenced.

Freud's account of this actual state of affairs, however, itself emerges from the sexualization of discourse — for it is caught up within the presuppositions of the production of discourse, presuppositions which Freud does not fully analyze. This demands a challenge to such philosophical discourse 'inasmuch as it constitutes the discourse on discourse' (Irigaray, 1991a: 122). The domination of this discourse derives, to a large extent, from its power to reduce all other discourses to the 'economy of the "Same" ' (Irigaray, 1991a: 123). Its fundamental power of domination is to eradicate the differences between the sexes in systems that are self-representative of the masculine subject.

Irigaray intends to disrupt such domination by opening up the main figures of philosophical discourse — substance, subject, absolute knowledge, etc. — in order to make visible what they have 'borrowed' — 'that is feminine, from the feminine, to make them "render up" and give back what they owe the feminine' (Irigaray, 1991a: 123). To accomplish this, the feminine must disrupt the coherence of discursive statements whose very coherence hides the conditions of their production. Coherence can only be maintained so long as it is not interrogated through the process of interpretive re-reading.

In order to open up the 'economy of the Same', Irigaray calls for a re-enactment of each figure of discourse. She argues that while woman as a 'residue' (Irigaray, 1985b: 114) is beyond a conceptual grasp — because she is defined as feminine by the masculine subject — she nevertheless possesses the facility ('of the "perceptible" of "matter" '; Irigaray, 1991a: 124) to recover ideas about herself which are elaborated in and by masculine logic. This responsibility to 'otherness' is accessed through playing the mime of the historically assigned feminine, which sees the feminine role assumed deliberately, so as to make visible, by repetition, that which is supposed to remain outside. By excessively interpreting and repeating the way in which the feminine finds itself defined as lack, deficiency, or as the imitation of the masculine subject, this gesture converts a form of exploitation into one of affirmation. For woman to play a mime is to try to rescue the place of her exploitation by discourse, while challenging the authority of discourse to be reproduced by it. Such a challenge makes visible 'residue', or 'excess' (Irigaray, 1991a) on the feminine side.

An 'extra-radical' intervention?

It can be argued that Irigaray's work presents the opportunity to develop what might be termed an 'extra-radical' intervention for organization theory. Theoretically this intervention sees excessive mimicry employed as just one medium for opening up the *extra* of social life.

The catalyst for this extra-radical intervention is Irigaray's comments on women's exploitation through the discourse of political economy. Irigaray (1991a) asks how can women analyze their own exploitation and inscribe their own demands within an order prescribed by the masculine? For Irigaray the demand for women's equality and difference cannot be articulated by the acceptance of a choice between 'class struggle' and 'sexual warfare'. This alternative serves only to minimize the question of the exploitation of women through a definition of power of the masculine type; it also implies putting-off a woman's politics until an unknown date.

Expanding upon this theme, Irigaray argues anyway that the relationship between economic class oppression and patriarchy has not been subject to sufficient dialectical analysis. She claims that the first class opposition was that between men and women in monogamous marriage. This opposition coincided with that of the oppression of the female sex by the male. Although this early antagonism signifies a first movement in class history, its associated oppression still remains normative. Through the established monopolization of private property, patriarchal order functions to the benefit of the head of the family. As a result, women are exploited in most exchange operations, be they sexual, economic, social or cultural. Irigaray writes: 'the use, consumption, and circulation of their sexualized bodies underwrite the organization and the reproduction of the social order in which they have never taken part as "subjects"' (Irigaray, 1991a: 131).

If this general relationship holds, how can women claim the right to speak and participate in non-exploitative exchange? A woman's social inferiority is reinforced and complicated by the fact that she does not have a language except through reference to masculine systems of representation. The feminine is never to be identified except by and for the masculine.

Such oppression does, however, present an opportunity for elaborating a feminist critique of patriarchal discourse. This is based on the disrupting enactment of mime outlined earlier. A radical mime of political economy holds that women are in a position 'outside' of the laws of exchange, even though they are included 'inside' them as commodities. This sets in train a 'discourse on discourse' by a residue, woman, who is ostensibly beyond the conceptual boundary of political economy (Irigaray, 1991a).

The mime is enacted through an excessive, yet seemingly playful, mimicking of the dominant patriarchal discourse. Otherness is accessed through disrupting the coherence of economic statements whose very coherence hides the condition of their production. A radical mime is accomplished through playing to excess the role of the historically assigned, exploitable female. The mimic muses excessively on what would become of the symbolic process that governs society if it were not for the metaphysical exploitation of the feminine 'other'? Through excessive gestures of the masculine subject, exploitation is converted into an affirmation of the economic position of the feminine. By mimicking personal economic status, the subject becomes knowing of, but not subjugated by, the objective situation.

Mimesis and organizational analysis

When this analysis is applied to what arguably has been a historically similar inequitable relationship — that between mainstream theory and attempts to establish radical separatism in organizational analysis — it charts an undecidable analysis through the residues of the former's representation of the latter. In concrete terms, these residues can be defined by excessively mimicking, for example, the various functionalist critiques of radical separatism (see e.g. Donaldson, 1985, 1996a; Pfeffer, 1993, 1997; McKelvey, 2003). As extravagant mimics of themselves — at least as understood by the academy of administrative science — radical theorists can become aware of, but not enslaved by, their own subordination. Excessive mimicry can convert its otherness into an affirmation. As the radical theorist sets in motion this process of self-radicalization, the authoritative conventions of functionalist organization theory are terrorized.

A reading of one of the best-known functionalist critiques of radical separatism scripts such a mime. The contingency theorist Lex Donaldson in his book *In Defence of Organization Theory: A Reply to the Critics* (1985) considered Radical Organization Theory and its associated sociological paradigm, radical-structuralism, actually to be commensurable with structural-functionalism (see pages 40–46). This representation draws on what he reads to be a contrary position within the writings of the 'critics' of organization theory — that factional and catastrophic models of change are not necessarily incompatible within the functionalist framework.

The critics' position is basically that 'radical' structuralism and 'functional' structuralism arise from distinct theories of society. The former suggests deep connections between social structures and radical change: the latter a relationship between social formations and regulated order (Burrell and Morgan, 1979: 400). Donaldson, however, counterpoises these differences with the actual comments made in the critical literature. Specifically, he cites Burrell and Morgan's (1979) continuum of change in system theory models, where: 'the mechanical, organismic and morphogenic models are consistent with a perspective characteristic of the functionalist paradigm; the . . . [factional and catastrophic models] . . . are more characteristic of the radical-structuralist paradigm' (Burrell and Morgan, 1979: 66).

It is the definition of factional and catastrophic models which provides Donaldson with the means to dispose of the radical 'other' through reconciliation of radical-structuralism and structural-functionalism. His vehicle for achieving this is a reading of Merton (1975), who argues that the concepts of contradiction (from Marxism) and dysfunction (from structural-functionalism) are complementary. To make these two concepts commensurable, and thus to bring change into the social system, Donaldson makes similar assertions. He begins by writing that the outputs of one sub-system may be dysfunctional for other parts. In this way, 'the essential notion of conflict has been *introduced*' (Donaldson, 1985: 40 emphasis added). Subsequently Donaldson postulates that such 'flows' of functioning between system parts will increasingly produce dysfunctions which 'overstrain' the system, the outcome being that the breakdown of the system is followed by its subsequent reorganization. This allows Donaldson to provide an account of contradiction and crisis in 'systems rather than Marxian terms' (Donaldson, 1985: 41).

It is Donaldson's next move, however, which opens his text for the enactment of a radical mime. Having reduced contradiction and dysfunction to comparable meanings, he ambitiously attempts to *subsume* radical-structuralism within a structural-functionalism framework. For Donaldson, radical-structuralism concerns the historically specific structures of feudalism and capitalism and the change from one to the other. As such, 'it should be seen as a *sub-type* of structural-functionalism which deals with those historical issues and which posits crisis and revolutionary change as the mechanisms of transition' (Donaldson, 1985: 41, emphasis added). Donaldson thus facilitates the incorporation of radical-structuralism as a *sub-set* into the structural-functionalist framework, the very notion to which the critics object.

Following the path laid by Irigaray (1991a, 1991b) it is possible to open this text to perceptible residues, so as to enable a responsibility to otherness in a way that disrupts the conventional discourse of orthodox organization theory. Here, that which is 'perceptible' is the conceptual mechanism of the 'flows' between systems parts. Donaldson's elucidation of flow begins with an attempt to make two quotations in Burrell and Morgan (1979) complementary — one by Radcliffe-Brown from the functionalist paradigm, the other by Rex from the radical-structuralist paradigm:

> The concept of function as defined thus involves the notion of a *structure* consisting of a *set of relations* amongst *unit entities*, the *community* of the structure being maintained by a *life process* made up of the *activities* of the constituent units.
>
> (Radcliffe-Brown, 1952: 180; quoted in Burrell and Morgan, 1979: 52 — emphasis in original)

> [S]ocial systems may be thought of as involving conflict situations at central points . . . The existence of such a situation tends to produce not a unitary but a *plural society*, in which there are two or more classes . . . The activities of the members [of the classes] . . . must be explained by reference to the group's interests in the conflict situation.
>
> (Rex, 1961: 129, quoted in Burrell and Morgan, 1979: 353 — emphasis in original)

For Donaldson, while these statements are not identical, once their terminological differences have been stripped away the only issue which remains is the pervasiveness of negative flows in the social system. The flows between parts can be positive or negative. Positive flows are those that assist the continuation and development of the recipient unit entity: negative flows impair continuation and development. A negative relationship between two entities amounts to a 'situation of conflict' (Donaldson, 1985: 42), with the entities involved in a conflict situation being classes.

Donaldson suggests that the only part of the radical-structuralist paradigm that now seems inconsistent with structural-functionalism is the argument that negative relationships between unit entities (classes) are a pervasive and persistent characteristic of the social system. To overcome this difficulty, Donaldson suggests that the problem is not a fundamental category difference, but is rather a 'matter of degree' (Donaldson, 1985: 43). Furthermore, he argues that this 'degree' — the balance of negative or positive flows, the variation between capitalist societies because of this balance, and its change over time — can apparently be tested empirically. To write, however, that change as flow is a 'matter of degree' is to close off or give value to the level of positive or negative flow. And yet to close off and give coherence to change cannot encapsulate all change. It is a reduction of that which is always a residue or excess.

Undecidability and the zero degree

To transform Donaldson's decidability into mimetic undecidability, we return to Cooper (1986, 1990), who — from a reading of Levi-Strauss (1950, 1966, 1979); Simmel (1965, 1980); and Derrida (1978) — offers an explanation of the undecidability of this excess, or the 'zero degree'.

The zero degree amounts to pervading undecidability: an excess 'of no specific order, organization or direction' (Cooper, 1990: 182). Cooper draws upon Derrida's (1978: see pages 278–293) notion that structure — and Cooper adds 'organization' — is conceived by tradition in a limited form, this being the presence of a 'fixed centre of point of origin' (Cooper, 1990: 183). In Cooper's reading of Derrida, this centre has two functions: one is to orient and balance the structure in a coherent way; the other, and more important, function, is for the principle of the structure to limit 'the *play* of the structure' (Derrida, 1978: 278, quoted in Cooper, 1990: 183). The centre's ability to organize the structure allows for the play of elements inside the 'structurality of the structure' (Derrida, 1978: 278).

The process of centring, however, both opens up and closes off play, in that to close off play it must exile from itself the play that is more than the 'structurality' of structure. As the means of a responsibility to act, the flows of negative change are played to excess as a responsibility to otherness. That is, the flow of change as a matter of degree is always, inasmuch as it is perceptible, an excess — the zero degree. Not everything, therefore, is carried along with the flow, for a residue or excess always remains outside the bounded frame of the inside of the organization.

Cooper (1990) suggests that the frame differentiates between an ordered inside and a disordered outside. The former corresponds to organization and the latter to disorganization. Cooper's specific working through of the framing of the boundary between the binary pairing 'system and environment' takes place within a clearly defined framework. The function of the frame is to privilege the system: 'the boundary belongs to the system and not to the environment' (Cooper, 1990: 170). Indeed 'in its most fundamental sense organization is the appropriation of order out of disorder' (Cooper, 1990: 172).

Through his reading of Derrida (1978), Cooper motions a further development: that the order of the inside of the boundary is attainable if the outside or disorganization is an excess or a supplement. In its desire to be complete, the order of organization discards the surplus. But this can never be complete, for without the surplus of disorder it has a lacuna. This lacuna can only be filled by the disorder of the undesired supplement necessarily constituting the meaning of the inside. Without the disorder of the outside, the order of the inside is meaningless.

In Donaldson (1985), however, we are confronted with the blunt, decidable assertion that when radical-structuralism is adopted as an organization theory it avoids any excess in terms of the ideological representation of organization. While this manoeuvre allows structural-functionalism and radical-structuralism to be presented as complementary, it also reveals the undecidable moment of their relationship. This attempt at commensurability or subsumption sets in motion the image of their incommensurability, which stems from the differing levels of analysis that each would address. While the index of orthodox organization theory primarily locates characteristics of administrative structures, that of radical-structuralism references economic and political change at the societal level. Thus as a form of organizational analysis, the dynamic of radical-structuralism is to establish significance in terms of large-scale political dislocation. Donaldson's argument falters in that the undecidable character of their reconciliation requires the subordination of orthodox organization theory to the principle of organizational analysis as a means of revealing conflict and change in the wider society. For Donaldson this is anathema.

The fate of radical separatism

Conversely, a reading of the attempt by radical separatists to develop an emancipatory organization theory also reveals similar mimetic tensions. Previously it was noted that Burrell (1980) made a series of exploratory moves in line with advocating radical-structuralism as a genuine paradigmatic alternative to an orthodox organization theory 'which ubiquitously confronts us' (Burrell, 1980: 98). For Burrell a radical-structuralist paradigm has no place for the notion of a social system which is open to its environment, or for related discussions of external forces and causal flows. This is because the totality draws the boundary around that which is theoretically relevant. The totality does not take recourse to that form of systems thinking which asserts that the social whole is greater than the sum of its parts. Instead an adequate theory of the part is a theory of the totality, just as a theory of the totality is a theory of the part.

Burrell's text, however, only rehearses the ideological conventions of the representation of bounded organization. He assumes that in 'late capitalism' the mechanism of totality integration is the organization itself, for it is currently found at the point of production where labour and capital meet. This mechanism has in fact taken various forms. Under early capitalism the role of integrating the social formation or social relations of production was fulfilled by the family. Just as the family was replaced as the primary unit of production, in the future organization may be replaced as the mechanism of totality integration.

Furthermore, as the current mechanism for totality integration, we know that the organization must create an inside-outside boundary of its own. Just as Donaldson's (1985) scripting of the mime of radical-structuralism could not account for the residue of flow, so this boundary cannot account for the excess of exploitation and oppression that radical-structuralism tries to give voice. Exploitation belongs to and is maintained by the 'inside' of the organization through the established social relations of capital and labour. The inside is privileged over the outside or other.

It can be argued, therefore, that radical separatism, in the form of the original project of Radical Organization Theory, ultimately failed its manifesto, for its rhetoric invoked the image of established and orthodox social systems concepts. Although radical separatists claimed to develop an autonomous political space, that space took recourse ultimately to many functionalist conventions. As its aim was primarily to change the distribution of organizational representation, it left the power structure intact (see Gergen, 1992). Because its discourse was structured essentially by systems concepts, radical separatism was largely 'intra-institutional' (Derrida, 1983) and could almost be described as an 'orthodox-radical' approach. In many ways the same accusation can be levelled at its direct descendent, Critical Management Studies, notably over its failure to influence organizational practice. In sum, although radical separatism has sought emancipation and otherness, it can be argued that it largely remains subject to the same institutional protocols and symbolic representations as the academy of 'orthodox' organization theory.

Conclusions

Developing a sensitivity towards the *extra*, *excess* or *other* of organizational life, the chapter has argued that the intellectual products of those who subscribe to a philosophy of radical separatism serve mainly to bolster the hegemonic conventions of orthodox/mainstream representations of organizational analysis. To a large extent this results from such writers failing to disrupt the inside/outside boundary of organization. It has been argued, theoretically, that a sense of self-emancipation can be achieved through disrupting orthodox conventions of representation and giving 'otherness' a voice. To achieve this, the circumscribed boundary of orthodox organizational analysis must be terrorized. Through reference to Irigaray's (1991a) work on mimicry, we have suggested that the excess which the boundary cannot contain informs a responsibility to act on behalf of those who are 'othered'.

Part II

Alternative concepts

4 Actor-networks and sociological symmetry (with Christine McLean)

In Part II, we consider a series of concepts and relationships for an alternative organizational analysis to explore and develop; these are namely, *actor-networks and sociological symmetry; fluidity and identity; time and temporality; decoration and disorganization;* and *governmentality and networks*. In the present chapter, we focus on actor-network theory (ANT). Following an introduction to ANT, the chapter discusses key issues which underlie the production of ANT accounts, such as, the inclusion and exclusion of actors; the treatment of humans and non-humans; the role of agency and structure; notions of ontology, space and time; and the nature of politics and power. In so doing we also discuss the relationships between such issues and one of the underlying aims of ANT in terms of achieving a sense of 'general symmetry' in the accounting process. This will involve noting how ANT authors are frequently chastised for either failing to take sufficient account of, or promoting too strong a sense of, analytical symmetry in their writing. Therefore, within this chapter we will explore a major challenge facing ANT research on organizations with regards to producing accounts that are robust enough to negate the twin charges of symmetrical absence and symmetrical absurdity.

What is actor-network theory?

Originating primarily in Science and Technology Studies, ANT is an increasingly popular analytical method used within a range of social science fields. This approach gains much of its notoriety through advocating a socio-philosophical approach in which, for example, human and non-human, and social and technical factors are brought together in the same analytical view. In attempting to comprehend complex social situations, ANT highlights the problems of sundering aspects such as the human and non-human, the social and technical, and the structural and agentic. In a much cited article, Michel Callon (1986) warns, for example, of the dangers of 'changing register' when we move from concerns with the social to those of the technical. The methodological philosophy is that all ingredients of socio-technical analysis be explained by common practices.

While issues of power are of central concern for ANT this area also raises complex problems. It is argued, when discussing the production and reproduction of networks of heterogeneous relations and 'actants' (this term being employed to suggest that both humans and non-humans be included in the analysis) there is often a war-like vocabulary with reference to trials of force, struggles and the assembly of alliances. Forces of the social and the technical are accounted for through a process of 'generalized symmetry', a method that employs a common analytical vocabulary for interpreting such phenomena. In this accounting process any *a priori* separation of the social and the physical world is prohibited (Callon, 1986). Thus, the actor-network (a purposively oxymoronic term) is realized through the common 'enrolling' of human and non-human participants into a network through processes of negotiation and translation.

When we seek to translate the ANT approach into the sphere of organizational analysis, we are involved in the analysis of alliances or networks that 'initiate and maintain the superordination of individuals or groups over others' (Grint, 1998: 142). We are thus reminded that many actors are locked into networks that may exist outside the focus of many organization studies. In addition, managerial networks take recourse not just to the network of peer managers and the control over material resources with the organization, but also, for example, to the resources of the legal system and domestic sources of support, which are 'invisibly meshed into the organization's disciplinary mechanisms' (ibid: 149). As Latour (1987) demonstrated similarly, scientists physically isolated from the rest of the world in their search for knowledge are actually highly dependent upon a large array of supportive networks 'outside' the laboratory.

In accounting for such processes, the character of the actor-network emerges as a contingent phenomenon. As noted, actor-networks are relentlessly produced and reproduced. The point here is not whether the actants of a network are social or technical, but, as Latour (1987: 140) points out, 'which associations are stronger and which are weaker'. In a later discussion Latour (1992) gives the 'mundane' example of hoteliers attempting to discipline their guests to leave room keys at the reception desk, rather than taking the keys outside with them. He explains that to make an impression on this practice the hotelier adds various elements to the key, including a verbal request, an inscription on the key and, if this still fails, increasing the weight or size of the key so that it becomes difficult to carry around. As the entities enrolled in the network have their own strategic preferences, the problem for the 'enroller', therefore, is to ensure that participants adhere to the enroller's interests and that in some way they can both begin to share similar interests. Such studies also enable the researcher to focus on these translating interests, delegations, and agency as an outcome of the process rather than existing in some *a priori* and coherent form.

ANT could thus be seen to provide specific conceptual tools that assist when studying the assembling and stabilization of diverse human and non-human entities, within diffuse socio-material systems (Hassard *et al.*, 1999; Law, 1999). In the field of management and organization studies, the use of these tools has been part of a movement away from a formal-functional emphasis on organization as an entity towards the study of processes and practices of organizing, and importantly socio-technical organizing (Bloomfield and Vurdubakis, 1999; Calás and

Smircich, 1999; Hull, 1999; Lee and Hassard, 1999; Newton 2002). ANT has been used by writers to examine a wide range of research issues within management and organization studies, and within the area of information systems and technology studies ANT has been applied in rather different forms (see Bloomfield *et al.*, 1992; Bowers, 1992; Bloomfield and Vurdubakis, 1994, 1999; Hine, 1995; Bloomfield and McLean, 1996; Boland and Schultze, 1996; Bowker *et al.*, 1996; Monterio and Hanseth, 1996; Vidgen and McMaster, 1996; Introna and Whitley, 1997; Silva and Blackhouse, 1997).

On introducing ANT we should note also that the research produced often differs markedly in terms of methodological approach and style of analysis. Even authors who are generally considered key figures in the ANT community differ in the way they see research activity progressing. For example, in *Actor Network Theory and After* (Law and Hassard, 1999) — a book which brought together many leading writers (such as Bruno Latour, Michel Callon and John Law) to debate key concerns — we find contrasting and divergent thoughts expressed on ANT and its future role in socio-material analysis.

Bruno Latour (1999a), for example, declares that for him there are four things wrong with 'actor-network theory' — actor, network, theory and the hyphen! First, he suggests that the term *network* is problematic in that it has been subjected to a process of 'transport with deformation'. As such, it is associated increasingly with 'an instantaneous, unmediated access to every piece of information' (Latour, 1999a: 15). For Latour, this rather ubiquitous view contradicts with *his* view of 'network', for it appears progressively to negate opportunities for critique (a point made similarly by Law, 1999, in reference to the metaphorical baggage carried by 'network' in its associations with computer networks, social networks, railway networks etc.). Second, Latour problematizes the notion of *actor*, especially with regard to its hyphenated connection to network. In particular, he highlights the way in which this coupling of terms has led to a number of misunderstandings, not least of which is the way the agency/structure debate has re-emerged within associated discussions of ANT (this issue will be addressed in greater detail later). Finally, Latour points out that ANT was never a *theory*, and in particular never a theory of the social, a theory of the subject, or a theory of nature. In contrast, Latour describes ANT as a 'very crude method to learn from the actors without imposing on them an *a priori* definition of their world building capacities' (Latour, 1999a: 20).

Michel Callon (1999: 194) similarly is ready 'not only to recall ANT, but possibly to change the model and to launch a new range'. While he agrees that the 'theory' part must go, he claims to be more 'optimistic' about actor-networks. Callon engages much less in critique and more on the contributions of ANT and a strategy for developing the approach. This includes an appreciation of the methodological power of concepts such as framing, disentanglement and the calculative agent. In particular Callon describes the complex tasks that underlie the making of economic simplicity (see also Law, 1999). Callon responds to the criticism that ANT is inadequate with regard to its theory of the actor by suggesting, like Latour, that one of ANT's strengths is that it has never been a 'theory' of the actor.

Finally, John Law's (1999) discussion of ANT begins with a set of stories in which the actor-network is converted into a smooth and consistent 'theory', but one that for him has been too easily 'displaced, criticised or applied'. Law (1999) notes the paradox he finds himself in with reference to producing ANT accounts. On the one hand he makes ANT a fixed point, and acts as a 'spokesperson for this name'; on the other, he argues 'against fixity and singularity'. Overall, Law suggests that ANT has been:

> a semiotic machine for waging war on essential differences … and has indeed helped to destabilize Euclideanism: it has shown that what appears to be topographically natural, given in the order of the world, is in fact produced in networks which perform a quite different spatiality.
>
> (Law, 1999: 4)

A major problem for Law (1999: 5), however, is that the topological assumptions underlying ANT have in turn been 'naturalized', limiting the conditions of spatial and relational possibility and 'tending to homogenize them'. While the approach is viewed as providing a significant contribution to the study of science and technology, for Law there remain grave concerns regarding its generic methodological application.

Constructing actor-network accounts

Having introduced ANT, we now turn to the main aim of the chapter, which is to examine a range of ANT issues, problems and criticisms in relation to the development of social theory and social science method. We will address, *inter alia*, concerns related to: the inclusion/exclusion of actors; the treatment of humans and non-humans; the agency/structure debate; ontology, space and time; and power, politics and distribution.

Examination of the literature suggests that these issues, which are of key concern to researchers interested in 'applying' ANT within the sub-fields of social science, can be handled in many different ways (or even be neglected) in terms of the research approach. Examples of the differential handling of such issues are witnessed, for example, in the range of ANT accounts in books on organization, work, and the management of technology (see Chia, 1996b; Grint and Woolgar, 1997; Grint, 1998) and in ANT-related articles published in leading management and organization studies research journals, such as the *Academy of Management Review* (see e.g. Calás and Smircich, 1999; Newton, 2002); *Journal of Management Studies* (see e.g. Knights *et al.*, 1993; Bloomfield and Danieli, 1995) and *Organization* (see e.g. Hansen and Mouritsen, 1999; Hull, 1999; Lee and Hassard, 1999; Munro, 1999c).

In the following sections, therefore, we discuss some of the critical issues at the heart of ANT accounting. We not only discuss each issue in its own right, but also acknowledge the analytical links between them, and highlight their respective relationships to the key ANT notion of achieving a sense of 'general symmetry' in empirical accounts. This analysis is offered primarily as a guide to those researchers in management and organization studies who as yet may be unfamiliar with ANT arguments and debates but who wish to pursue ANT-related empirical work in the future. In particular it is for those who wish to consider, in detail, certain ontological and methodological issues underlying the production of ANT accounts.

Issues of inclusion and exclusion

The first concern of the ANT accounting process is that of the so-called 'inclusion/exclusion' debate. Whereas Callon suggests that an observer needs to be agnostic to ensure that 'no point of view is privileged and no interpretation is censored' (Callon, 1986: 200), Latour asserts the need to make a 'list', no matter how long and heterogeneous, of those who do the work (Latour, 1987: 258), and Callon and Law (1997) call for the inclusion of the vast number of entities that they argue are missing from many social science stories (such as 'nature and animals', 'angels and fairies'). However, many of the criticisms expressed by writers dissatisfied with ANT are directed towards the need for a firm decision on who to include and exclude in ANT studies. For Strathern (1996) this is essentially a question of when and where to 'cut the network', and involves a continual process of deciding which actors to follow and how we are to represent them.

The issue of where to cut the network has also been raised by Miller (1996) in his review of Latour's book *Aramis* (Latour, 1996). Rather than slavishly following a manual that instructs which 'Big Actors' to take into account (such as the technological infrastructure, the corporate culture, the global economy, etc.), Miller suggests that investigative work should be directed at contextualizing the specific event. Rather than 'Big Actors' being disregarded, the focus is on a careful process of unpacking in order to understand how 'the dreams and schemes of the different actors proliferate' (Miller, 1996: 362).

Among Miller's list of management and organization studies groups who are likely to be 'banging on Latour's door' are the accountants. For Miller this group in particular will want more information about the way in which projects are economized and made calculable. This includes gaining a greater understanding of how such a notion as 'economic viability' is made visible, operable, and amenable to intervention as well as providing linkages between different parts of the network (e.g. by examining the assemblages of programmes and technologies). Furthermore, as Miller (1996: 358) indicates, the general advice to 'follow the actors' and to 'stop when the contextualizers stop' leads to a whole range of related questions:

> It's fine to tell us that we should believe them when they speak to us, that we should refrain from judging them, but we have to know who to speak to in the first instance, which meeting to attend, who to call on the telephone, who to email, and who to ask for an interview!
>
> (Miller, 1996: 363)

It should be noted that even if the researcher focuses upon the project itself and the activities of the contextualizers, this is problematic as it assumes that the boundaries of the project are given and knowable. In addition, Miller suggests that the linkages are not as clear-cut as they appear in *Aramis*. They do not end at a certain point, but just get flimsier and become more difficult to discern, even though their influence may be significant (Miller, 1996). Thus, for Miller (1996: 363) 'the trick is to select the paths you wish to follow, and those which you wish to ignore, and do so according to the assemblage you wish to chart'. In practice, however, (and especially for new researchers) this process is far more uncertain than even Miller's statement suggests. As an academic biographer cannot follow actors everywhere, s/he engages ultimately in a practice of ordering, sorting and selection. In this regard, Law (1991a) suggests there is always a 'price associated with following actors'. This includes the problems associated with maintaining analytical distance as we begin to see the world through their constructs, experiences and practices. Law also suggests that certain distributions may ultimately become invisible, for 'those that are of no concern to the actor who is being followed tend to melt from view' (Law, 1991a: 11).

As we will see later, this issue also links to the more metaphysical concern of how we study complex and messy objects. For instance, one way may involve recognizing how 'things' can coexist in many forms and can be mobilized through a variety of ways (e.g. through inscriptions). However, this again raises the question of how we represent those who are viewed as unrepresentable. Do we exclude them as 'monsters' (see Law, 1991b) — as not providing an acceptable attribution of agency? Or do we include them through our role as the political representative of these entities, and reintroduce them through semiotic processes? The problem of what counts as a *relevant* actor still remains. Even if the observer is encouraged to be 'agnostic', to make 'long lists', and to avoid stipulating his or her own authority, the process of selecting between actors in terms of relevance relies on assumptions concerning what is 'out there' and how it can be known and communicated (see Bloomfield and Vurdubakis, 1999: 8).

Some of the conceptual tools underlying ANT can, therefore, provide for a confusing ontological mix with regards to this issue of inclusion/exclusion (and also to related dichotomies such as absence/presence, human/non-human, subject/object etc.). Bloomfield and Vurdubakis' (1999) analysis of Law's (1987) study of fifteenth-century maritime expansion provides some interesting reflections in this respect. First, Bloomfield and Vurdubakis consider the inclusion/exclusion issue through analyzing Button's (1993) critique of Law, with regard to the way in which the latter defines various associations and selects his actors. Button, for example, suggests that if we are willing to take on board Law's approach in its entirety, why should we stop with the actors he has selected? Could we not extend this further to, for example, the air the men breathe, the food they eat, the sea, the earth, the daylight etc. until we reach the situation of trying to include *everything* (see the later section on Ontology, Space and Time for further discussion of this issue)?

In this critique, Button claims that while Law highlights the process by which the galley emerged from the 'association of elements', he fails to provide 'any understanding of what that association consists of in the production of the particular object "the galley"' (Button, 1993: 24). For Button the problem concerns the way Law abandons the idea of actions in favour of processes. Button provides an alternative perspective through a more ethnomethodological approach, one that positions the embodiment of skilled working practices as the major theme of enquiry. Here the importance of studying techniques and embedded (human) working practices should not be negated by positioning these practices in some privileged status, as if they exist independent of the world in which they operate. For example, in Law's description of the constitution of a network of artefacts and skills for 'converting the stars from irrelevant points of light in the night sky into formidable allies in the struggle to master the Atlantic', he not only examines the process of translation in terms of stars, instruments and inscriptions, but in addition, provides a discussion of the working practices of the mariners and the creation of a new social group in the form of the astronomical navigator (Law, 1987: 124). While they are seen as part of the network of entities, such working practices are not examined as if they exist within a privileged or independent state in relation to other entities.

The humans/non-humans issue

Having introduced issues of the inclusion and exclusion of actors, we now move towards our major concern relating to ANT accounts: assessing the application of the notion of 'general symmetry' in their production. Basically, this includes the symmetrical treatment of such seemingly dichotomous factors as humans and non-humans, society and nature, and the social and technical. We must note, however (as with other sections of this chapter), that this is not necessarily a 'concern' for proponents of ANT, only for those who would call the approach into question.

Collins and Yearley (1992), for example, have criticized what they see as a 'radical' form of symmetry, notably for the way in which it attempts to 'suspend all dichotomies'. While appearing radical in attempting to 'dissolve dichotomies', Collins and Yearley suggest that the work of the actor-network theorist is essentially conservative, and results largely in impotence in the form of prosaic case studies. Collins and Yearley liken writers on ANT (citing in particular Bruno Latour and Michel Callon) to players in a game of 'epistemological chicken' (the term 'chicken' refers to a game played by children in which each child seeks to be the last to move off the road before a car arrives) in terms of who is bravest when it comes to epistemological brinkmanship. The attempt by ANT to decentre the social, is seen by Collins and Yearley to result instead in a form of political impotence. Rather than waiting for the car to arrive and rush across the road, they describe how the actor-network theorist 'turns out to have crossed the road well before the traffic was in sight, leaving only their ventriloquist's voices echoing between the curbs' (Collins and Yearley, 1992: 323). Collins and Yearley suggest, for example, that while the scallops in Callon's (1986) well-known study of St Brieuc Bay are to be treated as actors, the creation of the symmetry between fisherman and scallops still appears to be in the hands of the analyst:

> The analysts remain in control the whole time, which makes their imposition of symmetry on the world seem something of a conceit. Would not complete symmetry require an account from the point of view of the scallops? Would it be sensible to think of scallops enrolling the scallop researchers so as to give themselves a better home and to protect their species from the ravages of the fishermen?
>
> (Collins and Yearley, 1992: 313)

Callon's (1986) study is criticized, therefore, for providing an essentially human-centred account. For Collins and Yearley the major problem within such ANT studies remains the way that humans (frequently in the form of researchers) have to represent non-humans, for the analysis appears to rely heavily on the human subject being centred, with little room for non-humans. Callon is taken to task, for example, on his lack of expertise in the area of 'scallop behaviour'. Collins and Yearley suggest that before Callon can enter into any discussion of scallop behaviour, he must first demonstrate his scientific credentials, that is, 'he must show that he has a firm grip on the nature of scallops' (Collins and Yearley, 1992: 318). The same accusation is aimed at Latour for his lack of technical knowledge (e.g. within the fields of mechanical engineering, materials science and architecture) in his well-known study of 'door closers' (Latour and Johnson, 1988), there being a similar credibility problem 'since doors have no social life in which we can participate in' (Collins and Yearley, 1992: 318).

But Collins and Yearley perhaps miss the point in their attempt to reinforce the separation of the social and the technical, for in their view each appears a discrete entity (such as a door with no social life). Under ANT the social and the technical are analytically composite for 'there is no thinkable social life without the participation … of non-humans, and especially machines and artifacts' (Callon and Latour, 1992: 359). Additionally, while Collins and Yearley question the appropriateness of trying to take the scientist's place (i.e. assuming that we should only talk on a subject if we become an 'expert'), the actor-network researcher does not seek to take the place of the scientist or engineer. Instead the primary role is to follow the various actors through the everyday practices in order to explore the diversity of positions entertained by scientists, attributions of agency, situations of controversy, and outcomes that are viewed in terms of their success or failure. This analysis relates to the way in which actors, entities, machines, forces, etc. *rely* on spokespersons and how the delegation of authority to speak on behalf of others is both an epistemological and political process. While some commend ANT for 'broadening the franchise to grant the right to representation to anything — anything at all' (Lee and Brown, 1994: 778), others suggest that 'spokespersons may indeed symmetrically speak for both people and things, but only humans can act (can be permitted to act) as spokespersons' (Pels, 1995: 138).

Some writers also question the way in which ANT sometimes appears to rate the status of non-humans too highly in relation to humans. Again Collins and Yearley (1992: 322) in describing the failure of ANT to distinguish between human action and the behaviour of things, question Callon (1986) for substituting non-humans for humans in the form of *specific* actors. Collins and Yearley suggest that under ANT material actors are granted 'reality' and 'potency' far beyond that which should be bestowed to them by humans. They describe this 'misconceived extension' of symmetry as actually taking a backward step 'leading us to embrace once more the very priority of technological, rule-bound description, adopted from scientists and technologists, that we once learned to ignore' (Collins and Yearley, 1992: 322). This resonates with their discussion of door-closers and scallops in terms of 'helping out' the natural scientists and engineers by siding with them and supporting their position. Callon and Latour (1992: 347) agree that at one level they have granted 'to nature and to artifacts the same ontological status that realists and technical determinists are used to granting to them'. However, they also state that:

> we wish to attack scientists' hegemony on the definition of nature, we have never wished to accept the essential source of power, that is the very distribution between what is natural and what is social and the fixed ontological status that goes with it … our general symmetry principle is thus not to alternate between natural realism and social realism but to obtain nature and society as twin results of another activity … network building, or collective things, or quasi-objects, or trials of force.
>
> (Callon and Latour, 1992: 348)

Walsham (1997) also advocates the strong empirical expression of general symmetry, in terms of conceptualizing things as actors, in terms of whose interests they inscribe, speak for and represent. He supports this conceptual position as a powerful analytical device and bulwark, especially within an age of complex hybrids and negotiable boundaries. For Walsham (1997: 475) this position has particular power in destabilizing studies of the IT-based vision of the virtual organization in which 'an objective central group is viewed to control the company's global operations, moving people, jobs and societies like pawns on a chessboard'.

Other writers, however, and notably Pels (1995) are concerned with the consequences associated with an 'extreme' position of symmetry for understanding people and things. As we know, Callon and Latour (1992: 359) highlight the importance of the symmetrical treatment of human and non-humans. They attempt also to alleviate methodological worries about this being viewed as 'extreme' by suggesting: 'it is not our intention to say that scallops have voting power and will exercise it, or that door-closers are entitled to social benefits and burial rites, but that a common vocabulary and a common ontology should be created'.

For Pels (1995), however, such an expression of general symmetry remains problematic. He states his desire for some degree of analytical 'privileging'.

While he supports the argument that we may have gone too far in erecting epistemological fences (to separate, for example, ourselves from nature, science from politics, fact from value) he makes a plea for 'weaker asymmetries', ones that enable us to maintain some of the 'crucial features of modernity'. Pels (1995) suggests that this includes its liberal complexity, web of differences, democratic separation of powers, and interests and competences. As Pels (1995: 138–9) notes: 'in a century which is presently drawing to a close, we moderns have also gone too far in erasing all such distinctions, in totally politicizing culture, science, and society, in massively reducing other people to the status of things'.

As we have noted, however, proponents of ANT do not *necessarily* deny such differences and divisions. Rather they question their *a priori* status and argue that these divisions should be understood as *effects* or *outcomes*. In other words, they are not given in the order of things. Entities achieve their form as a consequence of the relations in which they are located and performed, that is, in, by and through these relations. Thus, in principle, everything is uncertain, although conversely the focus of many ANT studies is the way in which durability and stability is performed and achieved. However, another concern relating to this issue of human and non-human concerns a central idea underlying ANT in terms of distributed action and the way in which distinctions such as human and non-human should also be treated as outcomes of complex networks of relations. This relates to the problems of focusing on being and identity as we then become locked into definitions of existence and problematic ontological and epistemological dead-ends. One of these dead-ends, for writers such as Latour, Law and Callon, concerns the focus on structure and agency, a theme which has been a central concern of several writers in management and organization studies (e.g. Reed, 1997; Clark, 1998; Mutch, 1999; Mingers, 2000).

The agency/structure issue

Our next issue relates to the claim that while ANT addresses the local, contingent and processual, it fails to attend to broader social structures that influence the local. Latour, Callon and Law (see chapters in Law and Hassard, 1999) have generally argued that the inclusion of an agency/structure dichotomy contradicts their work (and indeed reference to this form of dualism is antithetical generally for those adopting an ANT position, for arguably to talk of structure in the same breath as ANT is to confound the approach). However, it remains an issue for writers who are critical of the method of general symmetry.

Habers and Koenis (1996), for example, suggest that Latour concentrates too heavily on the contribution of 'things' to the production of social order. By failing to address the sociality of the stability of things, this leads to an asymmetrical reading of the mediation process. Reed (1997) also appears dissatisfied with a lack of appreciation of the impact of social structures on micro events and processes. He argues that ANT tends to neglect the impact of institutionalized structures on social interaction and socio-material practices. Although Walsham (1997) broadly sympathizes with this view, he suggests a resolution to this apparent failure of ANT to account fully for the impact of broader social structures by synthesizing the approach with the work of Giddens (1990, 1991). However, for reasons outlined above, such an analytical trajectory is not feasible, let alone beneficial or desirable, for structuration theory and ANT are largely antithetical. In short, being drawn constantly into a debate over structure/agency is one which Latour, Callon, and Law would certainly view as unproductive (see Law, 1999, for a discussion of centred actor and decentred network in relation to agency/structure).

In response to related sophistic and largely paralogical comments that his approach concentrates on the 'micro' at the exclusion of the 'macro', Latour (1991) describes how (for sake of argument might be termed) the 'macro-structure' of society is made up of the same basic connections as the micro-structure, and thus can be examined in much the same way in order to provide descriptions which 'take into account the social structures which influence the course of local history' (Latour, 1991: 118). In a later work, Latour (1997) suggested, in relation to this issue, that 'Big', does not mean 'really' big or 'overall', or 'overarching', but 'connected', 'mediated' and 'related'. With regards to this reverse reductionism he refers to the similarities between ANT and the work of Tarde (1962) and the need to dismantle the setting up of this distinction between the macro and micro. For Latour (2002), Tarde prefigured ANT in his refusal to view society as more complex and higher order than an individual monad, and the individual human agent as the basis upon which society is made. Rather than following Durkheim's train of thought, in treating social facts as external things, society can be any form of association and all things are societies (Tarde, 1962). Thus, for Tarde, there is no collective self in the sense of something which exists external of such associations: no macro society; and what is considered as macro, bigger, and whole should actually be viewed as a simpler, more standardized version of one aspect, or as possessing a fraction of the properties of the monad — those which manage to make part of its view shared by others (Latour, 2002). The monad aspires to become a universe in itself, as every other thing resides 'within', both real and possible (Latour, 2002). For Deleuze (1994) this concern about the use of the 'possible' directs his focus to the virtual and actual (both considered as real) although in practice you would expect Latour to share similar concerns and interests with regards to this matter. We, therefore, need to explore how to 'exist is to differ' (Tarde, 1999) and how monads, which are already richer in difference through such diverse engagements and via complex assemblages, are seen to repeat themselves into 'existence' (Latour, 2005; McLean and Quattrone, 2005).

'Macro' factors should, therefore, be viewed as provisional and the picture of order portrayed should be one constantly under threat, as no one component is fully part of it and each monad overspills in the sense that only a tiny part, a facade of itself, is imparted in the temporary achievement of 'existence': monads (which could also be replaced with the term 'actor-network') cannot be 'dominated', as you can only enroll some sides of the monads. As Latour (2002: 120) states, 'Revolt, resistance, break down, conspiracy, alternative is everywhere'. In fact, differences, diversity and alterity could be seen as enabling order particularly as existence, however provisional and partial, relies on engaging diversity, and provides occasions for more differences to be generated (Jones *et al.*, 2004). In addition to noting that smaller parts do not join to make wholes, as no framing can contain all others, we will explore later how inclusion relates to the issue of alteration and difference. Thus, when exploring the 'social', rather than being directed away from the local, one gets closer to it. While Latour argues that the most 'useful' contribution of ANT has been to transform the social from a 'surface, a territory, and a province of reality' into a 'circulation', he also suggests that this highlights yet another area which requires examination, that of the 'empty space' between networks.

Although writers interested in the Sociology of Scientific Knowledge (SSK) initially appeared close allies of ANT, Latour claims that due to problems associated with this issue of structure/agency some have become its harshest critics (e.g. see debates between Latour and David Bloor in the journal *Studies in the History and Philosophy of Science*). For example, the social explanations underlying SSK examine epistemological issues relating to society, psychology, politics and theology, etc. as *separate* problems (Latour, 1999a). For ANT though, components need to be tackled simultaneously in order to explore 'alternative' understandings of the types of connection between them. To say that something is 'socially constructed', made of 'social' stuff — 'a kind of fabric to account for the fabrication of facts' (Latour, 2002: 2) — is also to assume this process is human-centred. Also, to be constructed is often viewed as not 'real', as construction is often perceived in opposition to reality (Latour, 2002, 2004a, 2005). This is clearly problematic and we need to reconsider our versions of the constructed and real in order to make more sense of this process. So while the real cannot be wished away, it is also something produced or made through social relations that are not merely centred on humans.

The oscillation between action as determined and action as determining, has of course been a major feature of the historical trajectory of social theorizing. However, rather than relating action merely to an individual human agent or member of the collective, or reducing it to the effect of the structure or system, under ANT, action is the *performance* of a specific collective (see Gomart and Hennion, 1999). Similar to writers who have undermined the notion that an external reality is a property of nature, those from a sociology of translation perspective have also examined the concept of subjectivity by highlighting the way in which it is not a property of humans, of individuals, or of intentional subjects (Latour, 1999a, 1999b); instead subjectivity is presented as a circulating activity:

> something that is partially gained or lost by hooking up to certain bodies of practice … the more we have socialized so to speak 'outside' nature, the more 'outside' objectivity the content of our subjectivity can gain. There is plenty of room now for both.
>
> (Latour, 1999a: 23)

For Callon and Latour (1997), therefore, each element of the network 'relays' and 'prolongs' the action of the collective without being the source itself. In this way, 'actantiality' is 'not what an actor does … but what provides actors with their actions, with their subjectivity, with their intentionality, with their morality' (Latour, 1999a: 18). The capacity to be strategic should then be described as the *effect* of an association of a heterogeneous network and not merely assigned to a human actor (Gomart and Hennion, 1999).

It could be argued that the work of ethnomethodologists developed similar themes, such as assuming that 'interests' and 'norms' are not stable but arise in local situations. This is clear in the work of Suchman (1987), notably in the way she produces accounts of situated action that emphasize collective action. However, Callon and Latour suggest that under ethnomethodology insufficient emphasis is placed on the presence of objects, and that ethnomethodologists are still concerned with the interaction of subject and object, human and non-human, agent and structure (see Gomart and Hennion, 1999). Moreover, for Gomart and Hennion, rather than undoing the model of human action, the situated-action approach merely allows the cognitive capacities of humans to migrate to objects. In addition, they suggest that ANT:

> seeks to describe the composition of heterogeneous elements in networks which produce emerging action from an indeterminate source … action is no longer the primitive unit of analysis, nor the only kind of event which might be described.
>
> (Gomart and Hennion, 1999: 225)

In other words, this involves a shift from action to a form of analysis which focuses on events, including those that 'just occur', or become viewed as non-events. This relates to the suggestion by Law (1997) that we need to examine non-strategic orderings, such as relations that take particular shapes or forms for other reasons. In addition, thc issue of being excessively strategic is considered within the work of Mol (1999) in terms of 'problems of difference'. This relates to the notion of mediation and the way in which object-mediators (which are rendered as prolongations of actions already initiated elsewhere) do not merely relay and repeat actions, but also transform them in different and sometimes surprising ways. Thus, events are not limited to origins, determinants or effects. As Gomart and Hennion, 1999: 226) suggest:

> Mediation is a turn towards what emerges, what is shaped and composed, what cannot be reduced to an interaction of causal objects and intentional persons. The network is not a black pool in which to drop, dilute, criticise, and lose the subject. It is on the contrary an opening — pried loose with a partly rhetorical liberation of things and an attentiveness to spaces, dispositions, and events — which releases us from the insoluble opposition between natural determination and human will. 'Mediation' allows the course of the world to return to the centre of analysis.

This suggests that certain concepts — such as mediation, framing, calculative agencies, etc. — can indeed provide an 'opening' through which to study spaces, events and non-events.

Issues of ontology, space and time

A major theme which needs further discussion concerns the issue of how we can produce accounts and represent actors from different 'places' and 'times'. For an illustration of this point we refer again to Law's study of Portuguese maritime exploration. To expand on a theme considered earlier, we note that for Bloomfield and Vurdubakis (1999), Law's selection of actors may have more to do with a present-day account of this period than how Portuguese sailors would have understood their world. In the case of the fifteenth-century shipbuilders, for instance, religious artefacts, symbols and acts of worship were all part and parcel of a Portuguese voyage:

> from what we know of the world inhabitated by fifteenth century ship builders and sailors, the construction and operation of the technological object 'galley' would also involve invocation of divine goodwill as an essential precondition of a safe and successful journey.
>
> (Bloomfield and Vurdubakis, 1999: 7)

Bloomfield and Vurdubakis ask whether heavenly hosts or the saints of passage should or could inhabit our actor worlds. They also ask does ANT have to 'bar its own monsters'? This highlights the problem of trying to provide a symmetrical treatment of past and present in terms that re-present other places and times: 'Again, this is the familiar problem — or rather paradox — of ethnocentricity: How can we re-present Other times and Other places with only the tools of Here and Now with which to do it?' (Bloomfield and Vurdubakis, 1999: 8).

So does Law's study of Portuguese expansion rely in part on a rather conventional (modernist) ontology and a traditional mode of social science accounting as suggested by Bloomfield and Vurdubakis. The potential problems of ethnocentricity associated with processes of network selection, extension and constriction are apparent. However, the distinction between 'relevant' and 'non relevant' actors is a difficult one. While some interesting points are raised in relation to those made on the basis of *current* conventions, in terms of what is recognizable to the modern(ist) social theorist, rather than to the fifteenth-century mariner, the problems of how we account for messy and complex objects still remains.

Issues concerning the production of accounts related to 'current' and 'historical' events have been addressed in studies of governmentality (see Chapter 8). Here writers have attempted to avoid producing accounts which search for origins or 'how it was', choosing instead to concentrate on the impact of the present. This involves gaining insight into current 'assemblages of language', the subtle and not so subtle shifts in meaning associated with taking a new direction for existing practices (Miller and Napier, 1993) and the redefinition of problems and solutions in the light of available techniques (Miller and O'Leary, 1993). Those adopting a governmentality perspective are likely to provide different interpretations of historical materials to historians who provide a 'traditional' form of analysis. However, this does not merely relate to a question of being more sensitized to the past, as this process of interpretation is considered to be motivated by different concerns (Hull, 1999). As Hull states, such governmentality studies are shaped by a desire to reach new understandings of the 'history of the present'. It should be noted, however, that such studies do not circumvent problems relating to whom or what is included/excluded in the accounts that are thus generated.

Finally, with regard to the way in which we are constantly revising our knowledge of the past in light of new developments in the present, Bowker and Star (1999: 40) suggest:

> This is not a new idea to historiography, or to biography. We change our resumes as we acquire new skills to seem like smooth, planned paths of development, even if the change had been unexpected or undesired. When we become members of new social worlds, we often retell our life stories in new terminology. A common example of this is religious conversion, where the past is retold as exemplifying errors, sinning and repentance.

Revisions can lead to new voices and interpretations of texts, categories, and artefacts, as well as new silences, as the repetitive traces associated with such classification devices can open up alternative realities, but these may be limited in terms of how they engage others. Therefore, when considering the ways in which accounts and classification schemes order the past, it is important to take stock of issues of inclusion/exclusion. For Bowker and Star, the indeterminacy of the past not only requires an understanding of how standard narratives (that seem universal) may have been constructed, but also of recovering 'multi-vocality' (Star, 1991).

Accessing the past thus requires some form of ordering and classification, a process that is far from unproblematic. Bowker and Star suggest two major historiographic schools of thought with respect to using classification systems on the past. The first relates to the use of 'real' classifications uncovered in the arts and sciences (e.g. work on genetic classification systems). The second claims that only classifications available to the actors 'at the time' should be used, on the basis that 'if a category did not exist contemporaneously, it should not be retroactively applied' (Bowker and Star, 1999: 42). However, Bowker and Star opt for what they refer to as a pragmatist point of view. This involves seeking to understand classification systems:

> according to the work that they are doing, and the networks within which they are embedded. That entails both an understanding of the categories of those designing and using the systems, and a set of analytic questions derived from our own concerns as analysts.
>
> (Bowker and Star, 1999: 42)

Rather than continuing to focus on finding ways of identifying objects existing in a particular space, perhaps we need to rethink how we study objects that are complex and messy, while also multiple and apparently stable (Jones *et al*., 2004; Law and Singleton, 2005). One of the main problems we encounter concerns trying to avoid an approach which assumes that objects exist 'out-there' in some independent and singular form and that reality precedes any attempt to know it, or that objects are social constructions based on human interpretations and meanings which construct the world, or finally an attempt to combine the two (e.g. structuration theory) (Jones *et al*., 2004). Through their reflections on alteration and difference, Tarde and Latour highlight the problems of relying on notions of identity, essentialism, and existence as relating to 'things in themselves', in such a search for difference:

> difference, in one sense, is the substantial side of things, what they have most in common and what makes them most different. One has to start from this difference and to abstain from trying to explain it, especially by starting with identity, as so many persons wrongly do. Because identity is a minimum and, hence, a type of difference, and a very rare type at that, in the same way as rest is a type of movement and the circle a type of ellipse. To begin with some primordial identity implies at the origin a prodigiously unlikely singularity, or else the obscure mystery of one simple being then dividing for no special reason.
>
> (Tarde, 1999: 73 as cited in Latour, 2002)

By exploring heterogeneous diversity, repetitions and difference, and by attending more to the active traces which 'existence' is seen to rely upon, we can attempt to avoid a subordination of alterity to identity (Jones *et al*., 2004). This relies on countering the assumptions that a human being imitates because s/he wishes to, or that action simply originates in some external source/object (Tarde, 1962). Thus, we need to oppose a focus on some external force acting upon individuals (in some Durkheimian sense) and through such an analysis we can seek to avoid an *a priori* distinction between self and other. By studying how imitation relates to the desire to imitate, with action being distributed through such imitative rays — we can also challenge such *a priori* notions such as identity, unity, and problematic divisions (e.g. macro/micro, subject/object, nature/culture). In other words, by reconsidering ideas of repetition and difference, and heterogeneity and homogeneity we can begin to shift our focus from 'being' and identity and explore others possibilities. For example, Tarde suggests that:

> From this principle 'I am', it is impossible to deduce any other existence than mine, in spite of all the subtleties of the world. But affirm first this postulate: 'I have' as the basic fact, and then the had as well as the having are given at the same time as inseparable.
>
> (Tarde, 1999: 86 as cited in Latour, 2002)

Movements from one difference to another thus shifts the focus from identity philosophy and identity politics towards possession, avidity and properties (Latour, 2002).

While in ANT there have been many attempts to address this issue of stability and change — and research continues in this area — there are specific problems with certain conceptual devices aimed in part at this theoretical and empirical puzzle. For example, the concept of the immutable mobile has contributed some important insights relating to mediation, translation and action at a distance by highlighting the reliance of many chains of associations. This approach, however, has been accused of effacing all sorts of arrangements and being too rigid in that it fails to account for the variability and multiplicity associated with such relations and associations (Law and Singleton, 2005). Mess, otherness, and invisible work could be seen as the alterity that plays a major part in the making of realities, even though fitting neatly or being in a unified and/or visible form within or between accounts may not be one of the properties of such aspects. For instance, Lee and Brown (1994) suggest that networks serve to colonize the Other in effacing all that cannot be accounted for in the talk of actor-networks and leaving little room for alterity. An alternative for Mol (2002) is by focusing on how accounts of realities — and the realities they describe — are performed together. For instance, De Laet and Mol (2000) make a case in favour of a more complex and fluid view of objects in relation to multiple ontologies and realties, with a shift in focus from representation to the object itself. An object is not merely a set of relations that shifts and stays the 'same', for 'staying the same' is actually reliant upon such changes, as objects do not exist by themselves or merely describe the visible realities out-there (Law, 2004).

Through their analysis of a water pump in Zimbabwe, Mol and Law (1994), for example, argue that a complex object such as a pump is made by different performances, enactments, practices and realities that coexist in the present: there is no singular object or reality 'out-there' as objects maintain a fluid existence with the capacity to exist in many different forms (not that this is unlimited, as this would merely fall into the relativist trap of 'anything goes'). Mol and Law (1994: 643) suggest that boundaries can allow leakage, and may come and go, or may disappear altogether, as relations have the capacity to transform themselves without fracture. This allows changes in shape both within Euclidean space (each pump looking different from its original design) and network space (in the way it works and the relations embedded in such change). Multiple objects thus exist through the different networks of relations — as the networks of relations change through these specific performances, so do the objects under scrutiny (Mol, 2002; Law, 2004; Law and Singleton, 2005). Thus, for Law (2004), rather than realities being explained by practices and beliefs, they are produced in them and have a life, in relations. Furthermore, there is a shift in the word 'is' to one which is situated, as it is not possible to say what something is 'in and of itself' as nothing is ever alone (Mol, 2002: 54). For Mol then, rather than 'to be or not to be' (which could sound more like a Derridian project, although this would require replacing the 'or' with an 'and'), there is a shift ('to be is to be related' but also 'more than one but less than many'), and this involves keeping 'present' the practicalities associated with enacting realities. This is an ontology that relies both on difference, multiplicity, and a political process of engagement.

Furthermore, Law and Singleton (2005) explore the issue of multiple realities using the spatial metaphor of 'fire', in order to examine the energetic and transformative aspects of multiplicity with a specific focus on issues of absence and presence. They argue that although certain methodological perspectives tend to silence this multiplicity and otherness, for fire objects this otherness is not only generative but also central to our understanding of complex objects. Here allegory, by making space for ambivalence and ambiguity, is seen as a way of manifesting what is otherwise invisible by extending fields of visibility and crafting new realities 'out-there' (Law, 2004: 90). Realities in allegory do not inevitably need to fit together; for such symbolism concerns holding together things that do not necessarily cohere. Representation, however, tends to deny the relationship with allegory (i.e. in terms of Othering, the mediations that produce its apparent transparency and detachment) (2004: 97). For Law, organizing could be seen in terms of allegory, as it is the process of holding together things that are not strongly consistent. 'Good' studies in organizational analysis are perhaps allegorical in that they avoid a focus on a 'single-version discursive consistency' — organizing is multiple, with multiple versions of repetition, and modes of Othering (2004: 112–13). For Mol (2002) similarly this requires a greater emphasis on the conflicts, tensions and struggles with regards to the many 'intersections', 'inclusions' and 'foldings' which underlie such complex relations. Thus, rather than relying on a 'single reality out-there' (whether in an objective or constructed form) we need to explore 'how multiple realities overlap' and the attempts to produce coherence along with the difficulties of such a reconciliation process (Law, 2004: 110).

For Latour (2002) an alternative to a universe is a multiverse. Occasions for coherence and unification may occur alongside much multiplicity, heterogeneity and mediations. This then returns us to the notion of repetition and alterity in the production of accounts with multiple versions of repetition in which absences overflow. Cooper (1998: 108) referred to this as the 'unknowable and excessive', which can provide sources of energy and possibilities through a 'flux and flow of unfinished, heteromorphic organisms' (see Law, 2004: 117). For Serres, a 'third object' is required to cope with the endless intersection of the two forms of metaphors for the real (i.e. the solid and the fluid) (Law, 2004). Similarly, for Latour, modernity (or non-modernity) grows out of the intersection between purity (regarding distinctions and forms) on one hand, and the proliferation of impurities, heterogeneities and hybrids, on the other (Law, 2004: 82). The desire for purity thus produces hybrids: with order comes mess. More sophisticated ways of re-enacting such associations and intersections are required and this involves attending to issues of intensity, quality and engagement (Jones *et al.*, 2004; Quattrone and McLean, 2005). This includes studying how 'things' are unable to 'travel' without chains that sustain them and how they require the support of many 'others' and acts of mediation to 'exist' (e.g. laboratories, knowledge, discourses, control, etc.).

For example, Latour describes how we need to explore the diverse sets of relays, mediations and chains of associations which underlie such a process and emerge from distributions elsewhere. Specific articulators or localizers are seen to engage in this continual process of assembling and redistribution. Moreover, in their role of enabling such dislocated actions to act (through indirect associations and circulations), they produce instances of multiplying in the sense of creating more closings and openings (Latour, 2005).

Accounting for such a fabrication process relies on alternative ways of conceptualizing such orderings and tracing, relations and actions. This includes avoiding an excessive desire for coherence and centring in which stability and multiplicity cannot easily coexist or overlap. For as Serres suggests (see Serres and Latour, 1995: 59), time and space are a 'multiple foldable diversity' and, therefore, we need to rethink how we consider such interactions in terms of multiplicity and existence. For instance, in Latour's (2005) discussion of interactions he states that time and space are always folded, and even though effects of isotropy or isochrony may be produced, interactions should not be viewed as isotropic or isochronic. He goes on to suggest that interactions are not synoptic; that is participants — in some stable/singular sense — may not be 'visible' in a course of action at the same time. In other words, it is not possible to see everything from one place as this fails to account for the issue of multiplicity and shifting agencies. Thus, there are no homogeneous interactions, as actions are never carried out by the same material all along. Rather than viewing interactions as homogeneous they should be seen as heterogeneous — as exerting different kinds and quantities of pressures (i.e. as interactions are not isobaric). As such, we need to gain an insight into relations, interactions and shifting agencies which are not always visible in the same time or place, do not exert pressure equally, and can lead to different outcomes in terms of stability and multiplicity. This requires a greater understanding of issues of quality, quantity, and effects (Latour, 2005) and an alternative view of otherness and difference, and how we understand organizing through alterity (e.g. in terms of considering how places and entities are 'framed' by actions/agencies coming from 'elsewhere'). If size, durability, universality and standardization all relate to many mediations and struggles, but in ways that often appear stable, this also raises questions concerning aspects of power and politics relating to such a process and how such issues are accounted for within ANT.

Heterogeneous engineering and the political issue

The final criticism aimed at those referred to as adopting an ANT position concerns an apparent failure to examine in detail the moral and political issues underlying the objects they study. In this section (which resonates with previous sections) we examine this issue in relation to the heterogeneity of socio-technical networks, and especially with regard to notions of power, ordering and distribution. For instance, Fuller (1999) calls for symmetry in the status of science as compared to social practices. While the actor-network researcher is encouraged to provide a description of the network without becoming too immersed in *a priori* distinctions and dichotomies, s/he does not exist in a vacuum, separate from the politics of everyday life. The actor-network theorist is embedded within the social world in which s/he is required to respond to 'differences' and make judgements.

Winner's (1993) description of 'the bridge' is often used to illustrate the way in which certain sociological approaches fail to account for the social consequences of technical choice. In particular, Winner criticizes the almost total disregard of this issue by the social constructivists, suggesting 'they have little to say about the deep-seated political biases that can underlie the spectrum of choices that surface for relevant actors' (Winner, 1993: 370). Likewise Latour responds to charges of apoliticism or moral relativism by suggesting that a refusal to explain 'the closure of a controversy by its consequences does not mean that we are indifferent to the possibility of judgement, but only that we refuse to accept judgements which transcend the situation' (Latour, 1991: 130). (nb some ANT articles appear to engage explicitly with what might be deemed as political implications and/or agendas: e.g. Star, 1991; Bijker, 1993; Boland and Schultze, 1996; Monterio and Hanseth, 1996). Latour (1991) reiterates the point made by Foucault (1977) that domination is an 'effect' not a 'cause', and suggests that making judgements does not lose any of its acuity once we let go of the need to transcend the situation.

Despite the range of problems associated with such positions of transcendence, it is hard to counter the argument that we need to find ways of keying into issues relating to politics and distributions. This relates to the methods we employ in the selection and positioning of actors and the ways we inscribe our accounts. However, clearly the way in which we attempt to respond to calls for politicizing our accounts is a complex issue that needs to be considered further (see Calás and Smircich, 1999). This is discussed by Star (1991) who argues that while we can all be described as 'heterogeneous engineers', heterogeneity is quite different for those who are privileged and those who are not. Star highlights the problem of 'hierarchies of distribution' being frequently ignored in the 'ordering' of actor-network accounts. By studying heterogeneity, or the way in which entities and perspectives are joined in the constitution of socio-technical networks — in terms of how things are brought together, how differences and similarities are constructed and maintained, and their distributive effects — it is possible to explore issues such as power with regard to the sets of relations that underlie the particular circulation of actors (Star, 1991). As Law (1991a: 18) has suggested similarly:

> No one, no thing, no class, no gender, can have power unless a set of relations is constituted and held in place: a set of relations that distinguishes between this and that (distribution), and then goes on to regulate the relations between this and that … power, whatever form it may take, is recursively woven into the intricate dance that unites the social and the technical.

For Fujimura (1992) the importance of understanding consequences and distributions also relates to the process of examining the practices, concerns, activities and trajectories of different participants, both human and non-human. This includes understanding: how some perspectives are more persuasive than others in the construction of truths; how some actors go along with the will of others; and how some appear to resist being enrolled. It is suggested that this can be partly addressed through an examination of the problem of standards and identity, and their relationship to 'invisible' work and marginality, although how we tackle such issues takes us down other ontological and metaphysical paths. In particular, the notion of 'irreversibility' is important with regard to the way in which 'facts' are constituted. As Star states, 'some truths and technologies, joined in networks of translation, appear to become enormously stable features of our landscape, shaping action and inhibiting certain kinds of change' (Star, 1991: 40). However, the reference to standards and identity returns us to the uncomfortable path of objects which we attempt to unpack from their black boxes, only to find them neatly packaged again when required in our accounts (see also the discussion of immutable mobiles).

Further, Bowker and Star (1999) suggest that whatever appears as normal, standard or universal is the result of organizational processes, negotiations and conflict. They ask a range of questions about this process, including: how do these negotiations take place? How does a classification system take a particular form? And what are the tradeoffs associated with visibility? Bowker and Star discuss how ubiquitous standards and classifications play a role in framing our representations of the past and the sequencing of events in the present. Through this ever-local and ever-partial work it can appear that 'science describes nature (and nature alone) and that politics is about social power (and social power alone)' (Bowker and Star, 1999: 46). No matter how dry and formal standards and classifications may appear, their development and maintenance is always a site for political decision-making and struggle. As Bowker and Star (1999: 320) suggest: '"moral" questions arise when the categories of the powerful become taken for granted; when policy decisions are layered into inaccessible technological structures, when one group's visibility comes at the expense of another's suffering'.

Law (1991a) also suggests that for critics of ANT the celebration of diversity is an empty gesture without the presence of a politics that establishes the conditions for its exercise. However, Law also states that he is personally committed to methods for obtaining 'the truth' in terms of political workability, and while standards for good knowledge may vary between academic groups this does not imply recourse to a philosophy of methodological and political 'quietism'. Law (1991a: 5) states that 'to accept the reality of epistemological relativism and deny that there are universal standards is not to say that there are no standards at all: and neither is it to embrace moral or political relativism'. Thus, at a local level, Law (1991a: 5) argues that we 'may seek to distinguish truth from power, persuasion from force, and what is right from what is wrong'.

Similarly, to return to an earlier theme, some ANT accounts have been accused of selecting and studying 'heroes' (business leaders, successful organizations, major projects, etc.) to the exclusion of relevant 'others'. Law (1991a: 12–13) outlines two possible reasons given for studying the 'big' and the 'powerful'. The first relates to the importance of debunking the idea that they are different to ourselves, for not to do so colludes in empowering them further (for 'like us … they have to pull their socks on in the morning': Law, 1991a: 12). In contrast, the second reason suggests that since they are 'bigger' and more 'powerful', they are likely to have a greater impact on organizing and ordering the shape of heterogeneous networks. We need, therefore, to look at both successes as well as heroic and large-scale failures (Latour, 1992).

Law (1991a) is at pains to state that while these reasons may seem sensible 'within limits', these limits are also important, especially to avoid succumbing to the perils of managerialism. As we focus on success and on the provision of extensive resources and strategies, we fail to consider those actors who may have fewer resources available to them and strategies that are restricted; that is, actors possessing a different set of expectations. For Law, the consequences may be 'fragmentation, pain and silence' — not possibilities which are usually entertained within a mangerialist perspective. Law argues, therefore, that we should not only look at heroes but also at 'victims' in terms of the differences between their fates. In other words, this involves reviewing the *distributive* strategies: 'the different kinds of discursive and non-discursive effects instantiated and reproduced in the process of heterogeneous engineering' (Law, 1991a: 15). (For Star, 1991, similarly, while ANT attempts to open 'black boxes' by examining previously 'invisible work', and tries to represent more than one view, studies within this area often describe political order as warlike and/or competitive, and tend to be biased towards the point of view of the victors [or management]. It should be noted, however, that such an agonistic view of the world has attracted much disquiet from feminist philosophers: see e.g. Irigaray, 1993a, 1993b.)

A kindred analysis of ordering and distribution also features prominently within Law's (1997) discussion of heterogeneity, notably in relation to architecture and minimalism. Law describes architecture as a structured order that might be seen from one place, a single location. It is concerned with aims, objectives, goals, fundamental laws, plans and blueprints, a search for success and failure, progress and redemption. In addition it could be seen to relate to centring and foundations, knowing and controlling, and about building materially diverse structures devised and controlled from a single place. This is a process that is goal-oriented and ruthlessly centred. In contrast, minimalism is described as ordering (a verb not a noun). It is an attempt to produce some kind of shape, a pattern, which in one way or another can be discerned and performed. It is ironic, as it knows and recognizes its incompleteness, that is, not all can be told and everything ordered, or centred, in one place. As Haraway (1997) suggests, to 'know well' is to be a 'modest witness'. Architecture and minimalism provide a basis for examining the issue of heterogeneity without being drawn into answering rehearsed questions of epistemology (e.g. which description is better, more accurate or corresponds more closely to reality). Law (1997) suggests rather than view, for example, different organizations as inhabiting separate and unrelated worlds, we seek to establish how they 'support, undermine and in general interfere with one another in complex and uncertain ways' (Law, 1997: 7) (see also Mol, 1997, on this point). In other words, they can be seen as 'partially connected' (Strathern, 1991). Within architecture this is unknowable and unperformable, because as Law (1997: 9) states 'that which is centring or foundational could not imagine that which might exist apart from itself'. For Law, 'the world is more than a singularity, but less than multiplicity. It is a fractionality of complex and partially connected space/times' (Law, 1997: 8).

But why should this interest someone who is concerned primarily with issues of politics and distributions? Well for Law (1997) politics is about distributions, especially hierarchical distributions. If heterogeneous engineering is about the making of distributions, the question arises of how is the process of exclusion (and thus of naming as impure, inverted, perverted, different and Other, etc.) to be adequately performed? This is 'where the Other becomes the mirror image of order, that which is told and performed into being as an exemplification of the evils of dis/order' (Law, 1997: 9) or what Lee and Stenner (1996) call 'belonging by banishment'. In order to deal with that which does not belong, or that which is not Other, a hierarchy, a larger, homogeneous context is created which is singular. It locates itself and those who *do* belong within a flat space. This may consist of a variety of singular contexts, viewed as making up the socio-material world. The making of this pluralist space is seen as the nearest that architecture, for example, comes to fractionality, and underlies the possibility of situations such as that of liberal democracy and the forces of the market. Pluralism is thus seen as the dream of singularity, the architect's answer to the uncertainties of Otherness (Law, 1997: 9).

In contrast, within minimalism orderings are partially connected, benevolently or viciously, with other orderings. It is impossible to grasp an ordering from one place or within one ordering. For Law (1997: 12):

> it is not a doctrine of flat spaces or conformable containers which hold separate but homogeneous entities. It is, rather an irreducible complexity of partial connections, which may be performed in one way or another, but cannot, as it were, be ordered, told, or performed from a particular place.

Law maintains that certain distributions cannot be 'seized' or 'drawn together' within the architectural attitude. He suggests instead that the best we can do is to adopt the incomplete and top-heavy attitude of minimalism, and thus find fractional ways of 'knowing' and 'telling' these distributions. This requires not only new skills, but also new ways of knowing and telling which are comfortable with the uncertainties of minimalism. That is:

> forms of knowledge that do not banish that which cannot be assimilated or told, but imagine and perform themselves instead in irony and ambivalence. Forms of knowledge that do not flatten differences into pluralism, but rather understand these — and themselves — to be partial connections in a fractional world.

> Such are the skills and knowledges appropriate to a post-architectural world, to a world of uncertainty.
>
> (Law, 1997: 12)

This also relates to the earlier critique of ANT and more specifically immutable mobiles where certain writers (Lee and Brown, 1994; Mol, 2002; Law and Singleton, 2005) have highlighted the ways in which such approaches can provide a rather standardized and limited analysis of particular objects. For Law and Mol, one possible solution to resisting such singularities and the pressure to render knowing simple, transparent, singular, and formulaic is through specific metaphors (as outlined earlier) which attempt to explore thinking which is lumpy, complex, heterogeneous and not strategically ordered.

While Latour (1997) has not followed the same path as Law, he also argues that while ANT has been accused of levelling human and non-human differences, this is not the same as ignoring political differences in terms of access and experience. Rather, the process of levelling seeks to break down reified boundaries that may prevent us from seeing how humans and non-humans are intermeshed. However, some of the consequences of these practices of intermeshing need to be examined, especially in terms of methods of accounting for exclusion and distribution. For example, a stabilized network is only stable for some — for those who are the ‘community of practice’ who form/use/maintain it (Star, 1991). Even for those who may be deemed part of this community of practice there may be occasions when some individuals have less access to particular strategies and resources, which may then limit their role in the formation and maintenance of networks (cf. the ‘marginal’ person who belongs and does not belong simultaneously). These are described by Star (1991) as ‘high tension zones’ and particularly relate to those actors who do not fit neatly into a certain category. (For example, she provides the moving illustration of the transsexual who is considering having an operation, to become a woman, but is in the stage ‘in between’, i.e. where she/he is being ‘told’ to act as a woman, for example, in how she dresses. Failing to wear ‘women’s’ clothes is viewed as a lack of conviction in actually wanting to make the change. There is a lot of pressure for those in a pre-operative stage to conform to a certain ‘image’ associated with women). While some form of ordering and classification is required in order to access past, present and future, it is important that the development and stabilization of standards and classifications are not taken as universal or given. In other words, there needs to be room to examine this process in more detail without relying on *a priori* notions of representation and universality.

Many have accused ANT of failing to give sufficient prominence to issues of power and politics. Even though the alternative path adopted by theorists such as Latour, Law and Mol may not fit comfortably with certain thinkers (e.g. with some researchers in labour process theory or critical management studies) these issues are in fact fundamental to their work. For Latour, in *Making Things Public* (Latour and Weibel, 2005), *Politics of Nature* (2004) and *Reassembling the Social* (2005), he recognizes the need for further reflection in this area and provides alternative ways of thinking about politics and relations. For instance, he notes that while talking politically may be viewed positively, it is often associated with negative connotations, something that slows things down, evades direct action, produces extra factors to consider and labour over, and involves deviations from faithful information and representation (see Latour, 2004b). Uttered talk, for example, does not belong to those who say it, thus the identification of origins in terms of which other agents who are involved in the process of talk is clearly a political issue. The continuous presence (and absence) of these others in the form of the 'irreducible multiple' or their 'indispensable unification', partly explains the slowness and curvature of political talk, but also the ways in which issues of authorship and authority are consubstantial to political ways of talking especially in terms of identifying in the name of whom we are talking (Latour, 2004b: 13). The delegation of the practices of speech to someone who speaks on their behalf could be seen as a shifting in spacing, timing and acting. Political talk is therefore similar to other talk in the sense that it is always the effect of engaging others: the multiplicity of many shifts in timings, spacing and actings. For instance, in addition to holding the position of the one to whom talk has been delegated, Latour describes how they also occupy:

> the position n^{-1} by prompting the speaker who makes her/him/it talk, to talk. "You don't make me say anything other than what I make you say; it is from this that we draw the possibility of our autonomy and hence our liberty". The "I-me" is thus both the one who delegates and the delegate: s/he has been given the right to speak and s/he gives it. There is nothing less authentic, primitive, natural, indigenous than the person who delegates. Like the "Me, I think" and for the same reasons, it is necessary for an enunciator of the first degree to have "sent her/him to say" something, for her/him to start talking. And, of course, this enunciator ranking n^{-1} is not a unit but a multitude. We now easily see why political talk arouses a feeling of discomfort every time political forms of talk are judged in terms of reasonable reason — which, remember, cannot either account for the real artifice of the sciences, for it always seems outrageous to those who believe they master what they say.
>
> (Latour, 2003: 14)

Political talk thus involves a complex positioning of the delegate and delegated, the enunciator and the enunciated, with much complexity underlying who 'makes' us talk, and for whom we talk. Resemblance is never possible from these contradictory positions, and neither is transparency, immediacy, nor mimesis (Latour, 2003).

Latour's notion of articulation also helps in exploring how articulations can proliferate through differences, and mediations and controversies. Articulations not only rely upon and create differences, but also occasions of repetition, stability and sameness. Clearly, articulation is not merely a logocentric term, for rather than locating articulations merely in words or things, Latour highlights the notion of propositions to describe what is articulated. The key difference is that rather than saying things are named in 'words' by the labelling activity of a human subject, the articulation does something to the 'things' themselves: a world made of articulated propositions. Again Latour attributes the term 'multiverse' to such a world, as the universe freed from its premature unification, by registering the many articulations. This is a multiverse affected by many others and 'put into motion by new entities whose differences are registered in new and unexpected ways' (Latour, 2004b: 3). Rather than talking with authority, this relates to being affected by differences, as differences are generative of meanings and leads to the creation of further spacings, timings and actings. However, this still raises the question of how we attend to this issue of good and bad articulations and fabrications, and the nature of objects (see Latour, 2004b).

Conclusions

The aim of this chapter has been to highlight some of the key issues and problems relating to the production of actor-network accounts, and to increase the awareness of these issues to writers and researchers not familiar with the approach, especially researchers in management and organization studies. Each of these issues — namely the inclusion/exclusion of actors; the treatment of humans and non-humans; the handling of agency/structure; and the nature of politics and heterogeneous engineering — is important for comprehending the notion of general symmetry in relation to the production of ANT accounts. We have seen how the concept of general symmetry is the focus for many of the criticisms directed at ANT: If an account appears to lack symmetry, or symmetry is brought in through the analytical 'back door', the ANT researcher is criticized for submitting to the demands of institutional empiricism at the expense of social theory. Alternatively, if symmetry is taken to its logical conclusion, the ANT researcher is taken to task for leading us into the realms of analytical absurdity, through providing 'unrealistic' accounts (where 'everything is seen as everything else and we become lost in a world of mirrors': Bloomfield and Vurdubakis, 1999: 8). These twin charges of symmetrical absence or symmetrical absurdity form the basis of a further challenge to ANT in terms of coping with the symmetry of homogeneity and heterogeneity, stability and multiplicity. In particular, this relates to how we attend to the multiplicity associated with organizational change while still attending to the complex interactions underlying ideas of endurance and subsistence. This is especially important when we consider the paradoxical situations in which ANT researchers find themselves when conducting field studies and producing accounts, notably in respect of notions of power, orderings and distributions, which are concepts that also require greater examination in terms of the research process.

In respect of the future use of ANT, it can be argued that despite its status as an 'unconventional' and thus perhaps peripheral approach in social science (and particularly so in management and organization studies) amongst other things it has provided us with new perspectives on sociological method, notably through analysis of construction and representation, reflexivity and 'otherness', managerial power and organizational technologies, and the ontological status of theories. As we increasingly confront the role of contemporary technologies in novel 'virtual' spatio-temporal configurations, and as our interactions with technological systems increasingly define our modes of existence, ANT can potentially offer new and meaningful ways of representing the associated processes and practices.

5 Fluidity and identity (with Beverly Metcalfe)

In this chapter we attempt to challenge dominant feminist philosophical debates on organization in order to develop fluid formations of a feminine symbolic imaginary. We map how the feminine symbolic is constructed and reconstructed through intertextual models of language so as to destabilize binary classifications of gender. Developing the analysis in Chapter 3, we draw on, and write through, the theoretical and poetical gestures of Luce Irigaray, a feminist philosopher frequently overlooked in contemporary critical debates on organization. In essence we argue that her writings can be a powerful medium for re-imagining organization practices by encouraging researchers to challenge taken-for-granted beliefs about gender structures, gender symbolism and gendering processes. Mindful of criticisms that Irigaray's work reflects a radical form of essentialism, we attempt to show, through dialogic engagement with her writings, a commitment to the fluidity of organizational identities. In so doing we argue that Irigaray's 'feminine' writings offer the opportunity to expand on feminist investigations of organization theory. In the feminist poststructuralist tradition we focus on the interweaving and overlapping aspects of her work. As in Chapter 3, we reveal how sexual difference is primarily based on a logic of the 'same' and how fluid forms of femininity can be imagined and (re)created. As part of this analysis we examine Irigaray's deconstruction of the sexuate structure of language; in particular we focus on two textual strategies — mimeses and dialogic forms of engagement. Unlike much poststructuralist work on organization, this form of analysis emphasizes intertextual forms of knowledge that weave together reader, writer and social text in moving interplay.

From body of woman to body of text: issues in feminist poststructuralism

Within feminist sociology there has been a burgeoning of literature seeking to cast a critical net over assumptions of gender hierarchies and unravel the nuances of gendered power relations and identities in organizations (Jackson, 1999; Halford and Leonard, 2001). Similarly, within critical management studies, feminist poststructuralists in particular, through deconstruction of taken-for-granted managerial and organization practices, have opened up several new knowledge territories (see Calás and Smircich, 1992a, 1992b, 1994; Mills, 1994; Fondas, 1997; Hardy, 2001).

Mumby summarizes what he sees as the six key themes underpinning such feminist poststructuralist modes of inquiry: a) a critique of dominant Western forms of rationality; b) a rejection of representational views of language in favour of a view of language and discourse as constitutive of reality and experience; c) a questioning of any universal truths; d) a decentring of the Western subject in favour of a subject who is fractured and discontinuous; e) a focus on power and domination; and f) a focus on difference and the 'other' embraced in a concern for marginalized groups (1996: 261).

We argue there is no single voice that situates poststructuralism and feminism in particular fashions, though there does seem to be consensus on a number of issues. First, the body is a central point of analysis amongst poststructuralist theorists. This is very much the case with Irigaray's writings, which attempt to redraw the polarities of patriarchal thought by positioning the female body as the locus of transformational possibilities. As McNay states:

> It is not necessary to posit a single cause of feminine subordination. Once the female sex has come to connote specific feminine characteristics, this "imaginary" signification produces concrete effects through diverse social practices. These concrete effects are not the expression of an immutable feminine essence. However, they react, in turn, by constituting the maintenance and reproduction of this symbolism and, thus, perpetuate the myth of immutable feminine qualities.
>
> (McNay, 1992: 22)

Second, many poststructuralist feminists situate the exercise of power at the local level. This means there are no overarching totalizing explanations of gendered relations of domination. Power is exercised not from above, but rather resides in the local and individual practices of institutional life and has multiple points of origin (Weedon, 1987, 1999).

And third, feminist poststructuralists are concerned with the role of discourse in the construction of the gendered relations of power. As such, subjectivities, power relations, forms of resistance and so forth all exist as discursive practices that are arranged in a complex system of signification (Butler, 1990; Gill, 1995; Mumby, 1996; Wetherell, 2001). As Weedon states: 'language is the place where forms of social organisation and their likely social and political consequences are defined and contested. Yet it is also the place where our sense of selves, our subjectivity is constructed' (1987: 21).

The idea of a unitary fixed sense of self is, therefore, rejected in favour of one that is fragile, fragmented and fluid. The effect of this is a move away from essentialist notions of subjectivity and to opening up the potential for transformation and change. These more fluid forms of subjectivity thus create the possibility for difference and otherness to become a primary focus in analyses in poststructuralist thought (Mumby, 1996).

These theoretical developments have been powerfully presented by Calás and Smircich who argue that poststructuralist modes of inquiry enable feminist concerns to move from '*the body of woman* to the *body of the text*' (1999: 660). They suggest that poststructuralist theorizing has argued that women's agency, and, therefore, their capacity to actively challenge dominant gender paradigms, is itself perceived as socially constructed, a product of highly gendered relations of power in society. In this respect it could be argued that a feminist poststructuralist framework is not tenable since it assumes *a priori* theorizing about femaleness and womanhood. This 'depoliticization' (Calás and Smircich, 1999), of course, poses several challenges. We would support the view of Riley (1988) who stresses that although women are 'historically' and 'discursively' constructed at different moments and in different situations, and that 'woman' is, therefore, an unstable category, nevertheless it is one we must continue to employ (1988: 23–24; see also Wolff, 1990: 7–9; Gherardi, 1995: 105–6; Calás and Smircich, 1992b, 1999). Many feminists concur with Toril Moi that 'it still remains politically essential to defend women as women in order to counteract the patriarchal oppression that precisely defines women as women' (1985: 13).

Butler argues similarly:

> Within feminism it seems as if there is some political necessity to speak as, and for women, and I would not contest that category … On the contrary, if feminism presupposes that women designates an undesignatable field of differences, one that cannot be totalized or summarized by a descriptive identity category, then the very term becomes a site of openness and resignifiability.
>
> (Butler, 1995: 49–50)

Thus, while disavowing the totalizing concept of 'woman', in favour of 'textual openness and fluidity' (Wolff, 1990: 9) we can still engage with a feminist politics, since feminist modes of knowledge inquiry are concerned with identifying dominant discourses and disciplinary practices so as to unveil new meanings, new voices and interpretations and to challenge the basis of existing knowledge. Butler suggests that: 'To authorise or safeguard the category woman as a site of possible significations is to expand the possibilities of what it means to be a woman and in this sense to enable an enhanced sense of agency' (1995: 50).

Calás and Smircich argue that poststructuralist feminism allows us to notice *how* the 'signs' of 'woman' and 'feminine' function as general limits in our discourse and institutions (1992a: 232). This approach enables one to unveil how is 'organization theorizing (male) gendered and with what consequences: And how may organizational theorizing be rewritten through gender' (1992b: 228).[1]

From the forgoing discussion one can argue that poststructuralist theorizing has advanced our critical understanding of feminist debates through disavowing universal concepts of woman, womanhood and femaleness. It can be argued also that such work has enriched organizational scholarship. However, we have some general concerns with aspects of this theorizing and draw upon Calás and

Smircich's work to illustrate these. We refer specifically to Calás and Smircich's writings because of the way in which critical organization theorizing has influenced academic scholarship, notably in America and Europe.[2] They also claim to be feminists. Our concerns with Calás and Smircich's work relate first to the fact that their writings appear to be disciplined within dominant modes of organization theorizing. Second, we feel there are lost opportunities in linking critical organization studies to wider debates within feminist sociological and philosophical scholarship, especially those that pay attention to how knowledge generation processes incorporate intertexual subjectivities (Jackson, 1999; Stanley, 2000; Webster, 2000).

If we review Calás and Smircich's writings one can see that their deliberations have been formed and fashioned in particular ways with critical positions established through recourse to the *fathers* of philosophy — especially Foucault, Derrida and Deleuze — rather than feminist philosophers who, like Calás and Smircich, have principally been concerned with challenging binary constructions of gender (see Braidotti, 1994; Benhabib, 1995; Fraser, 1995). In addition it can be said that their work rather skims over feminist literary/women's studies, which has paid special attention to exploring the way in which text and author are interwoven as part of knowledge-generating processes (Moi, 1985; Jackson, 1999; Stanley, 2000; Webster, 2000). Marshall (2000) comes to a similar conclusion in her editorial of feminism and organization studies research in the *Journal of Management Inquiry*. She notes how the well-known *Handbook of Organization Studies* (Clegg and Hardy, 1996) provides an illustration of how: 'there are substantive sections of mainstream conversation that focus their referencing on a relatively small band of scholars and do not incorporate pluralist appreciations' (2000: 171).

Turning now to our concerns with writing and reflexivity one is struck by how little feminist organization scholarship has taken up the significance of 'writing theory' in detail despite its central significance highlighted in postmodern organization analysis. We would argue that Calás and Smircich do not adequately engage with issues of reflexivity and the process of writing research. They highlight how poststructuralist approaches depict the author as 'embedded in the text', and argue that by thinking through, and with the author, newer meanings may be produced (see Calás and Smircich, 1999: 553–54). In addition, they posit the key to 'success' and 'identity' within an academic's work is personal engagement with 'writing' (1999: 665). As such, they claim:

> Writing while incorporating undecidability of meaning, the crisis of representation, and the problematisation of subject and author locates the moral responsibility of the scholar, who cannot claim innocence from the representational force that she or he brings to the text.
>
> (Calás and Smircich, 1999: 665)

Calás and Smircich thus allude to the way in which writing and writing theory are interlinked but do not promote those feminist literary scholars and philosophers who have been concerned to bring meaning to the embodied experiences of those they research and who expose the intertextualities between subject and author (e.g. Irigaray, 1985a, 1985b; Benhabib, 1995; Lengel, 1998; Stanley, 2000). That is, they do not elaborate on the fluidity of textual constructions as reader, writer and text come together, nor detail reflexive engagements. Is this perhaps due to the way in which they and other writers on postmodern organization theorizing have been entombed by the rush to incorporate Foucault, Derrida, Lyotard and Deleuze within their work? We emphasize that this argument is made not to cast doubt on the intellectual integrity of Calás and Smircich's work, but to give voice to arguments such as Irigaray's (1985a) concerning the way in which, for example, the philosophical academy in France has been so dominated and controlled by men (see also Whitford, 1991). The corollary perhaps is that theorizing that rests outside the realm of dominant organization studies is rendered less meaningful and relevant (or is indeed meaningless and irrelevant).[3]

Failing to respond to the growing concerns within broader feminist scholarship to unravel the living textualities — the embodied experiences of men and women that 'writing differently' produces — is perhaps bizarre when one considers that Calás and Smircich acknowledge the lack of 'solid ground' (1999: 649) and elusiveness of poststructuralist debates. They ask: 'but once you've deconstructed, then what? How can we reconstruct, or get anything positive from this?' (1999: 649). As feminist literary scholars note (in particular Jackson, 1999 and Cameron, 1998) is it necessary to distinguish between the applications of discourse analysis and the theory itself? Among the potential problems identified (and to some extent already alluded to here) are that discourse-based approaches deny anything that is extra-discursive, such as the materiality of women's oppression (Jackson, 1999), the moral and political relativism that marginalizes questions of value, and the absence 'at the end of a hard day's deconstruction', of any clue as to what, in the realm of feminist politics, might actually be done about anything (Cameron, 1998: 965).

Of course, it could be argued that all politics is discursive politics, and that discourse is all there is, and that when the social scientist has taken a text apart and understood how it works then it has somehow been changed. The process of discourse analysis is resistive: isn't that enough? Cameron argues not, since new meanings and interpretations, upon which a 'new reality' is based, do not necessarily move us towards, for example, 'taking different actions (including discursive ones) such as defining a particular experience as sexual harassment' (Cameron, 1998: 966).

Specifically, it is the engagement of the author with the subject matter, in, around, at the margins, of the text, as the author impinges on, and shapes knowledge production, but also acknowledging the fleshy passions and embodiment of the organizational actors which are studied, that is at the heart of Irigaray's theorizing. In the following we will promote Irigaray's insights into the materiality of discursive discourse practices, notably in relation to feminist poststructuralism. We suggest that Irigaray's writings permit a fluid dynamic way of understanding organizational relations, and in particular gendered power relations. In essence Irigaray is concerned with writing in the *fluidity of gender in process*. We cannot hope to do justice to the richness of Irigaray's contributions and here focus on just two aspects that have been relatively unexplored in organizational analysis. First, how fluidity is central to Irigaray's deconstruction processes, thereby disavowing claims of essentialism which she has frequently been targeted with (as in Chapter 3, we show how Irigaray's appropriation of the feminine is a purposeful textual strategy — mimesis). And second, by examining how the dialogic engagement of reader/writer and text is significant in forming and reforming fluid identities and relations.

Specularizing fluid forms of femininity

In *Speculum of the Other Woman* Irigaray (1985a) provides a probing retrospective analysis of the phallogocentric epistemological assumptions in Western thought, commencing with Freudian theory and ending with Platonic philosophy. In this and her other key works she is concerned to spell out the consequences of defining sexual difference by recourse to masculine systems of representation. Irigaray discusses the particularities of the feminine world — a world different from that of men with respect to language, with respect to the body, with respect to work and with respect to nature and the world of culture. In relation to work she attempts to show:

> that socioeconomic justice does not consist of merely putting a rule into practice — "equal work for equal pay" — but consists of respecting and valorizing women in forms of choice in the ends and means of production, professional qualifications, relationships in the workplace, asocial recognition of work and so on.
>
> (Irigaray, 1995: 13)

Irigaray's questioning is structured as a reflective mirroring, hence the *Speculum*.[4] She mirrors these theories by entering into close dialogue with the fathers of philosophy, deconstructing them not only through her own, but also through their, often paradoxical, words. Hence there is a Derridean deconstructive influence informing her writing structure, though she does not directly acknowledge Derrida's influence.[5] Above all she provides a flexible theoretical framework where masculinity and femininity function as fluid psycho-linguistic structures instead of being static definitions. For Irigaray the other cannot be touched, for it remains at the margins — 'the other is always the other of the same and not an actual other' (1995: 10).[6]

This logic of the 'same' results in the perpetuation of binary classifications of sex and gender so rendering the feminine and female as distorted, lesser than masculinity: 'What is women? But rather, repeating/interpreting the way in which, within discourse, the feminine finds itself defined as a lack, deficiency, or as imitation and negative image of that subject' (1985b: 78).

Irigaray makes the distinction between speaking 'as' and 'like' a woman (1993b: 51–59) to illustrate how the female becomes entombed within masculine systems of representation, since 'the *feminine occurs only within models and laws devised by male subjects*' (1985b: 86, emphasis in original).

To resist this masculine sameness Irigaray articulates a feminine symbolic order, or a new economy of sexual difference, one that opens up spaces for feminine sensualities. This is not to suggest, however, that in creating feminine spaces she is tied to an essentialist logic, rather, as we will show, in mimicking masculine representations she seeks to disrupt binary constructions, thus elevating the feminine as constitutive of a social order dedicated to ongoing (identity) change (see Chapter 3). But this is not only to recognize the female but to 'bring into play the multiple connections among persons of one's own and other sex, an entire people and people in general' (1993a: 67). Given her commitment to fluidity and analysis at the localized and individual levels, it can be argued that Irigaray's work has much significance for an 'alternative' literature on organization and management. How then does Irigaray re-imagine these new formations and reformulations?

This essentialism which is not one

Schor (1994) notes that the label 'essentialism' conflates a variety of positions that are not always mutually compatible, thus concluding that 'essentialism is not one' (1994: 60, see also Fuss, 1996).[7] This enables essentialism to be read as a 'position rather than an ontology' (Whitford, 1994: 16).[8] This is apparent when one seeks to unravel Irigaray's attempts to 'define woman'. Whitford's critique illustrates that Irigaray 'does not want to tell us what "woman" is: this is something which women will have to create and invent collectively' (Whitford, 1991: 9). Rather, by interrogating the ethical, ontological and social status of women, Irigaray wants to move towards the creation of a powerful female symbolic so as to represent the *other* of sexual difference. In this sense Irigaray is trying to 'imagine the unimaginable'; she is suggesting social transformation, 'a state beyond sexual difference'. Without rearticulating the dualistic classification of male and female, this would be to merely reaffirm the deceptive universality of the male, while the status of women in our society would continue to be secondary (see Whitford, 1991: 22; also Benhabib, 1995). Throughout her work Irigaray makes clear that she does not advocate a theory of woman, nor universalizes womanhood. When asked the question 'Are you a woman?' Irigaray replies:

> A typical question. A man's question? I don't think that a woman — unless she has been assimilated to masculine, and more specifically phallic models — would ask me that question. Because "I" am not "I", I am not, I am not *one*. As for woman, try and find out … In any case, in this form, that of the concept of denomination, certainly not … So the question "Are you a woman" perhaps means there is something "other". But these questions can probably be raised only on "on the man's side" and, as all discourse is masculine, it can be raised only in the form of a hint or suspicion.
>
> (Irigaray, 1985b: 120)

Irigaray's (1985b) concern, therefore, is to show the exclusion of women via discursive strategies, but also at the same time to note the female is 'not one' — *This sex which is not one, has not become, yet.* The charge of essentialism is forcefully raised when she talks of women's sexual anatomy and *her two lips.* Irigaray's 'labial politics' powerfully and poetically expresses multiple identities and their fluidity: 'Between our lips, yours and mine, several voices, several ways of speaking, resound endlessly back and forth. One is never separable you/I are always several at once' (1985a: 209).

Thus Irigaray's writings of 'two lips' is not an attempt to construct a true theory of sexual difference starting from the foundations of female biology, rather it is a challenge to the traditional construction of feminine morphology where the bodies of women are seen as receptacles of masculine completeness (see Schor, 1994: 48–51). In other words, the structuration of a phallocentric discourse shows up in the non-representative nature of the *feminine* in male discourse, and as such, must be investigated. Irigaray is aiming to *unveil* and *make visible* what was supposed to remain invisible — the *feminine*:

> the issue is not one of elaborating a new theory of which woman would be the subject of the object, but of *jamming the theoretical machinery itself*, of suspending its pretension to the production of truth and a meaning that are excessively univocal, repeating/interpreting the way in which, within discourse, the feminine finds itself defined as lack, deficiency or imitation and negative image of the subject, they would signify that with respect to this logic a disruptive excess is possible on the feminine side.
>
> (Irigaray, 1985b: 78 — emphasis in original)

Diverging from a pure Derridean approach that emphasizes difference, Irigaray postulates *sameness* as the constrictive omnipotent intent of prevailing discourse systems. Since philosophical discourse has set forth the laws of the order of discourse it will be necessary to unveil how the domination of the philosophic logos stems in large part from its power to reduce all others to the 'economy of the same' and thus to eradicate the differences between the sexes in systems that are self-representative of the masculine subject (1985a: see 133–51 and 227–40, also Chapter 3). Irigaray (1985a: 227) states: 'So woman has not yet taken (a) place … Woman is still the place in which she cannot take possession of herself as such. She is experienced as all-power-full precisely as her indifferentiation makes her readily power-less'.

From the forgoing discussion it is clear that Irigaray is committed to fluidity of the identity process and is concerned with unveiling how all language use/construction has gendered implications, most notably that the feminine is repressed and censured through recourse to a philosophical logic of male sameness. This perspective provides a theory of gender which proposes that gender subjectivity is constructed through the individual's experience of a variety of subject positions which are created in discourse and constructed in language. This feminist imagining is thus more than mere unveiling of dualistic gender constructions, as evidenced in dominant organization works on gender and sexuality; rather Irigaray hints at political, social and thus gender transformation and becoming (Irigaray, 1985b; Braidotti, 1994).

This view acknowledges the way in which the gendered subject and his or her representation of reality are constructed within a 'social field' (Fournier, 2002). As Nelson argues 'there is a distinction to be made between the subject position described by a text and thus with the subject position it offers' (1999: 34). Similarly Irigaray notes the significance of acknowledging agency: 'There is no simple manageable way to leap to the outside of phallogocentrism, nor any possible way to situate oneself there, that would result from the simple fact of being a woman' (1985b: 162).

And as Weedon (1999) argues, while the individual is never a fully coherent intentional subject, as in the liberal tradition, the individual *is* the site for competing and often contradictory modes of subjectivity which together constitute a particular person. She claims that: 'Modes of subjectivity are constituted within discursive practices and lived by the individual as if he or she were a fully coherent intentional subject' (1999: 104).

Thus Weedon, like Irigaray, concludes that feminist poststructuralist accounts are 'not bereft of agency' (1999: 104).[9] This is significant because this position acknowledges that individuals have a *choice* in the way that they negotiate competing and contradictory discourses.

Playing with text/identity

While noting that female identity is multiple and fluid it is important to note also that Irigaray's use of the word *feminine* is intentional and playful (Kozel, 1996). As we argued in Chapter 3, Irigaray is in fact *mimicking* the discourse that has always been fabricating essentialist sexed facts and truths about female (and male) sexuality.[10] As Butler (1993: 45) argues: 'This textual practice is not grounded in a rival ontology, but inhibits — indeed penetrates, occupies and redeploys — the paternal language itself'.[11]

With this *penetrative* textual strategy Irigaray is able not only to unveil the essentialist and 'sexed' nature of the masculinist tradition, but also at the same time prevent herself from being reabsorbed into the reductive phallocentric order. In other words, to assume 'the feminine role deliberately' (1985a: 76) Irigaray transforms woman's masquerade, her so-called femininity, into a means of appropriating, and playing with, the feminine (see Burke, 1994; Schor, 1994). Through this 'playful repetition' (Irigaray, 1985a: 76), that is, assuming a seemingly essentialist but truly sexed gesture, Irigaray is able to achieve the sexual difference against the sexual indifference characteristic of the phallocentric tradition, so resisting dominant modes of masculine heritage and history, thereby opening up a site for destabilizing binary constructions of gender/sexuality. Irigaray, following Derrida, argues that 'the logic of the same' cannot maintain its supposed self-identity (see also Butler, 1993: 36–53; Schor, 1994: 65–67). Through the interplay between textuality and physicality she attempts to identify how materiality is filtered through and constructed by a set of discursive strategies. To play with Irigaray's text we will state again: *This sex which is not one, has not become, yet.*

The *feminine*, then, is not to be understood as opposite to the masculine: the genderizing of the term should be understood in a broad sense (Kozel, 1996). Mimesis is a purposeful tool to subvert the social order as it is presently defined and preserved by patriarchal structure. Irigaray emphasizes the parodic and playful character of the mimetic role:

> To play with mimesis is thus, for a woman, to try and recover the place of her exploitation and discourse, without allowing herself to be simply reduced by it. It means to resubmit herself … to ideas about herself, that are elaborated in/by a masculine logic, but so as to make "visible", by an effect of playful repetition, what was supposed to remain invisible … It also means to "unveil" the fact that, if woman are such good mimics, it is because they are not simply resorbed in this function. *They also remain elsewhere.*
>
> (Irigaray, 1985b: 76 — emphasis in original)

Je, tu, nous

Braidotti (1994) argues that Irigaray's mimetic strategy is successful because she refuses to separate the 'symbolic discursive dimension' from the 'empirical material and historical dimensions'. In so doing she connects together epistemological questions of the feminine with embodied experiences thereby permitting investigations of embodied subjectivities. The way in which she weaves together the symbolic construction of gender identities and their material positioning is particularly powerful when we explore a central literary strategy running throughout her work — dialogic play. Throughout much of her work Irigaray enacts a dialogic female voice to express the passions and emotions of women as a means of exploring silence. These 'spaces of femininity' (see Irigaray in Hirsch and Olsen, 1995) or individual resistances, can be unveiled, surfaced and articulated through the 'performances of writing', that is by situating as a living place on the borders between feminist thought and masculine traditions. This writing performance is unquestionably sexuate (1993a) and wrapped up with bodily sensitivities and desires. Irigaray states:

> The whole of my body is sexuate. My sexuality isn't restricted to the sexual act … Not to contribute making language and its writings sexed is to perpetuate the pseudo-neutrality of those laws and traditions that privilege masculine genealogies and their codes of logic.
>
> (Irigaray, 1993a: 53)

By challenging masculinist orthodoxy and spirit and drawing attention to the female process of text making, Irigaray's 'embodied performances of writing' aim to make productive spaces for a female voice. Irigaray mingles her voice with the voice/text of male philosophers, searching for an 'entre-nous' — what can we do together? Her writings can be read as being beyond the reach of binary sexual differences as articulated via masculine languages, and so connecting you and me (text and reader) — a form of performative textual engagement. This is effectively articulated by Monteiore:

> Irigaray's insistence on women's fluidity and plurality of speech is, then, as much a prescription for the reader's response as a description of female identity: It describes an approach as well as the thing being approached. Correspondingly, her discursive method very often consists in offering and at the same time withdrawing a list of definitions of the feminine, none of which quite fit.
>
> (Whitford, 1991: 23)[12]

Irigaray's concern to performatively engage with her readers resonates strongly with poststructuralist concerns to encourage the reflexive processes of the writer as she/he is involved in knowledge construction and interpretations. As Whitford convincingly argues of Irigaray:

> her work is offered as an object, a discourse for women to exchange among themselves, a sort of commodity, so that women themselves do not have to function as the commodity, or as the sacrifice on which sociality is built … Her work is for symbolic exchange only.
>
> (Whitford, 1991: 52)

Thus Irigaray is committed to an intersubjective economy that permits equitable symbolic representation and exchange. Her relational figuration of pronouns enriches a reading collaboration with *you* and *us*. She states:

> I am not a simple subjectivity which seeks an object in the other. Belonging to a gender allows me to realize, in me, for me — and equally towards the other — a dialectic between subjectivity and objectivity which escapes the dichotomy between subject and object.
>
> (Irigaray, 2000: 21)

These intertextal exchanges enable both genders to be represented in the structures of language as active, transitive and *reflexive* (or in other words as the *specularization of subjectivity*). Put simply by Derrida 'Everything is reflected in the medium of speculum of reading-writing' (1992: 177), since 'reading is transformational' (Derrida, 1981a: 63), thus text/identity is always unfolding. Conceived in this plural and dynamic fashion woman can never be identified as static and foundational, or as Irigaray states, paraphrasing Aristotle's formulation, 'as place, matter, envelope for the erection of the content of conversation, its form and shaper-man' (1993b: 12). In her texts the influential Aristotelian dichotomy between feminine matrix (inert envelope, passive matter, malleable body) and masculine form (active soul) crosses its hierarchical boundaries, reemerging as embodied ethical relations of gendered intersubjectivities.

Thus in dialogic engagement women and men perceive the differences that unite and separate them. Irigaray's approach rests on multiple and fluid definitions of class, race and gender identifications and divergences that are discontinuously and diversely reinforced by particular responses to the other rather than being essential and constant. Hence, although our symbolic order may always be coded by signifiers such as gender, race and class this does not necessarily mean that all subjects will be aware of these social markers in similar ways or at all times.

The relevance of Irigaray to organization analysis

By extension our analysis would position feminine and organizational analysis within a new symbolic order, one that seeks to re-imagine gendered relations in an organizational setting. Our discussion of Irigaray brings to the fore the inadequacies of all-encompassing organizational frameworks and extends to the localized and personal dynamics of (intra)organizational relations (Hearn, 2000). Similar to Burrell's (1988) observation (when reviewing Foucault's contribution to organization analysis) that the linguistic category 'organization' attempts to reduce difference to sameness, Irigaray posits that knowledge constructions are built on a masculine logic, reflecting its own alter ego — unable to reflect any other image than that constructed within masculine systems of representation. So while symbolically, organization, managerial and social practices reproduce the hierarchization of the disciplinary gender order, the logic of the same masks other subjectivities. By unveiling the sexualization of discourse, Irigaray (1985a, 1985b) urges us to look for new structures of meaning, a vision that embraces a redefinition of gender relations between men and women, a vision that acknowledges the existence of two sexes, not one. Quite simply it concerns envisioning a social order where *To Be Two* (Irigaray, 2000) is linguistically represented. Through her mimetic interrogations Irigaray hopes to bring about a change in discourse (see 1985: 191) and for the feminine to *become*, 'This sex which is not one, has not become, yet' — since 'women lack a mirror for becoming women' (1985a: 79). Women must come to speak 'as' women (Irigaray, 1985b) according to their own definitions and desires, not as mirror reflections of men.

From a feminist poststructuralist position this would permit the unveiling of the complexity, contingency and fragility of organizational forms as 'transitory manifestations of relationships of dominance-subordination — and as mere embodiment of an underlying relationship of forces' (Burrell, 1988: 231). Work by Ely and Meyerson (2000) could be seen to take this approach. In their work on evaluating gender identities and organizational restructuring programs they have suggested the use of 'narrative revision', which encourages organizational actors, especially those in marginalized groups, to 'name themselves, speak for themselves, and participate in defining the terms of interaction' (Ely and Meyerson, 2000: 28) thus bringing to the fore those voices that have been silenced and conflicts that have been suppressed. This process is not intended to generate a single, coherent narrative, but rather to disrupt and modify dominant narratives, opening up new knowledge territories.

While not wanting to underplay the significance of undoing binary constructions, what is key to engaging with Irigaray's writings are the fluid (re)formations of intertextual territories and corresponding embodied subjectivities (Braidotti, 1994). While reflexivity is part of poststructuralist organization modes of inquiry, within feminist organization research reflexivity assumes a greater significance in view of the ways in which gender symbolism and gendered power relations inscribe meaning and value to masculinity and femininity — rendering femaleness, femininity and womanhood in organization spheres as problematical — something to be managed (Hearn, 2000). The opening up of marginalized and silenced voices is therefore essential as part of feminists' reconstructive aims, especially when we can only express organizations and ourselves through a masculine literary logic and form. Through her dialogic strategies Irigaray alerts us to the *fluidity of writing gender in process*, and following feminist literary traditions instills a sense that 'writing differently', writing femininity and writing organization can unsettle and destabilize a masculinist orthodoxy (Lengel, 1998; Webster, 2000). We write with who we are (see Irigaray, 1993a: 52–54). We write differently, within, and through organizational texts. Je, Tu, Nous. If one looks to the future development of organization theory within what is often termed the 'postmodern debate' the message is that we invite her, the other in, so as to re-imagine new organizational formations and new identities. As Irigaray argues: 'Don't cry. One day we will succeed in saying ourselves. And what we shall say will be even more beautiful than our tears. All fluid' (1985b: 215).

Conclusion

Advancing a feminist poststructuralist organization theory, this chapter has again drawn upon the theoretic and poetical writings of Luce Irigaray to show how organizational and managerial practices can be re-imagined. We have focused upon three aspects of her work — the fluidity of identity construction as an ongoing change process; her mimetic strategies for unveiling sexuate language structures; and her dialogic mode of reading/writing texts. Emphasizing the transformational possibilities of intersubjectivities within shifting textualities, we have suggested that organization modes of inquiry can benefit from an Irigarayan lens — by inviting the feminine, the 'other' in, we can begin to open up new knowledge territories and unveil the writing of the fluidity of gender in process.

6 Time and temporality

In this chapter, we explore a set of alternative concepts of time and temporality as they apply to organization theory and analysis. Specifically the chapter offers a historical review of paradigms of temporal structuring and experience in the evolution of work organizations. The chapter is developed in three parts. Initially we outline some key images of time and temporality to emerge from philosophy and social theory. In particular, we discuss images of temporal structuring reflected in the two key time metaphors, the line and the cycle. Second, we examine some of the main time paradigms to emerge from the history of industrial organization. While initially the focus is upon those modernist linear time images that stem from the progressive *commodification* of the labour process, subsequently this analysis is juxtaposed with time images that reflect the social *construction* of organizational culture and meaning. Here an examination of the homogeneous time-reckoning systems of Taylorism is contrasted with examples of heterogeneous time-reckoning from anthropological traditions and ethnographic studies. The final part of this historical review, discusses what can be termed, basically, the postmodern debate in the sociology of time. Having devoted much of the foregoing analysis to issues of modernist and industrialist 'clock-time', this section sees discussion of what has been referred to variously as postmodern or postindustrial 'instantaneous-time', whereby organizational practices are based on time-frames that lie beyond conscious human experience. This concept is associated historically with the purported complex shifts from Fordism to the flexible accumulation of post-Fordism. Central to this debate is the notion of the time-space *compression* of physical processes and human experiences.

Social philosophy

A common starting point for those wishing to explore sociological and organizational paradigms of temporal structuring and experience is within the long and sophisticated tradition of temporal analysis in the literature of social philosophy. As Jaques (1982: xi) notes, the concept of time has been a central and continuous subject for philosophers for over 2,000 years. Debate is found at a number of abstract levels, ranging from ontological concerns with time and existence, to epistemological concerns with time and understanding. It is a tradition that has yielded a wealth of abstract, complex, yet unresolved questions (see Gale, 1968). Although a detailed analysis of such questions is beyond our scope, we can at least note some of the main issues that confront the philosopher of time.

To achieve this, we turn briefly to the excellent analysis of temporal philosophy presented by Heath (1956). On introducing the philosophy of time, Heath asks three questions central to discussions in the field. First, at the level of ontology, he asks whether we should regard time as an objective *fact* located 'out there' in the external world, or as a subjective *essence* which is constructed via a network of meanings; that is, should we think of time as real and concrete or essential and abstract? Second, he asks whether we should think of time as *homogeneous* (time units are equivalent) or as *heterogeneous/epochal* (time units are experienced differentially); is time continuous and infinite, or atomistic and divisible? And third, he asks whether time can be *measured*, and if so, whether we can have more than one valid time; should time be regarded as a *unitary quantitative commodity* or as a *manifold qualitative experience*? In many ways, the manner by which we answer these questions will determine how time is conceptualized in relation to organization, organizations and organizing. Heath's antinomies represent basic constructs for interpreting much of the nature and history of time paradigms in organizational analysis. Moreover, they provide a set of tools for dissecting many of the sociological concepts relating to temporal issues of organization, and lay conceptual foundations for several associated research perspectives.

Metaphors of time

Sociologists have argued that a metaphor is a powerful tool for the analysis of social and organizational phenomena (Manning, 1979; Pinder and Moore, 1979; Tinker, 1986). In particular, it has become popular to use metaphors, or other related tropes, when illustrating the imagery of sociological concepts (Lakoff and Johnson, 1980). Morgan (1986), for example, has shown the power of metaphor for interpreting organizations as 'systems', 'machines', 'dramas', 'organisms', and even 'psychic prisons'. For concepts of time, however, relatively few robust metaphors have been refined to conceptualize what is, like organization, an abstract and elusive notion. Of those that have, the most ubiquitous historically have been those of the 'cycle' and the 'line' (see Jaques, 1982).

For the metaphor of cycle, one of the best-known analyses has been that provided by Eliade (1959), who describes how the cycle was the basic time metaphor of what he calls 'archaic' or 'pre-Christian' man. Eliade suggests that for 'archaic man' events unfolded in an ever-recurring rhythm; his sense of time was developed out of his struggle with the seasons; his time horizon was defined by the 'myth of the eternal return'. Eliade argues subsequently that when 'Christian man' abandoned this bounded archaic world for a direct, linear progression to redemption and salvation, then for the first time he found himself exposed to the dangers inherent in the historical process. Since then humankind has tried to master history and to bring it to a conclusion, as, for example, Marx and Hegel sought to do. In the 'modern' world, he suggests we seek refuge in various forms of faith in order to rationalize a historical process that seems to have neither beginning nor end (see also Park, 1980 and Fabian, 1983).

An argument similar to that of Eliade is provided by de Grazia (1974) in his analysis of 'linear-time'. De Grazia suggests that whereas primitive concepts of time are dominated by the metaphor of the cycle, for 'modern' societies Christian beliefs give the image of time as a straight line — as a testing pathway from sin on earth, through redemption, to eternal salvation in heaven. He argues that in the evolution of modern culture the idea of irreversibility replaced that of the eternal return. The distinguishing feature of 'ultimate progression' led the way to a new linear concept of time and with it a sense of firm beginning. de Grazia suggests for example that in Book Two of *Confessions*, Augustine 'broke' the circle of Roman time. In contrast to Herodotus and his notion of the cycle of human events, Augustine dispelled 'false circles' and instead purported the 'straight line of human history'. In particular, during the eighteenth century the Anno Domini chronology became culturally widespread, with history being dated primarily from the birth of Jesus Christ (de Grazia, 1974).

The commodification paradigm

The linear metaphor of time became hegemonic for organizational analysis because of its link with a further concept — time as a commodity of industrialism. This link is central to the development of what can be termed the 'linear-quantitative' paradigm of temporal imagery in industrial and organizational sociology. In terms of the modernism-postmodernism debate, this paradigm reflects a classic modernist grand narrative and trajectory (see Ermarth, 1992; Macnaghten and Urry, 1998; Casey, 2002).

To expand, during the rise of industrial capitalism this sense of unilinearity was to find time equated with value (E. P. Thompson, 1967; Thrift, 1981; Nyland, 1986). Technological and manufacturing innovations saw the concept become closely aligned with that of industrial progress. Time, like the individual, became a commodity of the production process, for in the crucial equation linking acceleration and accumulation, a human value could be placed upon time. Surplus value could be accrued through extracting more time from labourers than was required to produce goods having the value of their wages (Marx, 1976). The emphasis was upon formality and scarcity. The images came from Newton and Descartes: time was real, uniform and all-embracing; it was a mathematical phenomenon; it could be plotted as an abscissa.

In this Newtonian/Cartesian tradition, modern industrial cultures were seen to adopt predominantly linear time perspectives. Here, the past is unrepeatable, the present is transient, and the future is infinite and exploitable. Time is homogeneous: it is objective, measurable, and infinitely divisible; it is related to change in the sense of motion and development; it is quantitative. Whereas in modern theology linear time has as its conclusion the promise of eternity, in the mundane, secular activities of industrialism temporal units are seen as finite. Time is a resource that has the potential to be consumed by a plethora of activities; its scarcity is seen as intensified when the number of potential claimants is increased. In advanced societies time scarcity makes events become more concentrated and segregated — special 'times' are given over for various forms of activities. Time is experienced not only as a sequence but also as a boundary condition. As the functionalist sociologist Wilbert Moore stated, time becomes: 'a way of locating human behaviour, a mode of fixing the action that is particularly appropriate to circumstances' (1963a: 7).

By uniting the ideas of linearity and value we begin to see time as a limited good — its scarcity enhances its worth. Lakoff and Johnson (1980) crystallize this idea by citing three metaphors to illustrate the dominant conception of linear time: time is money; time is a limited resource; time is a valuable commodity. Graham (1981), likewise, suggests that time and money are increasingly exchangeable commodities: time is one means by which money can be appropriated, in the same way as money can be used to buy time; money increases in value over time, while time can be invested now to yield money later.

This quantitative, commodified image is thus primarily a by-product of industrialism. Mumford (1934) for instance emphasized how 'the clock, not the steam engine [was] the key machine of the industrial age' (1934: 14). He argued that rapid developments in synchronization were responsible for organizations of the industrial revolution being able to display such high levels of functional specialization. Large production-based firms required considerable segmentation of both parts (roles and positions) and activities in time and space. Such specializations set requirements for extensive time/space co-ordination at both intra- and inter-organizational levels; as high levels of co-ordination needed high levels of planning, so sophisticated temporal schedules were necessary to provide a satisfactory degree of predictability. The basis of fine prediction became that of sophisticated measurement, with efficient organization becoming synonymous with detailed temporal assessments of productivity. As the machine became the focal point of work, so time schedules became the central feature of planning. During industrialism the clock was *the* instrument of co-ordination and control. The time period replaced the task as the focal unit of production (Mumford, 1934).

In another landmark study, E. P. Thompson (1967) argues that industrialism sees a crucial change in the employment relation, as it is now time rather than skill or effort that becomes of paramount concern. In large-scale manufacturing, the worker becomes subject to extremely elaborate and detailed forms of time discipline (E. P. Thompson, 1967). Whereas prior to industrialism 'nearly all craftsmen were self employed, working in their own homes with their tools, to their own hours' (Wright, 1968: 16), with the factory system came temporal rigidity. Before the industrial revolution the prime characteristic of work was its irregularity. Periods of intense working were followed by periods of relative inactivity. There was the tradition of 'St Monday', with Mondays often being taken as a casual day like Saturday and Sunday (E. P. Thompson, 1967). Similarly, the length of the working day was irregular and determined largely by the time of the year. Thompson's quote from Hardy complements his analysis well: 'Tess ... started her way up the dark and crooked lane or street not made for hasty progress; a street laid out before inches of land had value, and when one-handed clocks sufficiently subdivided the day' (1967: 56).

The linear-quantitative tradition thus emphasizes how, in contrast to the task-oriented experience of historical and developing economies, under industrial capitalism not only does the workforce become subject to rigidly determined time schedules, but it also becomes remunerated in terms of temporal units — paid by the hour, day, week, month or year. The omnipresence of the factory clock brought with it the idea that one is exchanging time rather than skill: selling labour-time rather than labour. The rise of industrial capitalism saw workers forced to sell their time predominantly by the hour (Gioscia, 1972). In sum, this modernist trajectory saw time become a commodity to be earned, saved or spent.

Out of this form of analysis industrial and organizational sociology came to view modern conceptions of time as hegemonic structures whose essences are precision, control and discipline. In industrial societies, the clock becomes the dominant machine of productive organization; it provides the signal for labour to commence or halt activity. Workers must consult the time-clock before they begin working. Although life in modern societies is structured around times allocated for many different activities, it is always production that takes preference: 'Man is synchronised to work, rather than technology being synchronised to man' (de Grazia, 1972: 439). Time is given first to production — other times must be fitted around the margins of the production process. Ideal productive organizations are those having temporal assets which are highly precise in structuring and distribution. As technological determinism dominates modernist perceptions of time, so correct arithmetical equations are seen as the solutions to time problems — there are finite limits and optimal solutions to temporal structuring. The basic rule is that a modern productive society is effective only if its members follow a highly patterned series of temporal conventions; each society's productive day must be launched precisely on time. In this process, clock-time holds advantages for capital as it is both visible and standardized. It has two strengths in particular: it provides a common organizing framework to synchronize activities, and it commodifies labour as a factor of production (Clark, 1982; Hassard, 1990; Thompson and McHugh, 1998, 2004).

It is indeed from this scenario that, for industrial and organizational sociology, Frederick W. Taylor was to emerge as the heir to Adam Smith's pin factory, and thus to become the high priest of rational time-use. It is in the manuals of industrial engineers following Taylor (e.g. Gilbreth, Gantt, Bedaux) that were found the logical conclusions to the ideas of Smith, Ricardo and Babbage. Scientific Management, and the time and motion techniques that were its legacy, established direct administrative authority that which the machine accomplished indirectly, namely fine control of human actions. In Taylorism we reach the highpoint in separating labour from the varied rhythms experienced in craft or agricultural work: clock rhythms replace fluctuating rhythms; machine-pacing replaces self-pacing; labour serves technology.

Thus, for modern industrial societies, the linear conception of time became 'commodified' due to a major change in economic development, that is, when time was discovered as a factor in production. Time was a value that could be translated into economic terms: 'it became the medium in which human activities, especially economic activities, could be stepped up to a previously unimagined rate of growth' (Nowotny, 1976: 330). Time was a major symbol for the production of economic wealth. No longer was it merely sacred, given, and reproducible through cultural notions of the 'eternal return', but represented instead an economic object whose production is symbolized. Under industrial capitalism, timekeepers were the new regulators and controllers of work; they quantified and transformed activity into monetary value (Nowotny, 1976). When time became deemed a valuable commodity then its users were obliged to display good stewardship; time was scarce and had to be used rationally (see also Julkunnen, 1977; Thrift, 1981).

This linear-quantitative thesis is powerful, therefore, because it describes how, under industrial capitalism, time becomes an object for consumption. Time is reified and given commodity status so that relative surplus value can be extracted from the labour process. The emphasis is upon time as a boundary condition of the employment relation. Time is an objective parameter rather than an experiential state (Fabian, 1983).

The constructionist paradigm

However, the standard linear-quantitative thesis is one needing sociological qualification. When taken up by industrial and organizational sociologists, especially those concerned with labour process analysis (see Thompson and McHugh, 1998, 2004), it is often used to overstate the quantitative rationality of production practices and understate the qualitative construction of temporal meanings. There is a tendency, for example, to gloss over the fact that the contemporary world of work and organization is composed not simply of external or paced control systems, but includes a wealth of processes based on self-determined production and service control.

Although temporal flexibility has been associated with the 'new times' of late twentieth-century structural forms of employment (see Pollert, 1988; Clegg, 1990; Thompson and McHugh, 1998, 2004; Jaffee, 2001; Casey, 2002), in the more subtle sense of social construction, it has long remained widespread in boundary-spanning organizational functions. Moreover, while professional roles retain flexible, event-based task trajectories, also many non-professional occupations have long operated within irregular, if not totally self-determined, temporal patterns (Smith, 2001). Further, event-based temporal trajectories have long been commonplace within service economies, while new forms of employment systems have violated the tradition of selling labour-time in the homogeneous sense of eight hours a day/five days a week/fifty weeks a year. An extreme example of this increasing heterogeneity in work-time arrangements is the system of 'no-hours' contracts in contemporary retailing, where employees can (in theory) decline to accept the work schedules offered by management.

We can begin to question therefore whether the linear-quantitative thesis should be applied so readily and exclusively as the basis for explaining the 'modern' organizational nature of time at work. Whereas many writers following the structuralist labour process formulae of Braverman (1974) suggest that a progressive temporal commodification accompanies progressive deskilling (Burawoy, 2001; Green, 2001; Gamble *et al.*, 2004; see also Thompson and McHugh, 2004), other writers (since Braverman) have argued that employers' time-structuring practices are far more complex and less deterministic than mainstream labour process theory implies (see Clark, 1982; Starkey, 1988; Clegg, 1990; Hassard, 1990; Beynon *et al.*, 2002; Graham, 2003, 2005; Barley and Kunda, 2004).

A quarter of a century ago, Clark (1982) for instance suggested that 'the claim that commodified time has to be transposed into a highly fractionated division of labour through Taylorian recipes is naïve' (1982: 18). Drawing upon socio-technical theory, he offered examples of 'rational' task designs that were not anticipated by the Marxian theory of the 'porous day' (Clark *et al.*, 1984). Clark argues that, for example, in socio-technical systems a major key to improving productivity — and also the quality of working life — is to permit bounded temporal autonomy. Here, elements of time structuring are taken away from the 'planners' and handed over to the 'operators', that is, to the 'quasi-autonomous' work group or work cell.

Indeed many of the scenarios that emerge from an unrestrained modernist linear-quantitative thesis require scrutiny. The standard image of post-Taylorist work practices is of homogeneous activities being measured in micro-seconds in order to form some optimal, aggregate, standardized production output. Although apparently a now 'neglected' (Rowlinson and McArdle, 1993) form of organizational analysis, production line ethnographies (e.g. Roy, 1960; Ditton, 1979; Cavendish, 1982; Kamata, 1982; Dudley, 1994; Delbridge, 1998; see also Smith, 2001) have documented how this image ignores the power of workgroups, on even the most externally determined task processes, to construct their own time-reckoning systems. Whilst in comparison to other forms of organization the collective temporal inventories of production are exact, they remain of bounded rationality when we consider contingencies such as technical failure, market demand and the psychological contract.

The identification of qualitative, collective experience has historically been a theme of both the French and American traditions in the sociology of time (see Hassard, 1990). In the French tradition, the writings of Hubert (1905), Hubert and Mauss (1909), Mauss (1966), and Durkheim (1915) all emphasize the 'rhythmical' nature of social life through developing a concept of 'qualitative' time, that is, an appreciation of time far removed from modernist writers who present it as simple, measurable duration. Hubert (1905), for example, defined time as a symbolic structure representing the organization of society through its temporal rhythms, this being a theme also developed by Durkheim who analyzed the social nature of time (see Isambert, 1979). Durkheim focused on time as a collective phenomenon; as a product of collective consciousness (see Pronovost, 1986). For Durkheim, all members of a society share a common temporal consciousness; time is a social category of thought, a product of society. In Durkheim we find a macro-level exposition of the concept of social rhythm. Collective time is the sum of temporal procedures which interlock to form the cultural rhythm of a given society. Durkheim argues that: 'The rhythm of collective life dominates and encompasses the varied rhythms of all the elementary lives from which it results; consequently, the time that is expressed dominates and encompasses all particular durations' (1915: 69). For Durkheim, time is derived from social life and becomes the subject of collective representations. It is fragmented into a plethora of temporal activities that are reconstituted into an overall cultural rhythm that gives it meaning (Pronovost, 1986).

In the American tradition, Sorokin and Merton (1937) also highlight this qualitative nature of social time. In so doing, however, they draw not only on Durkheim, but more significantly on the works of early cultural anthropologists such as Codrington (1891), Hodson (1908), Nilsonn (1920), Best (1922) and Kroeber (1923). This synthesis allows Sorokin and Merton to identify qualitative themes at both micro and macro levels. Whilst, at the micro level, they emphasize the discontinuity, relativity and specificity of time ('social time is qualitatively differentiated', 1937: 615), they also suggest, like Durkheim, that: 'units of time are often fixed by the rhythm of collective life' (1937: 615). Indeed, they take this position a step further. Whereas Evans-Pritchard in his studies of the Nuer (1940) illustrated how certain activities give significance to social time, Sorokin and Merton adopt a position more characteristic of the sociology of knowledge. They argue that meaning comes to associate an event with its temporal setting, and that the recognition of specific periods is dependent on the degree of significance attributed to them. Drawing on Gurdon's (1914) anthropology, they argue that 'systems of time reckoning reflect the social activities of the group' (1937: 620). They show that the concept of qualitative time is important not only for primitive societies, but also for modern industrial states. They suggest that, 'Social time is qualitative and not purely quantitative … These qualities derive from the beliefs and customs common to the group … They serve to reveal the rhythms, pulsations, and beats of the societies in which they are found' (1937: 623).

Perhaps the most ambitious attempt to outline the qualitative nature of social-time, however, has been made by Gurvitch in *The Spectrum of Social Time* (1964). In a sophisticated, if at times rather opaque, thesis, he offers a typology of eight 'times' to illustrate the temporal complexity of modern, class-bound society (i.e. enduring, deceptive, erratic, cyclical, retarded, alternating, pushing forward, explosive). Gurvitch illustrates how cultures are characterized by a melange of conflicting times, and how social groups are constantly competing over a choice of 'appropriate' times. Like earlier writers, he distinguishes between the micro-social times characteristic of groups and communities, and the macro-social times characteristic of, for example, systems and institutions. Gurvitch makes constant reference to a plurality of social times, and notes how in different social classes we find differences of time-scales and levels. He suggests that through analyzing time at the societal level we can reveal a double time-scale operating — with on the one hand the 'hierarchically ordered and unified' time of social structure, and on the other the 'more flexible time of the society itself' (1964: 391).

This literature suggests, then, that contemporary societies — as well as primitive ones — hold pluralities of qualitative time-reckoning systems, and that these are based on combinations of duration, sequence and meaning. Unlike homogeneous time-reckoning, there is no uniformity of pace and no quantitative divisibility or accumulation of units. The emphasis is on collective cultural experience and sense-making: on creating temporal meanings rather than responding to temporal structures. The goal is to explain the cyclical and qualitative nature of social time.

The compression paradigm

Finally, we have noted in previous chapters that much attention has focused in recent decades on the notion of the postmodern 'turn' in social and organizational theory. This 'turn' is predicated on the view that many of the symbolic boundaries between, for example, art, high culture, and the academy, on the one hand, and everyday life and popular culture on the other, are dissolving. The postmodern is said to bring with it more open and fluid social identities, as compared with the traditionally fixed ones of the 'modern' period, and in particular those related to family, work and career.

For the analysis of the relationship between time and organization, it can be argued that, under postmodernism, the theoretical sociological hegemony of the linear-quantitative 'clock-time' paradigm is becoming replaced with what Macnaghton and Urry (1998) describe as that of 'instantaneous-time'. The basic argument here is that decision-makers who respond to an increasing complex and risky organizational world are required to do so 'instantaneously'. Whereas in decades past technologics such as telephones and fax machines reduced human response times from months, weeks and days to that of seconds, in recent times advanced computer technologies have contracted them into nanoseconds, to even times of a billionth of a second. As such, contemporary social and organizational practices can be based on time-frames that now lie beyond conscious human experience. Time can be organized at speeds beyond the feasible realm of human consciousness. To deploy a scientific metaphor, instantaneous time is based on a shift from 'the atom to the bit', with decisions being made by computer technology in 'nanosecond time'. As Macnaghton and Urry (1998: 149) argue, 'the new computer-time represents the final abstraction of time and its sequestration from social experience and the rhythms of the social world'. The following list (abridged from Macnaghton and Urry, 1998: 150) sets out some of the sociological indicators of an associated collapse of 'waiting culture' and the increasing permeation of 'instantaneous time':

- organizational changes which break down distinctions of night and day, working-week and week-end, home and work, leisure and work;
- the increased disposability of products, places and images in a 'throw-away society';

- a growing volatility and ephemerality in fashions, ideas and images;
- a heightened 'temporariness' of jobs, careers, values and personal relationships;
- the proliferation of flexible forms of technology and huge amounts of waste;
- the growth of 24-hour trading;
- the increased rates of divorce and other forms of household dissolution; and
- an increasing sense that the 'pace of life' has got too fast.

Offering a theoretical underpin for this notion of instantaneous-time are works that document changes in the connections of time, space and technology. Perhaps best known amongst this literature is Harvey's (1989) work on 'time-space compression'. Harvey has argued that the advance of capitalism entails different 'spatial fixes' within different historical periods. Within each capitalist epoch, space is organized so as to enable the continued growth of production and the maximization of profit. Indeed, it is through the reorganization of spatio-temporal arrangements that capitalism overcomes its periods of crisis and lays the foundations for the next period of capital accumulation.

Harvey in particular examines how the notion of the 'annihilation of space by time' can be used to explain the shift from Fordism to post-Fordism, the latter involving new ways in which time and space are represented. Crucial here is the notion of time-space compression of physical and human processes and experiences. Harvey argues that in contemporary society instantaneous mobility has been carried to extremes, so that time and space appear literally *compressed*. He suggests that as we are forced to alter how we represent the world to ourselves, then

> Space appears to shrink to a "global village" of telecommunications and a "spaceship earth" of economic and ecological interdependencies … and as time horizons shorten to the point where the present is all there is … so we have to learn how to cope with an overwhelming sense of *compression* of our spatial and temporal worlds.
>
> (1989: 240)

Various transformations characterize this socio-economic-spatial compression of time. Products, places and people go in and out of fashion with ever-increasing rapidity. At the same time, products become instantaneously available everywhere (but most notably in the West). Thus the time-horizons for decision-making shrink dramatically, being in minutes or less on the major international financial markets. Contracts are increasingly 'temporary' due to a general culture of short-termism and the decline of the 'waiting culture'.

Conclusion

This chapter has reviewed some of the main time paradigms and metaphors associated with the study of industrialism, work and organization. Initially drawing upon philosophy and social theory, the historical roots of the key metaphors of line and cycle were examined in order to lay the ground for a more detailed understanding of time-use and experience in organizations 'under capitalism'. Initially this analysis witnessed a preoccupation in industrial and organizational sociology with the paradigm of temporal *commodification* and in particular with examination of the homogeneous time-reckoning systems of Taylorism as the basis for organization and control. It was argued subsequently that necessary as this 'linear-quantitative' tradition is for explaining the evolution of industrial and organizational behaviour, it alone does not provide the complete story of temporal structuring and experience. The chapter attempted to contrast a review of the commodification literature with an appreciation of work that documents the anthropological and ethnographic 'real world' of time-use and experience through emphasizing the qualitative experience of temporal social *construction.* Research in this tradition describes how our 'everyday' understanding of work is based frequently upon the construction of recurrent 'event times'. Finally, the last stage of our historical review argued that in recent decades much attention in the sociological study of time has been concerned with issues of postindustrialism and organizational flexibility. The argument was made that decision-makers are required to respond to an increasing complex and risky organizational world 'instantaneously'. In examining issues of time structuring and experience from this paradigm we suggested that the metaphor of increasing time-space *compression* of physical and human processes has come to challenge the long-standing hegemony of the linear-quantitative thesis of clock-time.

7 Decoration and disorganization (with Stella Minahan)

While organizational decoration has been of interest to those who study organizational artefacts, in this chapter we suggest four ways in which decoration is worthy of fuller attention in 'alternative' organizational studies. First, decoration, ornament and embellishment are not only what we see but also what we do as managers, consultants, writers, and designers of both physical and project spaces. Second, and drawing on the art/craft debate, we note that decoration occupies a contested and even liminal aesthetic position and that 'decorative art' lies betwixt and between fine art and craft. Neither fully accepted nor fully marginalized, decoration is 'only applied' and embodies shifting tensions between form and function. Third, we review the particular negotiations of these tensions at the Bauhaus, a controversial and highly influential aesthetic organization in early twentieth-century Germany. Fourth, and importantly, we suggest that decoration, like disorganization, provides a source of complication for organizational studies that are neither pure nor parsimonious.

Just decoration?

Decoration is a subject that has been variously trivialized, discounted, and admired and we discuss its status, particularly in relation to craft activities which are, themselves, often marginalized within aesthetic debates. In contrast, we suggest that the decorative is worthy of attention in both aesthetic and organization theory. We propose that organization theorists should consider themselves as decorators working with peripheries, often violating contemporary standards of taste, repeating and elaborating the traditions of the past, causing much discussion and disagreement, and sometimes leaving material traces of their contributions.

For some, decoration should be celebrated. Drawing on the examples ranging from the decoration of a soldier to the 'strained relation' of ornament to the Christian spirit, the Australian commentator Robert Nelson has suggested that ornament is a metaphor for dignity and value (see Nelson, 1993: 9). In his (1993) essay, Nelson discusses the Latin origins of the terms 'ornament' and 'decoration' and suggests that there are physical and moral associations for both. The latter are perhaps most evident in the noun *decus*:

> The term *decus* means ornament, grace, embellishment, splendour but also glory, honour, dignity and so on. The verb *decoro* means I adorn or decorate or beautify … But the adjectival form (*decorus*) is more exclusively moral, paralleling our contemporary "decorous" and readily translating the Greek term for "the appropriate (*euprepês*)".
>
> (Nelson, 1993: 8)

Nelson goes on to point out that this association means that decoration and ornament 'harbour not only an onus of conformity but institute an uncritical dictatorship of the appropriate' (Nelson, 1993: 13). Depending on the values of the time, the appropriateness of particular amounts and styles of decoration is, of course, a matter of aesthetic judgement. In one extreme, the Victorian era in arts and crafts had been known for its obsession with decoration, detail and excess ornament. From doileys to chair legs, the 'lace' on terraces, and to the finials of curtains, all items in the built environment displayed decoration.

For Nelson, ornament and decoration are both material manifestations of convention and indicators of value. Ornament can even be practical where decorations are applied to 'solve problems of finish and save the expense of perfection in fussy assemblies' (Nelson, 1993: 3). In addition, and rather than being merely 'unnecessary features in a design' (Nelson, 1993: 2) or a 'pure aesthetic' (Nelson, 1993: 6), decoration can also signify the necessary, the functional, and the stable in architectural construction as it 'celebrates the presence of things' (Nelson, 1993: 4). For example, Nelson discusses how wooden motifs on Greek stone temples helped the temple to 'look strong' and to 'argue its own structure' (Nelson, 1993: 2), and how brackets in Chinese temples celebrated their engineering even after the brackets were no longer structural requirements. Thus, ornament can be seen as 'an artifice for claiming space as meaningful' (Nelson, 1993: 5) and as 'a language of pattern which ritualises function and structure within a design' (1993: 6).

The decorative can also fulfil a real structural role. For example, Japanese farmers' jackets are usually made of two layers of indigo-dyed cotton material, hemmed and bound together by stitching in very thick thread. This needlework looks like added decoration but it is nothing of the sort. Its charm is in its appropriateness to use and the strength of the stitching. The delightful patterning is incidental and utterly suitable. There is no concept of décor for its own sake (Yanagi, 1989).

In contrast to such celebration, and in a reference to the legacies of the Viennese architect, Adolf Loos, Nelson points out that ornament has also been derided as 'a device for soaking up meaningless space' (1993: 5). According to Kleinert (1992: 119), Loos 'suffered the modernist's usual aversion to decoration' and led a campaign against decoration that would influence architects for many years into the future. For Loos, decoration was 'a sign of degeneracy and immorality in a rational, civilized society' (Kleinert, 1992: 119). Only 'others' — children, criminals and primitives — would be interested in decoration and were denigrated for 'their obsessive desire to in-fill space with decoration' (Kleinert, 1992: 119, with reference to Black, 1964: 49–50). Loos' (1908) paper titled 'Ornament and Crime' is also discussed by Fuller (1989), who comments that Loos' rejection of the decorative arts was based on arguments that they were not only erotic and regressive but also uneconomic (see also Pevsner, 1991: 30).

Nelson suggests that part of this disdain is due to ornament being 'paradigmatic of craft in general' (1993: 12) and to craft's association with traditions from the past which, under modernism, are identified with a backward commitment to outmoded precepts (Nelson, 1993: 12; cf. Metcalf, 1993: 40, 44). As a result:

> Ornament still finds itself oppressed by prejudices of the Modernist tradition. Never far from the opprobrium heaped upon it by Adolf Loos, ornament languishes under the doyley of quaintness and ineffectualness in all things emotional and spiritual. One speaks of "surface decoration" as though superficial in the aesthetic sense, if not the moral sense as well.
>
> (Nelson, 1993: 4)

Similarly, Kleinert (1992: 116) cites Alberti's (1957) view that:

> Ornament is painting and concealing anything that was deformed, trimming and polishing what was handsome; so that the unsightly parts might have given less offence … A kind of auxiliary brightness and improvement to Beauty. So that then Beauty is somewhat lovely which is proper and innate, and diffused over the whole body, and Ornament somewhat added on or fastened on, rather than proper and innate.
>
> (Alberti, 1957: 230–31)

Alberti argued that beauty conformed to the classical ideal of *decorum* where 'all parts fitted together with such proportion that nothing cou'd [sic] be added, diminished or altered but for the worse' (Alberti, 1957: 230; see also Pevsner, 1991: 28–32). As a result, this essentialism resulted in the association between decoration and decorum becoming inverted, and 'the concept of "decorative" still carries pejorative associations which relegate "the decorative" to a position of marginalisation, spuriously associated with superficial ornamentation and the utilitarian' (Kleinert, 1992: 115).

Thus beauty became associated with an *absence* of decoration in modern architecture and design. However, while modernism has been regarded as 'a final nail in the coffin' for decoration (Collins, 1987: 6), it was certainly not the first. For example, it is perhaps ironic that John Ruskin's early rules for craft included: 'Never demand an exact finish for its own sake, but only for some practical or noble end' (Lucie-Smith, 1981: 209). Decoration could, however, pursue such ends and mark the importance of the individualism that Ruskin saw as so threatened by the advance of industrial capitalism and the associated advance of mechanized production.

In this context, Fuller (1989: 133) discusses Ruskin's admiration for Gothic ornament where 'every jot and tittle, every point and niche affords room, fuel and focus for individual fire'.

In marked contrast to Ruskin and to the 'horror vacui' of William Morris' densely decorated textiles (Collins, 1987), the 'chaste priests of the Bauhaus … banish[ed] ornament from their credo' (Nelson, 1993: 3). The Bauhaus' first director, Walter Gropius, sought a new society that would embrace machine production and efficiency and would be 'ruthlessly modern' (Metcalf, 1993: 41). He contrasted the Bauhaus emphasis on true form with the decadence and deceit of traditional style (Pier, 1999: 13, 15). Whereas Ruskin had stated in 1853 that 'ornament is the origin of architecture' (Zerbst, 1988: 10), Gropius regarded decorated buildings as 'lies' and derided those who disagreed with him (see Pier, 1999: 16, 17). For example, the buildings he created for the new were of 'clear, organic (form) whose inner logic (is) radiant, naked, unencumbered by lying facades and trickeries' (cited in Roper, 2000). Bauhaus style was typified by machine technology, good design and affordability (Greenberg, 1996), and the celebration of pure function even became the 'new beauty':

> The Bauhaus attempts to find the functional form for the house, as well as for the simplest utensil. It wants things clearly constructed, it wants functional materials, it wants this new beauty. This new beauty is not a style, which matches one object with another aesthetically by using similar external forms (façade, motif, ornament). Today, something is beautiful if its form serves its function, if it is well made of chosen material. A good chair will then "match" a good table.
>
> (Fleischmann, 1924, cited in Whitford, 1984: 210; cf. Strati, 2000b: 20)

Thus, 'Form without ornament' was the name of a Bauhaus exhibition that both heralded and embodied the era of modernism (Collins, 1987: 14), and the Bauhaus' Mies van der Rohe praised the decline in the significance of the individual and the growing trend towards anonymity (Fuller, 1989). Similarly, and in the context of his protest against the elitism of Art Deco, the architect Le Corbusier intended 'to "purify" architecture of ornament to reveal the hidden structure and function' (Roper, 2000) and to show that 'by virtue of … standardization … industry creates pure forms' (cited in Lucie-Smith, 1981: 252; cf. Pevsner, 1991: 37).

Although decoration has since been celebrated under feminism and postmodernism (Kleinert, 1992), its banishment had long-lasting effects. For example, Fuller (1989: 136) referred to the triumphant advance of 'the anaesthetic International Style' from the 1930s onwards and Greenberg (1996) suggested that the pervasive influence of the modern Bauhaus affected American resistance to decoration and ornament on design even until the 1980s. However, modernism is not *necessarily* associated with a lack of decoration. Powers (2000) has argued that modernism was both a rebellion against Art Nouveau and an extension of Art Nouveau and that modernism 'was deeply engaged in the issue of nature and was as much a return to ancient sources and standards as it was driven by progress and technology' (Powers, 2000: 28; see also Fuller, 1989). For example, while the growing emphasis on modernism in the works of the architect Charles Rennie Mackintosh has led Collins to the opinion that Mackintosh 'helped to cause the downfall of Art Nouveau simply by using an architectural style that was too rectilinear to accommodate it' (Collins, 1987: 48), Pevsner (1991) illustrates how Mackintosh's earlier Glasgow School of Art embodied a combination of Art Nouveau and modern styles, among others. Further, and in what might otherwise seem a rather unlikely combination, Ramirez (2000) has suggested that both Gaudí and Le Corbusier evoked images of bees and the beehive metaphor in their architecture, despite Le Corbusier's emphasis on the man-made and the machine aesthetic (Lucie-Smith, 1981).

More generally, art nouveau was even known as *modernisme* in Spain (Permanyer, 1999), and in Barcelona *modernista* architects such as Gaudí both embraced the new and drew on the city's craft tradition to display the 'characteristic aesthetic of restless movement' (Permanyer, 1999: 10) in their highly decorated facades:

> *Modernisme*'s movement is highlighted everywhere with the *fueteda* (*coup de fuet* or whiplash), that interminable stem-and-flower motif that meanders through and fills modernista spaces; it also appears in less descriptive form, such as in the triumph art curves of La Pedrera, the sinuous stone that dominates the whole façade.
>
> (Permanyer, 1999: 10; see also Howard, 1996)

Just as Ruskin had argued for the imitation of nature in decorative works, Gaudí's works were also imitative. For example, Sweeney and Sert (1960) comment that the glazed tile 'skins' of Gaudi's later buildings resembled the texture of local rock formations and that his use of colour was also inspired by nature. While decoration was supplemental to his interest in architectural structure, Sweeney and Sert (1960) suggest that Gaudí's naturalism was derivative of the Romantic movement in architecture.

In summary, while the worth and even existence of decoration is highly contested, even apparently strong positions on the subject belie unexpected associations and contextual subtleties. We argue that attention to such (figurative) twists-and-turns is not only of relevance to the study of art, architecture and design but also to organization studies, where decoration has received little attention.

Organizational decoration

Within the arena of organizational culture studies, organizational decoration has perhaps been most closely associated with signification. For example, in one of the most influential popular texts on organizational culture, organizational artefacts are presented as superficial, material manifestations of 'deeper', more fundamental values and basic assumptions, or taken-for-granted beliefs about reality and human nature (Schein, 1985). Cultural artefacts such as interior design, artwork, office size and employee dress, therefore, give some indication of what is important to an organization, but because they occur only 'at the surface' they are not particularly important or reliable indicators of underlying meaning structures (see Mohr, 1998).

Some attempts have been made to complicate the study of organizational artefacts. For example, Hatch (1993) introduced a variant of Schein's (1985) model of organizational culture that articulated particular cultural dynamics and gave greater attention to the importance of cultural artefacts in the constitution of organizational culture. Further, Gagliardi (1996) presented a different view, suggesting that:

> Artefacts do not constitute secondary and superficial manifestations of deeper cultural phenomena … but are themselves – so to speak – primary cultural phenomena which influence organizational life from two points of view: (a) artefacts make materially possible, help, hinder, or even prescribe organizational action; (b) more generally, artefacts influence our perception of reality, to the point of subtly shaping beliefs, norms, and cultural values.
>
> (Gagliardi, 1996: 568)

For example, Munro (1999) has examined how organizational artefacts may be exhibited or 'managed' in order to present the semblance of a certain type of organization, or a certain type of manager. In addition, Strati (2000c) has argued that while artefacts, even photographic artefacts, may be limited in their ability to represent the real, their presence may create enjoyment and pleasure both for their viewers and for their creator/s, who may, in turn, be able to respond to the responses of the viewers.

Artefacts, therefore, are of interest not merely as decorative signifiers but as aesthetic actants, whose constitutive roles allow greater attention to the relevance of decoration for aesthetic organizational studies. In the following sections we briefly outline some arenas for such attention. First, decoration, ornament and embellishment are not only what we see but also what we do as managers, consultants, writers, and as designers of both physical and project spaces. Second, and drawing on the art/craft debate, we note that decoration occupies contested and even liminal aesthetic position and that 'decorative art' lies betwixt and between fine art and craft. Neither fully accepted nor fully marginalized, decoration is 'only applied' and embodies shifting tensions between pure form and pure function. Third, we review the particular negotiations of these tensions at the Bauhaus, a controversial and highly influential aesthetic organization in early twentieth-century Germany. Fourth, we suggest that decoration, like disorganization, provides a source of complication for organizational studies that are neither pure nor parsimonious.

Organizational decorators

Our first suggestion is far removed from the notion that organization theory can (or should) emulate some form of administrative science. If not lesser scientists, perhaps organization theorists can be considered as consultant designers and decorators of discursive space, reproducing, translating, extending and guiding the organizational tastes of (often) elite consumers. Their efforts in grouping and partitioning, including and excluding, smoothing or elaborating the contours of what is noticed, discussed and diffused as legitimate may be highly influential (cf. Clark and Salaman, 1996, 1998; Kieser, 1997).

This is not to suggest that such efforts do not have material effects and consequences, but to draw attention to the styling of organization within paradigmatic boundaries, narrative genres, and feature themes, devices and topics. For example, and with respect to the latter, the diverse topics of empowerment, psychological contracts, benchmarking, emotional intelligence and the balanced scorecard are among many that the contemporary consumer of organizational knowledge would include within his or her discursive repertoire. And each of these has been embellished such that it can be applied at multiple levels of analysis. Empowerment, for example, is relevant to both individual and group applications; emotional intelligence has been deemed important for organizational leaders, individual managers, managerial groups and children; and benchmarking has been promoted for operations, human resource management and strategy. While the theoretical and empirical justifications for such extensions and embellishments are, of course, quite varied, our interest is in the nature of their enhancement and application. We suggest that such mimetic processes can be compared with the skill of patterning and repetition in craft where a finished design may be copied, altered, reformed and realigned in different media, the surface creating effect rather than representing essence.

More generally, organizational decorators may well be informed by others who have worked with aesthetic peripheries rather than functional fundamentals of organizational life. In a book directed to what he has termed *paraesthetics*, Carroll (1987) examines:

> art in terms of its relations with the extra-aesthetic in general. I am, for example, interested in the philosophical, historical, and political issues raised by the question of form or the problem of beauty rather than form and beauty as narrow aestheticist questions.
>
> (Carroll, 1987: xiv)

At its theoretical boundaries, Carroll sees paraesthetics as 'a faulty, irregular, disordered, improper aesthetics – one not content to remain within the area defined by the aesthetic' (1987: xiv). For example, he discusses Jacques Derrida's work on art and argues that it is paraesthetic in that it ' "mobilizes" both theory and art by rethinking each in terms of the frames that both separate them and link them together, that both block and permit passage or movement between them' (1987: 144). In addition to Derrida, Carroll argues that Michel Foucault and Jean-Francois Lyotard have also been concerned 'with how art resists (even its own) theorization, and for this reason they attempt through various strategies to push the question of art beyond itself and its theoretical representation' (1987: xiv). As all of these theorists have had much influence on organization studies over the years since the publication of the series on 'Modernism, Postmodernism and Organizational Analysis' in *Organization Studies* in the late 1980s (Burrell, 1988; Cooper and Burrell, 1988; Cooper, 1989), it is perhaps timely to remember that they shared a common concern with aesthetics. For Carroll (1987: xi), they are 'critical philosophers whose awareness of the limitations of theory has led them not to reject theory but rather to work at and on the borders of theory in order to stretch, bend, or exceed its limitations'. For us, they are theoretical decorators.

Positioning decoration

We now turn to a discussion of why such a categorization may be classed as superficial. Aside from the obvious limitations of any overly deliberate attempt to summarize the thesis of a major work in a few lines, it is worth noting that decoration itself occupies a borderline position within the art/craft debate. This debate concerns whether or not there remains a hierarchy of distinctions between art and craft, where art is fine and perceived to be at the 'high' end of the aesthetic ladder of preference and taste (Editor's introduction to Marincola, 1995; Kuspit, 1996; Ioannou, 1997/1998). Because of 'our tendency to value what is distinctive about paintings over what is distinctive about pots' (Markowitz, 1994: 67), *fine art* is distinguished from *applied*, more utilitarian art (see Osborne, 1970: 12), and art further marginalizes and excludes *craft* as a lowly pursuit (Metcalf, 1994; Ioannou, 1997/1998).

Drawing on Aristotle and Aquinas, Kuspit argued that before the concept of 'fine art' arose in the eighteenth century, craft and art were regarded as 'inseparable' (Kuspit, 1996: 16). However, and in contrast to craft, Kant claimed that the viewer of art experiences a universal, *common sense* that ignores tradition and transcends material existence. Thus, as Metcalf (1994: 16) has argued, 'Kantian notions of the aesthetic experience … exclude function — and thus much of craft — from the possibility of having an aesthetic component'. The art/craft debate stems from Kant's argument that an aesthetic experience could be supported only by an autonomous art object, and that the disinterested gaze of the art spectator is elicited only when art is removed from moral, social and religious values and from ordinary life (Metcalf, 1993).

While it is often argued that an object becomes *art* when decoration, special processing or the inclusion of precious materials takes place, decoration occupies contested and even liminal aesthetic position and *decorative art* lies betwixt and between craft and fine art. Kleinert (1992) has discussed the positioning of the decorative arts with particular reference to Australia and to the efforts of the artist, Lucien Henry, who wanted to improve the perception of decoration and went so far as to suggest that the decorative arts 'constitute the substrata of civilization; the rich soil from which the other arts draw their sap' (Smith, 1979: 242, cited in Kleinert, 1992: 123). Kleinert has presented arguments that Australian decorative art has legitimized space both for women and for Aboriginal culture, although that legitimation was only ever partial. For example, the superficial appropriation of

Aboriginal motifs without reference to their symbolic value 'was closely linked to the widely held belief that the Aboriginal race was doomed to extinction' (Kleinert, 1992: 125) and assisted the status of neither Aborigines nor 'the decorative'. In addition: 'To be criticized as "decorative" (as many women artists found) was to imply that one's work was superficially concerned with pattern, with a consequent disregard for structural form and content' (Kleinert, 1992: 125).

Decorative debates

Thus, neither fully accepted nor fully marginalized, decoration is 'only applied'. Decoration also embodies shifting tensions between pure form and pure function. For example, one of the most well-known sites for the negotiation of such tensions was at the Bauhaus where, despite Gropius' distaste for architectural decoration, there was, supposedly, equal regard for fine, decorative and industrial arts (Greenberg, 1996: 69) and, despite the supposed emphasis on the new beauty and form following function, there were many instances of aesthetic debates.

Introduced briefly above, the Bauhaus was established by Walter Gropius in 1919 in the Weimar Republic when Van de Velde's School of Applied Art was amalgamated with the Academy of Fine Art (Rowland, 1997). After being given notice after a conservative local election win, the Bauhaus moved to Dessau and then to Berlin, where it was closed in 1933 (Greenberg, 1996). There were many differences and difficulties within the Bauhaus. Its predecessor organization, the Art Academy, had been a site for extensive debate on art and craft and the various stakeholders argued for four years 'over whether the Academy should be an art school that taught craft or one school that taught both' (Hochman, 1997: 31). Difficulties in finding any unity were apparent prior to the opening of the Bauhaus (see also Naylor, 1990), and only six weeks into its life the internal politics were described by Feininger (a staff member) as 'a hornets' nest' (Hochman, 1997: 86). Many students were angry with the notion that art was not a higher pursuit than craft and resented the attempt to transform what was an art academy into a craft school.

Walter Gropius was committed to the teaching and creation of craft as part of a broader social agenda to create a better world. He acknowledged Ruskin and Morris 'who consciously sought and found the first way to the reunification of the world of work with the creative artists' (Whitford, 1984: 23; see also Pevsner, 1991: 38–39). He argued: 'Let us create a new guild of craftsmen without the class distinctions which raise an arrogant barrier between craftsman and artist' (Gropius, 1919, cited in Lucie-Smith, 1981: 251–52; see also Whitford, 1984: 202).

Around 1921, Gropius became concerned with both the increased politicization in the Bauhaus workshops and with the sense that handcraft was being seen solely as art (Roper, 2000). His master Laszlo Moholy-Nagy moved the workshops away from self-expression, and traditional craft was superseded by modern geometric designs that used contemporary manufacturing techniques using accessible, manufactured materials such as tubular steel. A well-known example is the chair designed by Marcel Breuer (Collins, 1987: 69).

In 1923, the Bauhaus mounted an exhibition entitled 'Art and Technology: The New Unity'. This was designed to celebrate the work of the Bauhaus students and to explore opportunities for mass production of the prototypes on display. The exhibits were harshly criticized by some as 'misleading' as 'most of the objects were bulbously curved and harshly angled, more revealing of Expressionistic angst than the stark, geometric simplicities of machine technology' (Hochman, 1997: 160).

Gropius resigned as director, tiring of the constant demands to protect the school and claiming 'that until now 90 percent of my work has been devoted to the defense of the school' (Ott, 2001: 2). His replacement, Meyer rejected any connection with art and was looking to mass produce domestic goods. However, the Bauhaus never managed to find an industrial manufacturer for its tableware (Rowland, 1997), and while the changing works of Marianne Brandt are often seen as an indication of the Weimar Bauhaus' transition from craft to industrial production (Lucie-Smith, 1981; Greenberg, 1996; Rowland, 1997), her hand-made tea sets, ashtrays and dishes include some that are decorated to look as if they were made by machine. Their smooth, apparently uniform finishes look undecorated and, therefore, 'modern', in contrast to their craft origins. Further, while the Bauhaus designs were supposedly based on function, the placing of the lids on tea and coffee pots drew comments as these lids were very close to the handles. Marianne Brandt even admitted that 'they were all obsessed with geometry' in the Bauhaus metal workshop (Rowland, 1997: 32).

At the Bauhaus building at Dessau, smoothness in appearance and absence of decoration became a material source of aesthetic disruption, for the 'new-style glass curtain wall' provided no insulation from heat or cold and it was claimed that no effort was made to respond to complaints and to solve this problem, or that of the building's poor acoustics. Indeed, Asendorf (1999: 80) argued that 'in the Dessau building practical efficiency was neglected in favor of the purity and smoothness of its technological appearance' and thus, at the Bauhaus, *absence* of decoration signified more an appeal to an aesthetics of function than any operational functionality. It was this *appearance* of functionality as signified by smoothness in form that was most important.

Decoration/disorganization

Accordingly, we argue that the study of both decoration and absence of decoration is, therefore, the study of interdependence and of complication. Not only does decoration (at least in most cases) literally embellish what may otherwise be seen as plain, its discussion triggers a further play of positions and counter-positions. At the Bauhaus, this play was often located around particular material artefacts that ranged from buildings to paintings to tea sets, but we suggest that the serious plays of organization theory are, in both senses, highly decorative.

For example, Weick (1999: 797) has discussed efforts 'to make the tacit craft of theorizing more explicit', giving particular attention to manifestations of Thorngate's (1976) discussion of tradeoffs among theoretical generality, simplicity and accuracy. Weick has argued that one of these three dimensions is often omitted in discussions of theorizing in organizational studies:

> Carried to the extreme, accurate-simple explanations say everything about nothing, general-simple explanations say nothing about everything, and general-accurate explanations say everything about everything but are unintelligible … Theorists may be better off trying to author relatively "pure" exhibits of general or accurate or simple explanations and leave the readers to embellish the text in ways that add in the two dimensions.
>
> (Weick, 1999: 801)

Perhaps Weick's search for a 'useful starting point' (1999: 801) for theory development can be re-read as an articulation of theoretical styles. While his references to the 'craft of theorizing' and to reader 'embellishments' display aesthetic references quite different from the science-based comparisons in Fabian's (2000) discussion of the more specific arena of management studies, Fabian, too, can be read just as much as a style guide as a representation of debates over various disciplinary approaches. Fabian (2000: 353) presents a 'conceptual framework of the kinds of standards the discipline should use to adopt, accommodate, or reject research as legitimate' and articulates a typology of nine disciplinary approaches that are differentiated in terms of their system of validation (universal or multiple standards), emphasis towards paradigm inclusion (solidarity, integration or segregation), and impetus for new research (knowledge development or knowledge breadth). Fabian's comparison of these centres on a distinction between scientific pressures for paradigm and theory proliferation and pragmatic pressures for consensus. While science rather than craft is her reference point, Thorngate's tradeoffs are clearly implicit in at least the first and third dimensions of her typology and, like Weick, she draws reference to the role of readers whom, 'it is hoped, will better discover their own predilections in these debates but also come to terms with why the discipline cannot move single-mindedly in their preferred direction' (Fabian, 2000: 366).

Within these debates on theory, readers, therefore, are presented variously as theoretical embellishers, theoretical consumers and arbiters of taste. In this reading, theory is not necessarily a representation of the real, just as decoration is not necessarily imitative of nature. Generality, simplicity and accuracy are of no particular interest except as theoretical styles. Theorizing, then, can be thought of as a decorative or ornamental art, and as means to complicate, attract attention and evoke response rather than to represent, control and predict.

However, this is not to suggest that the decorative is purely pleasurable or occasionally entertaining (cf. Weick, 1979: 264). First, it is never purely anything. As Nelson (1993) has argued:

> Ornament always assists another structure: it is never the total structure; there has to be a more fundamental structure which it does not circumscribe

> but which it inscribes with various intonations. Ornament presupposes a difference between itself and the design to which it is applied .... The reason why ornament can never be the totality is because it expresses difference; it functions by contrasts and, as it goes distinguishing its support and its own motifs, it can never arrive at autonomy.
>
> (Nelson, 1993: 15)

Second, decoration, like disorganization, provides a source of complication for organizational studies that are neither pure nor parsimonious and that are also informed by attention to difference. For example, in his landmark paper on the subject of 'Organization/disorganization', Cooper (1986) discusses the 'illusory edifice' of notions of structure and organization (Cooper, 1986: 317). Such notions represent the privileging of unity and order where 'what lies outside the system – or more accurately, what is said to lie outside the frame that creates the system – is viewed as less ordered and less unitary than what is included' (Cooper, 1986: 302). For example,

> Traditional conceptions of system are ... structured so as to give preference to the idea of systemness, of articulated unity and order. The system (with its boundary) becomes conceptually detached from background or environment and this takes on a life of its own. This has the effect of diverting attention from the all-important function of the frame.
>
> (Cooper, 1986: 303)

Drawing on the work of Saussure, Bateson and Derrida, Cooper (1986: 303) conceives of the boundary or frame between the inside and outside of a system as 'an active process of differentiation', and suggests that:

> attention to the divisionary nature of the boundary reveals that the work of organization is focused upon transforming an intrinsically ambiguous condition into one that is *ordered* so that organization as a process is constantly bound up with its contrary state of disorganization.
>
> (Cooper, 1986: 304–5; emphasis in original)

Cooper argues that the 'struggle for the "superior" position necessarily requires the "support" of an "inferior" position inasmuch as the latter is what defines the former' (1986: 328). Thus, in the context of organization studies 'it becomes impossible to disentangle the "content" of organization studies from the theory or methodology that frames it' (Cooper, 1986: 331). In terms of this discussion, the boundary is more than 'purely ornamental' for it conducts a censuring function and requires 'a certain force or violence ... for the act of separating the decidable from the undecidable' (Cooper, 1986: 314). As ornament, it certainly assists structure. But as a frame it may also direct attention, inhibit debate and artificially stabilize centre-periphery relations.

The power of decoration

Our call for attention to organizational decoration is thus also a call for disorganization. It includes greater reflexive consideration of organizational decorators; their roles, their reception, and, in a few cases, their legacies. It recognizes the liminal aesthetic position of decoration, and the associated placement of decoration as a highly contested site for aesthetic debates. It allows for the consideration of style in theoretical debates, and for the consideration of organization theory as an ornamental art. And it recognizes the power of decoration as a framing process where marking and boundary setting are not just 'purely decorative' but may be thought of as processes of violence.

Accordingly, this last emphasis draws our attention to the context for decoration, and to the impossibility of either organizational or aesthetic purity. With reference to the latter, it should be noted here that even Kant's (1952) requirement for the autonomy of fine art has been disputed by Slater (1997) who argued that:

> It is a matter of plain historic fact, however, that Kant held … that art involved the perfection of a concept, the achievement of a function, and so was a matter of what he called dependent beauty, not independent beauty, which was free of concepts, as with nature … Moreover it was free beauty which alone required abandonment of self-interest and attachment to objectivity.
>
> (Slater, 1997: 230; see also Wicks, 1995)

In tracing the history of aesthetic thought, Kelly (2000), too, has questioned the possibility of art's autonomy, but from a different position and with particular attention to the thesis that 'the arts-politics choice is false' (Kelly, 2000: 223). For example, Kelly (2000: 225) argues that Kant's insistence on the autonomy of aesthetics 'was possible only in a social world in which autonomy of freedom was a prominent, if as yet largely unrealised, political (and moral) concept' and that Kantian autonomy 'does not separate art/aesthetics and politics, it actually unites them via a common philosophical presupposition and historical condition' (Kelly, 2000: 227).

Within a more contemporary context, the claim for the autonomy of art has itself been complicated in the work of the modern critical theorist Theodor Adorno. Adorno's (1997) *Aesthetic Theory* discusses the position and operation of autonomous works under advanced capitalist conditions. As interpreted by Zuidervaart (1991: 32), Adorno's position was that the autonomy of art 'can be equated … with freedom of art from religious, political and other social roles'. It is through art's very autonomy that art can be critical, for 'art criticizes society just by being there' (Adorno, 1984: 321):

> Indeed, [Adorno's] account of advanced capitalism as a function of exchange and domination leads him to attribute unusual social significance to autonomous art, a significance tied to the position and operation of

> autonomous works under advanced capitalist conditions. Where cultural commodity fetishism and domination in exchange prevail, autonomy enables art to mount critical resistance. Autonomous art is one part of the totality that challenges the totality from within.
>
> (Zuidervaart, 1991: 87)

Further, Adorno's reasoning was that: 'By appearing to be detached from the conditions of economic production, works of art acquire the ability to suggest changed conditions. And by appearing to be useless, works of art recall the human purposes of production that instrumental rationality forgets' (Zuidervaart, 1991: 89). However, Adorno does not idealize art's autonomy, regarding it as 'illusory' (Zuidervaart, 1991: 182). His argument for autonomy is, instead, a resistance against simple historicist determination (Horowitz, 1997), a comment on the artwork as 'the literal embodiment of the distance between where we are and freedom' (Huhn, 1997: 249) and as afterimage, 'a response to socio-historical conditions that have since changed' (Harding, 1997: 12). Adorno has argued that while 'every advance in political freedom is accompanied by repression', the dialectic of semblance allows for a possible reconciliation of reality with itself in a utopian future (Kelly, 2000: 232; see also Zuidervaart, 1997: 6). With reference to the particular importance of modern art:

> art's task (even its truth) is to sustain the dialectic of semblance: "Through the irreconcilable renunciation of the semblance of reconciliation, art holds fast to the promise of reconciliation in the midst of the unreconciled". Which in turn accounts for art's mimetic function; it "imitates" reality's non-reconciliation while holding up a mirror to the possibility of reconciliation.
>
> (Kelly, 2000: 232–33, quoting Adorno, 1997: 33; see also Bernstein, 1997: 179; Huhn, 1997)

In Adorno's writings, the notion of mimesis means more than imitation. In contrast to the Platonic definition of mimesis as copy, Adorno's mimesis is not defined by reason and is 'a truly protean concept, refer[ring] to an archaic openness to the other' (Zuidervaart, 1997: 7; see also Schultz, 1990; Bubner, 1997: 175; Hansen, 1997). Art is mimetic but does not imitate. As explained by Jay (1997: 35): 'by refusing to imitate, or be assimilated entirely to, a bad external reality … works of art hold out the hope for a more benign version of mimesis in a future world beyond domination and reification'.

While Adorno's praxis has drawn criticism from both Marxist and postmodern thinkers, it is perhaps surprising that his aesthetics has received such little discussion in organization and management studies. We suggest his discussions of mimesis and semblance could contribute to contemporary discussions on representation, on emancipatory potential, and on materiality (cf. Alvesson and Willmott, 1992a, 1996; Calás and Smircich, 1999; Alvesson and Deetz, 2000). Of particular interest to us is his emphasis on the autonomy of art in contrast to recent calls for attention, instead, to craft as historically and culturally embedded and as a tangible way of considering marginality (see Wolfram Cox and Minahan, 2001, 2002). In this context, it is important to examine Zuidervaart's (1991) review of Bürger's (1984) criticisms of Adorno's autonomy of art, and Zuidervaart's own discussion of the distinction of autonomous art from 'heteronomous art'. The latter includes both traditional folk art and contemporary popular art and 'has not become relatively independent from other institutions of bourgeois society and whose products are produced and received to accomplish purposes that are directly served by other institutions' (Zuidervaart, 1991: 227). Zuidervaart discusses the proposition that autonomous art must be useless to be critical and the implication that 'major works' of autonomous art 'have greater social significance than any works of heteronomous art' (Zuidervaart, 1991: 233), suggesting that 'heteronomy need not keep a work from challenging the status quo and disclosing human aspirations' (1991: 231). Zuidervaart concludes that 'the criteria of truth and significance need not be restricted to autonomous art' (1991: 233), and that Adorno's aesthetics are 'inadequate with respect to popular art' (1991: 234).

Conclusion

In this chapter we have examined the effect of historical context on the aesthetic positioning of decoration and ornament, both generally and within the specific institutional setting of the Bauhaus. We have argued that this positioning has been highly contested and have argued that attention to the figurative twists and turns of debates over decoration is just as relevant to organizational studies as to studies of art and design where decoration embodies shifting tensions between pure form and pure function. In a world where the decorative can be both functional and violent, the autonomous is an illusion and not only the useless may be critical, we conclude that the search for organizational and representational purity, therefore, be abandoned on aesthetic as well as linguistic grounds (cf. Cooper, 1986). Disorganization and decoration have much greater appeal and warrant further attention in organizational analysis where organization theorists can be seen as organizational stylists and as consultant designers of discursive space.

8 Governmentality and networks

Our final chapter on alternative concepts discusses the notion of organizational network, but specifically connection to the Foucauldian theory of govermentality (see Foucault, 1991a). In so doing, we shift tack from the largely theory-based explorations of previous chapters to a more empirical form of organizational case analysis. In so doing, we explore in a more tangible sense some of the issues of discourse raised in Part I.

Networks and change

Networks have attracted much theoretical interest in organizational analysis. For example, in their review of theoretical explanations for the formation of inter-organizational relationships, Barringer and Harrison (2000) discuss joint ventures, networks, consortia, alliances, trade associations and interlocking directorates from the (diverse) perspectives of transaction cost economics, resource dependency, strategic choice, stakeholder theory, organizational learning and institutional theory, and outline the potential advantages and disadvantages of participation in each type of inter-organizational relationship. Networks, which are constellations of businesses that each focus on a distinctive competency and are organized through social contracts (Atler and Hage, 1993; Bluedorn *et al.*, 1994; Jones, 1995), tend to emerge where there is both high demand uncertainty and stable supply and where complex tasks must be completed under time pressure (Jones *et al.*, 1997).

From a more critical perspective, Buttery *et al.* (1999) have argued that the study of networking has been dominated by efforts to classify different types of networks (see Shortell *et al.*, 2000 for a classification of American health networks), to identify costs and benefits of networking, to explain the competitive advantage of networking, and to develop theories of trust in cooperation and collaboration. Despite the distinction between fragile/opportunistic and resilient trust based on norms of equity and reciprocity (Ring, 1997), and despite the recognition that cooperation is not necessarily trust-based (Hardy *et al.*, 1998), inter-organizational networks are represented as real, progressive, postcorporate organizational forms (see, for example, Clegg, 1990; Jaffee, 2001; Limerick *et al.*, 1998; cf. Strati, 2000a) rather than as discursively constituted social objects (cf. Lawrence *et al.*, 1999).

In this chapter, the aim is to examine the representation of network changes in public hospitals. In particular, the chapter focuses on the discussion of network change in published government reports and in so doing examines organizational networks as 'discursive' rather than 'objective' phenomena. As such, we are concerned with the documentation of change and how the purpose and nature of organizational networks is constituted (and reconstituted) across public texts. In sum, we wish to examine the relationship of networks and change in terms of a movement from inter-organizational forms to intertextual constructions.

Network reorganization as discursive change

With reference to the latter, this study of organizational change is of the constitution and re-constitution of network discourse rather than of the causes, nature and consequences of any objective actuality. First, it must be acknowledged that the much-used term *discourse* has been the subject of many interpretations (see Grant *et al.*, 1998), ranging from the wide 'system of statements that constructs an object, supports institutions, reproduces power relations and has ideological effects' (Elliott, 1996: 65 with reference to Parker, 1990) to the narrower system of texts that brings an object into being (Parker I., 1992). Consequently, discourse analysis is concerned with 'the constructive effects of texts' (Hardy and Phillips, 1999: 2), and critical discourse analysis (Fairclough, 1992) with 'the role of discursive activity in constituting and sustaining power relations' (Hardy and Phillips, 1999: 2). Further, 'discursive activity is a form of political activity because of the way in which it changes understandings of a social situation which, in turn, shape particular experiences and invoke certain practices' (Hardy and Phillips, 1999: 6).

Foucault (1991b) comments that discourses undergo constant change through formation, transformation, and correlation or situation alongside other types of discourse (e.g. clinical medicine alongside biology or chemistry) and within a non-discursive context of 'institutions, social relations, economic and political conjuncture' (1991b: 54). Similarly, Linell (1998) suggests that there is never a pure transfer of a fixed, context-free meaning, but that the study of recontextualization, or of discursive change and 'travel across situations', can be *intratextual* (within the same text; for example, within a conversation), *intertextual* (between texts), or *interdiscursive* (between activities or genre types). Drawing on Bakhtin's (1981) discussion of polyvocality, Linell (1998) commented that individual texts and discourses embody features of previous texts and discourses 'that partly merge, partly stay on to compete with each other' (Linell, 1998: 150; see also Boje, 1995).

Foucault's interest in discursive change lay not in the 'abstract, general and monotonous form of "change" which so easily serves as our means for conceptualising succession' (Foucault, 1991b: 55) but in emphasizing discontinuities and examination of particular sets of rules that define the limits and forms of the *sayable* (what it is possible to speak of), of *conservation* (disappearance, memory, reuse, circulation, or repression and censorship of utterances), of *reactivation* (retention, reconstitution, transformation, appreciation and role of previous or foreign discourses), and of *appropriation* (differential access, institutionalization, authorship and control of discourses). Accordingly, the study of organizational change moves from the progressive assumptions of organizational 'development' (see, for example, Harvey and Brown, 1996; French and Bell, 1999; Waddell *et al.*, 2000) to the textual changes of simplification, condensation, elaboration and refocusing (Bernstein, 1990):

> In Goffman's (1974) terms, recontextualization usually amounts to reframing. Aspects of discourse which can be recontextualized include linguistic expressions, concepts and propositions, 'facts', arguments and lines of argumentation, stories, assessments, values and ideologies, knowledge and theoretical constructs, ways of seeing things and ways of acting towards them, ways of thinking, and ways of saying things.
>
> (Linell, 1998: 145; cf. Palmer and Dunford, 1996)

One way of examining such changes is through the study of intertextuality between texts. Itself a term that has various definitions (see, for example, Fairclough, 1992; Keenoy *et al.*, 1997; Grant *et al.*, 1998 on relations between text and context), intertextuality in the (narrow) sense used here refers to 'the examination of any document in light of similar, related documents from the same setting, created previously, contemporaneously, or perhaps afterwards' (Hansen, 1995: 103). In extending this definition beyond the analysis of documents alone, Hansen (1995: 104) draws on the work of Witte (1992) to argue that intertext is longitudinal, for 'our text has been affected by previous texts and will affect future acts of communication'. This intertextual analysis can include 'examination of written and spoken communicative acts over an extended period of time' (Hansen, 1995: 105), and the study reported here concerns an intertextual analysis of the discourse of organizational networks and examines the particular formation, reorganization and 'disaggregation' of the Australian state of Victoria's public hospital networks through the lens of governmentality.

Governmentality

> Government has as its purpose not the act of government itself, but the welfare of the population, the improvement of its condition, the increase of its wealth, longevity, health, etc.
>
> (Foucault, 1991a: 100)

> Government lies between domination and those relationships of power that are reversible; it is the conduct of conduct, aiming to affect the actions of individuals by working on their conduct – that is, on the ways in which they regulate their own behaviour.
>
> (Hindess, 1996: 97)

In two lectures at the Collège de France in Paris in 1978 and 1979, Michel Foucault discussed what he termed the rationality, or art, of government. For Foucault, government was concerned with the broad conduct of conduct, 'that is to say, a form of activity aiming to shape, guide or affect the conduct of some person or persons' (Gordon, 1991: 2), and he introduced the word *governmentality* to describe an era since the eighteenth century in which there has been both expansion of and reflection on government (Foucault, 1991a; Hindess, 1996). In addition to the gradual *governmentalization* of the state and the formation of specific state apparatuses pertaining to government, Foucault argued that this era had seen increasing attention to the security and conduct of the subjects of the state rather than to *ad hoc* interventions, law enforcement or 'straightforward domination' (Hindess, 1996: 108). Ensuring the security of a population includes predicting possible and probable events, calculating comparative costs, and prescribing what is optimal 'within a tolerable bandwidth of variation' (Gordon, 1991: 20). Since security involves leading or controlling a series of actions, governmentality includes:

> the ensemble formed by the institutions, procedures, analyses and reflections, the calculations and tactics that allow the exercise of this very specific albeit complex form of power, which has as its target population, as its principal form of knowledge political economy, and as its technical means apparatuses of security.
>
> (Foucault, 1991a: 102)

Our analysis follows a particular line of argument in which governmentality is addressed within the context of healthcare. For example, Turner (1997) discusses the importance of Foucault's (1991a) work on governmentality as a mechanism for regulating and controlling populations through security, and argues that this work has both 'placed power and knowledge at the centre of the sociological understanding of medical institutions' (Turner, 1997: xiv) and allowed the sociological study of health to be seen as a contribution to the study of power. Important within the contemporary context, Turner (1997) discusses tensions between Foucault's analysis of governmentality, with its emphasis on security, and Beck's influential (1992) work on risk society, which is marked by managerialism, privatization and deregulation in an uncertain, contingent and flexible world (see also Petersen, 1997). Turner suggests five possible resolutions of such tensions: first, that 'macro-risk' in the global environment of political and economic uncertainty between nation-states may necessitate greater investment in internal systems of governmentality and intensified micro-surveillance and discipline; second, that 'a risk society, based on deregulation and devolution, often requires more subtle and systematic forms of control' (Turner, 1997: xviii); third, that despite ideological commitment to privatization and deregulation, governments may intervene to save major companies and public institutions; fourth, that McDonaldization (Ritzer, 1993, 2000), based on principles of cheapness, standardization and reliability, is a response to the growth of risk and uncertainty, and has extended to the health industry to the extent that 'the welfare and health system is now a complex mix of risk culture and McDonaldization of services' (Turner, 1997: xviii); and fifth, that greater control through the promotion of preventative medicine and associated self-regulation may be a response to generalized environmental risk.

This chapter concentrates on the fourth of these through examination of subtle shifts between localization and centralization in public healthcare policy (see Powell and Wessen, 1999a). The particular context discussed here lies within the Australian state of Victoria between 1995 and 2000, when the organization of public health underwent three organizational changes and also a change in state government from a conservative to a more liberal regime. The aim of this chapter is to review the documenting of those changes as one local example of tensions between risk and governmentality, and also to call for greater attention to the analysis of documentation (rather than facilitation, implementation or evaluation) in the study of organizational change.

Governmentality and health

Referring to Foucault (1989), Osborne (1997) has commented that government tends to problematize, or to put into question, the relation between those who are governed and those who govern. Osborne links Foucault's discussion of a historical shift from concern with sovereignty over territory to concern with population 'above all else as the ultimate end of government' (Foucault, 1991a: 100), and, in particular, with population augmentation and productivity. Similarly, Gordon (1991) pointed out that:

> Whereas sovereignty has as its object the extended space of a territory, and discipline focuses on the body of the individual (albeit treated as a member of a determinate collectivity), security addresses itself distinctively to "the ensemble of a population". Foucault suggests that from the eighteenth century onwards, security tends increasingly to become the dominant component of modern governmental rationality.
>
> (Gordon, 1991: 20)

As can be seen from the quotation that introduces the section on governmentality, health policy is clearly relevant to this emphasis on population, and Foucault's work on governmentality has been influential in the study of changes in healthcare (see, for example, Petersen and Bunton, 1997). As a result of this influence, and because 'health' is an indeterminate rather than absolute concept, Osborne (1997: 181) suggests a focus on 'diverse technologies of health; that is, all the diverse means, projects and devices through which the impossible dream of a healthy population has been made an object of realisation'. In particular, Osborne distinguishes a *liberal*, or indirect, government of health as a by-product of general policy from *neo-liberal* government, which acts more directly on health in order to achieve goals and targets 'relating to finance, pharmaceuticals, recovery rates, operations, patients, waiting-lists and so-forth' (Osborne, 1997: 185) within a limited set of objectives. Osborne (1997) distinguishes his discussion of liberalism from party-political allegiance, and suggests that the logic of a socialized health policy can be seen:

> either *beyond* liberalism towards a properly socialised – that is, something like a *socialist* – service; or – as seems to have been the case in Britain and in most of the English-speaking countries since the 1980s – *away* from liberalism and in the direction of something like a neo-liberal government of health.
>
> (Osborne, 1997: 184 — emphases in original)

The latter is certainly the case in Australia, where there is a mixed public and private health system that supplements the Commonwealth-supported Medicare program for universal health coverage (see Short and Palmer, 2000 for a review). Funding for health delivery operates on a state system, and since 1993 a Casemix (capitation-type) funding system based on hospital activity types or *diagnosis-related groups* has operated in the state of Victoria in Australia's southeast (Duckett, 1994; cf. Covaleski *et al.*, 1993; Bazzoli *et al.*, 2000). While this system was introduced following the election of a conservative Liberal Party government in 1992, Casemix-based public hospital funding 'is now implemented in every [Australian] state and territory to a greater or lesser degree' (Short and Palmer, 2000: 451) and is widely accepted in several OECD countries (Kimberley *et al.*, 1993; Wessen, 1999b). As Osborne (1997: 186) points out, 'it would be a mistake to regard the neo-liberal approach to health policy as being the exclusive property of the Right (even if in most countries this so far has, in fact, been the case)'.

Petersen (1997) points to a direct link between public health, Foucault's (1991a) work on governmentality, discussion of risk and such neo-liberalism (Castel, 1991), and presents the position that the notions of reflexive self-governance and regulated autonomy for subjects so important under neo-liberalism illustrate a new form of population regulation. Rather than control of dangerous individual subjects through direct repression or welfare intervention, this regulatory form is closely associated with control of risk through market regulation, objectified performance indicators, and through the individual-as-enterprise (see also Gordon, 1991; Rose, 1993; Hindess, 1996; Lacombe, 1996).

For example, Petersen (1997) discusses the refinement of national health goals and targets in Australia in 1993 in order to extend the government's 'framework of action' to health promotion and also to facilitate people's ability to care for themselves (Commonwealth of Australia, 1993). Accordingly, the emphasis shifts from distinguishing healthy and unhealthy populations to ensuring population security through extended prevention and self-management of risk (see also Wessen, 1999a), and the study of how such self-government shapes subjectivity can be informed by Foucault's earlier studies of discipline, and of the association between disciplinary refinement and changes in fields of knowledge such as the social and behavioural sciences that constitute the subjects of that knowledge (Hindess, 1996; see also Rose, 1990; Foucault, 1991a: 101; Gordon, 1991; Reed, 1998).

Similarly, Turner suggests that governmentality is seen as a 'regime which links self-subjection with societal regulation' (1997: xv). This self-government complements the activities of the state in gathering detailed measurement data on its subjects, and this gathering is a manifestation of what Foucault has termed *pastoral power*. In its modern secular form, pastoral power assures individuals of goods such as health, well-being and security, if not liberty as defined in other, contractarian and republican traditions of Western thought (Foucault, 1988; Hindess, 1996; Nettleton, 1997). It also retains an emphasis on self-examination that, Foucault argued, had been appropriated into the Christian modification of the shepherd-flock metaphor from earlier, Stoic practice (Gordon, 1991; Hindess, 1996).

Associated with such an emphasis, and of particular relevance to this study, is both an extended possibility for social control and for inter-organizational alliances. With specific reference to the promotion of health, Petersen (1997) argues:

> An important health promotion concept is that of 'intersectoral collaboration', the forging of alliances between different levels of government, private bodies, non-government organizations and community groups, to create, in effect, a multi-levelled and multi-organisational network of surveillance and regulatory practices.
>
> (Petersen, 1997: 196)

Petersen goes on to point out that this extension of governmentality does not assume complete and coercive domination, but that it 'allows one to acknowledge the complexities, subtleties and micronegotiations of relations of power' (1997: 203; see also Lacombe, 1996). Petersen has called for further critical work on the complexities and micro-dynamics of relations of power in the new public health, in line with Foucault's concern with the means by which the effects of power are produced (Hindess, 1996, see also Gordon, 1991).

This chapter is a response to Petersen's (1997) call. The shifts discussed here are not in terms of the broader liberal/neo-liberal distinction, but in terms of organizational change within the Australian hybrid system as an example of 'the continual definition and redefinition of what is within the competence of the state and what is not, the public versus the private, and so on' (Foucault, 1991a: 103). In recognition that forms of power may be socially dispersed as well as concentrated and hierarchically organized (Hindess, 1996), the particular focus here is on how governmentality matters in the shifting organization of inter-organizational hospital networks in the Victorian public health system.

Method

Eight government reports were examined, representing the major public health documents published over the period that included the formation of seven Victorian Health Care Networks in 1995, subsequent amalgamations among those networks, and their 'disaggregation' into 12 Metropolitan Health Services in 2000. The reports included:

(a) *Victoria's Health to 2050* (January 1995), which set the strategic direction for implementation of the networks;
(b) *Phase 1* and *Phase 2 Metropolitan Hospitals Planning Board Reports* (February 1995), which recommended formation of the seven networks from 35 independent public hospitals;
(c) the operational *Plan for Metropolitan Health Care Services* (October 1996);
(d) the *Ministerial Review of Health Care Networks* (also known as the 'Duckett Report'), which took place after a change of state government from the more conservative Liberal Party to the more liberal Labour Party recommended disaggregation of the Health Care Networks and formation of the Metropolitan Health Services, and included:

    a. an *Interim Report* (Duckett, 2000a);
    b. the *Final Report* (Duckett, 2000b); and
    c. the *Government Response* (May 2000).

(e) the quarterly *Hospital Services Report* (June Quarter 2000).

As part of the document analysis (Sommer and Sommer, 1991; Forster, 1994; Lee, 1999; Flick, 2003), the reports were analyzed by inductive content analysis (Gephart, 1993) based on open coding or fracturing (Strauss and Corbin, 1990) of themes and sub-themes and emergence of recurring links (Creswell, 1994). The analysis presented below is the result of constant comparison and editing techniques, in which a reduced summary is the result of a cyclical process of comparison between themes and original textual data (Miller and Crabtree, 1992). In this presentation, particular attention is given to intertextual simplification, condensation, elaboration and refocusing (following Bernstein, 1990); and on the language with which the organization and reorganization is presented.

From responsive regionalization to responsible localization: discursive change in healthcare networks

In this section, a summary of results of the intertextual analysis is presented. Results are first discussed following the sequence of reports that were analyzed, and then summarized according to the shifting themes across the reports.

(a) Victoria's Health to 2050: Developing Melbourne's Hospital Network (January 1995): From inefficient, uncaring hospitals to modern networks

This report presented an overview of strategic directions for healthcare in Victoria for the next half-century, providing a summary of the current scene, trends and forecasts, and impediments to change. The shift in emphasis from the public hospital to hospital networks is heralded both through the use of the term *network* in the subheading to the report and in the association of individual hospitals with the old, the inefficient, and the uncaring. Additional support for this shift was gained through the use of particular terminology; for example, there was seen to be a need for 'modern practices' to replace 'traditional, hierarchical systems'. External environmental analysis that included reference to Australia's aging population among other 'pressures for change' suggested a decreasing role for the institution of 'the hospital' and an increasing role for contracted services and networks. The modern concepts of the *boundaryless hospital* (with frequent reference to Braithwaite *et al.*, 1994), and of *managed competition*, which is an application of the influential ideas of Alain Enthoven (see Enthoven, 1985, 1993; Wessen, 1999b), gave external legitimacy to the call for changes (see also Brunsson and Sahlin-Andersson, 2000).

In addition, there was a call for individual patient 'health gain' rather than the health system to be of central importance, and this, together with the suggestion that there were too many hospitals, particularly in the 'outdated' inner city areas of Melbourne, supported a shift in emphasis away from the public hospital as principal health provider (cf. Wessen, 1999a).

(b) Metropolitan Hospitals Planning Board Reports (February 1995): Invisible changes toward better (and more efficient) care

In recommending the formation of the Health Care Networks, the emphasis of these reports was on the provision of care (rather than the earlier idea of 'gain') to the patient. Thus, instead of individual public hospitals, there was to be a 'network of care', which was defined as a 'collection of health care providers under common governance, possessing a wide range of health care facilities and attuned to meeting an individual patient's needs with appropriate medical response'. Supplemental to this rhetoric of care was also a rhetoric of efficiency, with references within these reports to 'commercial orientation', to the optimization of physical plant, to downsizing, and to hospital relocations away from the inner suburbs and closer to where patients live.

The new networks were to provide an invisible framework for the management of health, and, as Adeney (1996) has noted, the term *invisibility* is repeatedly mentioned in the Phase 1 report. Adeney discussed the subsequent legislative changes that decorporatized public hospitals such that they were no longer individual legal entities, suggesting that the government aimed to keep the changes invisible in order to reduce resistance to hospital amalgamations without undermining public confidence or affecting the level of (tax exempt) funds donated to the individual hospitals. Relevant to discussions of the technologies of government through the increasing roles of government agencies, market rationality, centralized decentralization and alliances (see, for example, Rose, 1996; Reed, 1998), shifts in the provision of service (including hospital closures) were now the responsibility of the networks rather than the direct responsibility of the state government. Indeed, Adeney (1996) argued that the invisibility of the shift from hospitals to networks continued an increase in external control and centralization of power that had started with earlier legislative changes in 1988 when public hospitals were no longer registered charities but became accountable to government.

(c) Plan for Metropolitan Health Care Services (October 1996)

This report further supported the shift in focus away from the public hospital. In particular, an introductory note from the then Government Minister of Health stressed the need to go 'beyond bricks and mortar' (i.e. the hospital) in addressing the health needs of an aging population and a population that was growing in the outer regions of the city. It was suggested that implementation of the plan would enhance the quality, efficiency and accessibility of Melbourne's public healthcare services in response to new demands on the health system, new capabilities, and changing community preferences for how and where services are delivered. The plan then included an overview of particular initiatives to take place within each of the new Health Care Networks.

(d) Ministerial Review of Health Care Networks: Rebalancing and realigning the commercial, the competitive, and the community

In the *Interim Report* (Duckett, 2000a) it was noted that due mainly to mergers among the networks, only three of the networks existed 'as originally envisaged'. Thus, it was argued, there was a need for 'reaggregation' or 'disaggregation' (both terms were used) of the networks into smaller groups, each with a community focus. It was assumed that such reaggregation would involve few major changes for staff involved in healthcare delivery, but would improve patient service. The primacy of the rhetoric of care over the rhetoric of efficiency in the first two reports was retrospectively reversed in this Interim Report, for here the *networks* were associated with an emphasis on efficiency over care that now needed remedy. For example, it was suggested that:

> the current undue emphasis on 'commercial' viability should be replaced by a more balanced requirement for sound financial management and accountability … [the] core purpose is to provide services to public patients in accordance with Medicare principles
>
> (Duckett, 2000a: 20)

However, by the *Final Report* (Duckett, 2000b), commercial viability became far more central, and the need to move away from a more narrowly defined commercial emphasis was replaced by a call to move away from an overly competitive emphasis. In other words, what was now used as a legitimation for (further) change was not the need to move *away* from an (over)emphasis on 'commercial viability', but, instead, the need to *emphasize* 'financial viability' and to reduce, instead, the (over)emphasis on 'competition' among the networks for services such as supplies. In this subtle elaboration, a distinction was, therefore, made between the significations of *commercialization* and *competition*: commercialization was now associated with the more positively valued term *financial viability* while inter-Network competition was distinguished from the higher values of *collaboration*. In addition, the individual health gains so important in Victoria's health to 2050 were now replaced with the emphasis on *community* that had first become evident in the 1996 plan.

Instead of the larger Health Care Networks, the new, smaller Metropolitan Health Services were to be financially viable, consumer-oriented, and focused on quality and service. What was now condensed as the 'disaggregation' of the networks would, it was argued, 'lower the cost of bureaucracy' and save A$18 million; focus attention on financial issues; be more in line with original intentions for network size; encourage collaboration rather than competition; and retain existing economies of scale for support services. Network aggregation was associated with network amalgamation, while the Health Services would be more responsive to local needs and offer closer services, shifting provision of services 'from institutional to community-based services' (cf. Wessen, 1999a).

In several ways, the rationale for the move away from the Health Care Networks echoes the same arguments that were important in their introduction. First, the need to progress from a more to a less institutionalized setting for healthcare was an important justification in both moving from hospitals to networks and also in moving from networks to Health Services. Second, the aim of providing closer services for patients was also important in both changes; hospital relocations from inner to outer parts of the networks were to bring services closer to Melbourne's outwardly expanding population, while the smaller geographical span of the Services would now mean reduced patient travelling time, except perhaps in areas where hospitals have been closed. Importantly, no mention was now made of the city's shifting population, and it should be noted that the context of public and provider resistance to planned inner city hospital closures and a recent growth in inner city residences may be relevant to this absence. Third, efficiency was still valued, and it was argued that the Health Services would reduce duplication. Fourth, and as in *Victoria's Health to 2050*, change is presented as progressive (cf. McKendall, 1993; Wolfram Cox, 2001). For example, there is a recommendation that new legislation should introduce the Health Services, but that these services and not single hospitals should succeed the Networks so as not to 'give rise to perceptions … [of] a return to the pre-Health Care Networks era' (Duckett, 2000b: 147).

What was different in the Final Report was its increased emphasis on financial viability, brought about by extreme (and increasingly publicized) problems within several Networks. Indeed terms used to describe these networks included 'precarious', 'destitute', 'crisis' and 'technically insolvent'. While this issue was mentioned in the Interim Report (Duckett, 2000a: 5), it receives much greater attention in the final report. Indeed, the authors of the Final Report are careful to 'focus attention' on the financial issue but not to 'create the issue', perhaps conscious of the use of financial crisis to justify major policy shifts during the term of the previous Liberal government under the then premier, Jeff Kennett. And by concentrating on the financial crisis, attention is shifted from other issues, such as the misuse of donations (Duckett, 2000b: 39), infection control, rural hospitals, mixed-gender accommodation, and the remuneration of boards and chief executive officers. Many of these latter issues have received substantial press coverage, but appear only towards the end of the Final Report.

By the time of the *Government Response* to the Duckett report (May 2000), there was yet another shift in (and this time a simplification of) the discourse. As noted above, the emphasis on community was an extension of the move away from competition (and towards financial viability) in the Final Report. While financial viability was the primary focus of the Final Report, and is still important in the Government Response, emphasis on community was now of utmost importance. For example, it was argued very early in this response (2000: 2) that 'the Bracks Labor Government's election commitment was to replace the large and expensive public hospital network with a system of governance more responsive to the community', and it was now the Networks rather than the smaller provider units that were associated with regressive descriptions of bureaucratic rigidity, for the 'large', 'remote', 'complex', 'bureaucratic', 'competitive' networks were to be replaced by 'smaller', 'local', 'collaborative', 'integrated' and 'accountable' Health *Services*.

(e) Hospital Services Report (June Quarter 2000): From inefficient, uncaring networks to modern services

The Hospital Services report for the June Quarter 2000 presents a further simplification of this discursive reversal. Here, the Metropolitan Health Services were seen to be representative of the 'new beginning' of the Bracks Labor (rather than the previous Kennett Liberal) government, of responsive and more representative boards, and of budgets brought 'into the black'. In contrast, the Health Care Networks were renamed 'the old hospital networks' without the reference to 'care' (2000: 1), and were presented as old, unwieldy, remote from the community, and associated with diseconomies and cash crises in certain hospitals.

In summary, the five years from 1995 to 2000 saw a change in the organization of health provision in the state of Victoria from individual hospitals to aggregated Health Care Networks, to amalgamations among those networks and subsequently to 'disaggregated' Metropolitan Health Services. While external population shifts, international practices and academic writings were used to justify what we term the *responsive regionalization* from individual hospitals to Health Care Networks, shifting internal competitive and financial network difficulties were initially presented as the justification for Network disaggregation, although that justification was itself the subject of a shift to what we term the *responsible localization* and community emphasis of the newly formed Metropolitan Health Services. Intertextual analysis between the major government reports published over that time has revealed a circular discursive pattern (see Figure 8.1), in which descriptions of the later shift from Health Care Networks to Metropolitan Health Services echo those of the earlier shift from individual hospitals to Health Care Networks. This pattern has been achieved through the combined processes of (a) *elaboration* of

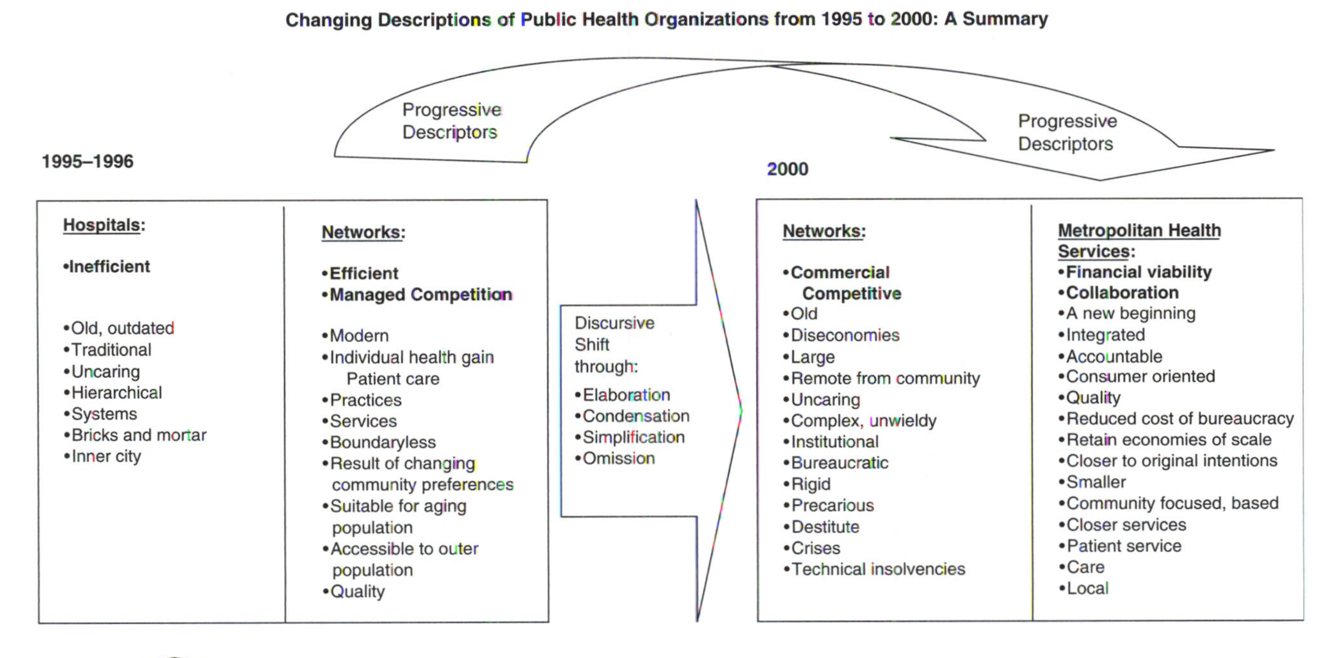

Figure 8.1 Government reports — discursive pattern

the signification of the term *commercialization* in order to allow separation of the positively valued term *collaboration* from the negative association of *competition*; (b) *condensation* of a mixed discourse of both *re*aggregation and *dis*aggregation to *dis*aggregation alone, which assisted the representation of the Health Care Services as progressive and Health Care Networks as regressive; (c) *simplification* of this progressive/regressive distinction in the period between the Final Report (Duckett, 2000b) and Health Services Report in June 2000; and (d) *omission* or *marginalization* of complications of and contradictions to this distinction, such as continuing public concerns with donations to hospitals, infection control, rural hospitals and mixed-gender accommodation.

Conclusion

While different theoretical frameworks (e.g. life cycle, teleological, dialectical and evolutionary change) can explain the reasons for and nature of organizational change (Van de Ven and Poole, 1995; cf. Weick and Quinn, 1999), Foucault's (1991b) emphasis on discourse encourages, instead, reviews of the micro-logics for causality, the importance of context rather than generality, and of discontinuity rather than progression. In this chapter, the emphasis was not on how to achieve progression, or on whether or not it has been achieved, but on how organization was (re)constituted and progression was represented in a series of public reports into the reorganization of public health institutions. From intertextual analysis across these reports, it was found that reference to bureaucratic rigidity consistently signified the old, the past and the need for change. In contrast, references to closeness of service, efficiency, and flexibility consistently signified the novel, progressive potential of the future. Importantly, subtle shifts within and between the particular reports discussed here reconstituted the Health Care Networks as progressive in 1995 but as regressive by 2000, and legitimated their 'disaggregation' into Metropolitan Health Care Services.

This reconstitution is particularly dramatic given the short time period over which it took place, and this study offers one example of how intertextual analysis can inform the study of organizational change. Following Bernstein (1990) and Linell (1998), particular discursive changes in the organization of health were analyzed through the concepts of elaboration, condensation, simplification and omission. Extension of this analysis to a longer time period, or across different health systems in which inter-organizational networks have been formed and reformed could inform both the understanding of those networks and of the types and sequences of intertextual shifts such as the one discussed here. Thus, such work could contribute further both to the development of intertextual methodology and to the further development of theorizing of inter-organizational forms, for the representation of forms such as networks is just as important as their actuality, and arguably of greater theoretical interest than further classifications by type, cause or consequence (cf. Buttery *et al.*, 1999).

The particular series of reports analyzed here has been discussed with reference to Foucault's notion of governmentality and, more particularly, within the domain of public health. Within this context, it must be acknowledged that Foucault's (1991a) work on governmentality has been conceived very narrowly here, for the conduct of conduct can extend well beyond the specific public domain. Similarly, the study of text can extend well beyond the written forms discussed in this study (see, for example, Hansen, 1995; Lawrence *et al.*, 1999), and could include media reports, written and verbal press statements, and submissions to the review of the Health Care Networks, among many others.

Within these limitations, this chapter opens up several issues that are worthy of further investigation. First, it was noted earlier that neo-liberal health systems offer a potentially fruitful setting for the study of governmentality in the form of self-government. In the case of Victoria, the inter-discursive association between health policy and aging is particularly interesting, for there has been a perceived need to increase the control and self-government of older people and to reduce their dependence on state institutions such as centrally located public hospitals. Translated as an increased community pressure for deinstitutionalization and localization of healthcare in the reports of 1995 and 1996 discussed here, self-government of the aging has partially legitimated the (initial) reorganization of public health from individual hospitals to Health Care Networks. Thus, self-government matters both between and within discourses, for increasing self-government in the constitution of the aging subject has affected the deinstitutionalization of the public hospital, and the subsequent constitution of subject positions for both patients/clients and health providers.

Second, this chapter is a call for further work on the documentation of organizational change and, in particular, how government documents matter in the changing constitution of subjects such as health, age and education. While attention to the discursive turn in organization studies has resulted in a growth in attention to change as conversation (see, for example, Ford and Ford, 1995; Ford, 1998; Roth, 1999), we argue for extending this attention to text (and intertext) as well as to talk. However, this emphasis on the representation and constitution of organizational change through text is not to deny the importance of studies of the lived consequences of the supposedly 'invisible' reorganization of healthcare discussed here. For example, in what can be interpreted as an example of virtual mobility between employers, workers at a single location within the Victorian health system may have been part of four different organizational arrangements within five years. Particular studies into shifting individual, professional and organizational identities in public healthcare are currently in progress as part of a larger study of which this analysis forms part of it.

Finally, comparison of such virtual experiences and shifts in identification with those of people experiencing actual relocation and even repatriation may well be a fruitful contribution to and extension of the literature in the field of international management. Such relaxation of the boundaries of the field of organizational development and change beyond the performative empirical study of change interventions in single organizations has plenty to offer, and this intertextual study of how governmentality matters in healthcare is but one exploration of the territory beyond objectivist approaches to change in inter-organizational forms.

Part III

Alternative methodology

9 Actor-networks, research strategy and organization (with Nick Lee)

In this, the first of three chapters dealing with 'alternative methodology', we return to actor-network theory (ANT) in order to develop two related ANT arguments for organizational analysis. The first concerns *research strategy* and draws upon Latour's (1999a) notion of definitional 'sliding' to describe how ANT overcomes its analytical limitations by removing conditions that exclude the 'other'. Through this discussion, we argue that, research-wise, ANT appears to be ontologically relativist, in permitting the world to be organized differentially, yet empirically realist in providing 'theory-laden' descriptions of organization. Our second argument concerns *institutional boundedness and flexibility*, and suggests that ANT's ontological slipperiness may actually be of value for studies of organizational form. Contrasting the critical theory contention that 'rational' organization has become progressively reified and disembodied, with the 'new flexibility' mantra that there is 'nothing but life' (i.e. boundaryless development), we take recourse to ANT's well-known treatment of human and non-human actors to elide this ontological discrimination of 'live' and 'dead'. We outline how, under ANT, the analytical focus shifts from structural prescription to processual deconstruction, the associated political dimension concerning where and for whom boundaries are produced/consumed. Overall the chapter argues for organizational field research that avoids any obligation to impose and defend its own theoretical discriminations.

Conceptualizing ANT

> From the very beginning, ANT has been sliding in a sort of race to overcome its limits and to drop from the list of its methodological terms any which would make it impossible for new actors (actants in fact) to define the world in their own terms, using their own dimensions and touchstones.
>
> (Latour, 1999a: 20)

In the quotation above, Latour portrays ANT as being in a state of permanent revolution. At every moment, it seeks to overcome its own limits. This description might, at first, lead us to draw comparisons with those imperialist revolutionaries of yesteryear who 'overcame' their boundaries by extending them; placing agents in key positions in neighbouring administrations, hurrying their neighbours' collapse and incorporation. No strategy could be more modern than that. But ANT's 'sliding' is no imperialist revolution. ANT overcomes its limits not by enforcing its boundaries — its view of what belongs and what does not — on others, but by removing from itself any terms and conditions that might serve to exclude others. ANT races against itself, against any tendency it might have to produce boundaries and thereby rule out possible future relationships.

At the outset of our discussion, then, we note that ANT is characterized by an antipathy to self-definition. This antipathy exhibits itself as ANT's habit of failing to forge its own internal and external boundaries. This is the key to ANT's 'success' (Law and Hassard, 1999). By making itself as blank as it can, it prepares itself to record the discriminations that are performed and the boundaries that are constructed in the activities it studies. Thus, rather than build its own discriminations, it pays attention to, for example, the emergence and deployment of centres and peripheries (Callon, 1986), the separation of ontological categories (Latour, 1994) and the relationships between boundaries and flows (Mol and Law, 1994) in the areas it is applied to. In short, ANT is *ontologically relativist* in that it allows that the world may be organized in many different ways, but also *empirically realist* in that it finds no insurmountable difficulty to producing descriptions of organizational processes.

Over the years, ANT has proved flexible enough to move from its origins in science and technology studies (see Callon *et al.*, 1986; Latour, 1988) into social science fields as diverse as sociology (Law, 1991b, 1994), psychology (Michael, 1996), anthropology (Strathern, 1996), politics (Mol, 1999) and economics (Callon, 1998). Latour (1999a) even holds out hope that it might yet bring something to theology! Sometimes, however, it appears as if ANT offers little more than analytical flexibility, since everything else, including methodological terms, seems expendable. Thus, as Latour reflects on ANT, he writes: 'I will start by saying that there are only four things that do not work with actor-network theory; the word actor, the word network, the word theory and the hyphen! Four nails in the coffin' (Latour, 1999a: 15).

So we turn to the task of aligning ANT and organization studies methodology with some trepidation. After all, our aim is to sketch out the relevance to organization studies of a research approach that, on some occasions, looks as imposing as Rabelais' Gargantua — the indiscriminately gluttonous, giant scholar/warrior — and, on others, as meek, defenceless and inviting as a blank sheet of paper. In this chapter, we focus on ANT's qualities of blankness and flexibility in relation to issues of research strategy. The chapter makes some speculative suggestions about how ANT can contribute to the general development of organization studies in the years to come; i.e. in the era defined as 'after ANT' (Law and Hassard, 1999). In so doing we tackle basic conceptual issues of ANT's research philosophy in relation to the study of organizational form.

ANT and research

Our first step will be to describe ANT as a *research strategy*. In so doing we will resist the temptation to draw up a list of key commitments, or even a glossary of key terms (see Callon *et al.*, 1986, for such a glossary and Latour, 1988, for worked examples of the use of such terms). In view of Latour's comments above, such lists and glossaries, as desirable as they may be, would clearly miss the point. But it is vital for our purposes that a clear picture of ANT as a distinctive research strategy comes across. This is because ANT's research strategy, as it bears on issues of expertise, boundedness and flexibility, appears peculiarly suited to the investigation of key contemporary developments in organizational thinking and practice.

We will argue that ANT represents an approach to field research that is well suited to contemporary conditions in which the expertise of the researcher is problematized (Jones and Munro, 2005). We argue also that this problematizing has taken place through two key developments: (a) growth of the 'risk society' (Beck, 1992) characterized not so much by the failure of expert knowledge to deliver on promises, as by the flourishing of rhetorical tools of expertise beyond the research context and the consequent dissolution of the expert/lay boundary; and (b) acceptance of reflexivity and empirical relativism into the 'common sense' of social scientific research, including that carried out in organization studies. In our view, reflexivity and empirical relativism are reflections of, rather than creative responses to, the dissolution of the expert/lay boundary (see Wynne, 1996 on this point, also Casey, 2002). They have the fortunate consequence of making the position of expert 'legislator' (Bauman, 1987) untenable, and the unfortunate consequence of removing any rationale for conducting field research.

We note also that in debates on the status of social investigation, the consensus appears to be that contemporary research strategy takes recourse increasingly to trajectories that are empirically relativist and ontologically realist (cf. sociological triangulation). In contrast, for us, the research strategies of ANT largely invert this position. ANT is empirically realist, in the sense that it leaves the task of challenging its empirical base to the research and user communities it addresses, and ontologically relativist in that it typically embarks on research without a clear picture of what sort of entities it will discover through interaction. This serves to distinguish ANT from both 'modern' and 'postmodern' research strategies (see Gergen, 1992, on this point).

ANT and flexibility

Beyond this introductory goal, however, we also want to use this discussion of ANT to focus attention on the themes of 'boundedness' and 'flexibility' as they are operationalized in the practices of organizations. We note that it was once deemed satisfactory for organizations to have a clear and coherent identity, guaranteed by a strong external boundary. The sheer coherence of the organization would serve to meet other organizational objectives such as efficiency, quality of decision-making and/or increased market share.

In the public sector, however, as deregulation has continued apace, the regulation of organizations has developed so as to allow the following: partnerships between state agencies which challenge existing organizational identities in the pursuit of efficiencies; internal purchaser–provider splits which fracture organizational identity so as to establish internal market relations; and, even, public/private partnerships, which erode the very distinction that has so long preserved the public sector's identity.

Likewise, in the private sector, the coherent bulk of the large organization, once a source of pride, now appears one of strategic, operational and frequently financial embarrassment. This is the era of organizational networks, strategic alliances, out-sourcing and business process reengineering. Core/periphery employment, zero-hour contracts, portfolio careers and, in particular, downsizing appear the strategic order of the day.

In short, economic conditions are such that strong organizational boundaries can no longer be treated as shorthand for success. Responsiveness to market conditions is the clarion call, and this responsiveness is sought by maximizing the flexibility of organizations' internal and external relationships. In this confusing scene, it may be useful to have at hand a research approach that is 'blank' enough to trace the production and removal of boundaries; an approach to research that does not come with an obligation to impose and to defend its own discriminations. We will argue that ANT's blankness or ontological relativism makes it flexible enough to chart such processes and practices.

So let us now turn to the task of introducing ANT in the context of contemporary debates on research strategy and philosophy.

Research strategy in an age of uncertainty

> The difference between "unenlightened mob" and "enlightened citizens" or, in more modern terms, between lay people and experts, shrivels and transforms itself into competition between different experts.
>
> (Bonß and Hartmann, 1985: 16, cited in Beck, 1992)

One of the basic questions that directs texts on social research methodology is what, if anything, distinguishes the 'expert' from the 'lay' commentator? There is one clear and positive answer to this question, which, though currently rather unfashionable in some circles, still makes its mark on the production and assessment of, for example, proposals for research funding. We will first give a brief account of this answer, and then turn to the objections that are most frequently raised against it in discussions of postmodern research strategy — objections from reflexivity and relativism. As we discuss these objections, we will suggest that the debate on research strategy, pitched between modern and postmodern approaches, appears to be grinding to a halt. The debate is not stalling through an exhaustion of the issues or through the collective and positive endorsement of an agreed settlement, but largely and simply through the exhaustion of the participants to the debate. As we proceed, we will indicate those points at which ANT may re-cast what has become this tired modern versus postmodern problematic in research strategy analysis. Our hope is that this re-casting may inspire some creative alternatives.

Let us first describe, however, the unfashionable answer to the question of what makes our work as social science researchers valuable and then turn to the alternatives. Those research practices that make social scientific research 'better' knowledge than lay comment are virtually identical to those that ensure discrimination between the expert and lay commentator. These practices produce an external boundary around social scientific enquiry by producing internal boundaries that demarcate stages of social scientific research activity. Inquiry that is demonstrably regular and sequential trumps the casual remark. Rigorous methods of research ensure that a researcher's access to the empirical is not impeded by 'irrational' forces such as, for example, subjective values, consensual preconceptions or personal opinions. Empirical domains are construed as offering raw materials for the research process. Such methodological rigour ensures the possible replication of research, which, in turn, ensures that empirical data can be shared within the research community (as if social data, once collected, stood patiently awaiting further processing). Once data have been isolated thus, they can be put to use either as inductive bricks with which to build theories, or as hypothetico-deductive cobbles, nicely rounded, for hurling at existing theories.

At the theoretical level, therefore, we are presented with much ground for establishing discrimination between expert and lay knowledge. Methodological operations allow for a working discrimination between relevant and irrelevant factors. We know what phenomena and which viewpoints we can either readily accept or safely ignore. This allows us to discriminate between cause and effect. Good method both reveals and preserves the *sequentiality* of empirical events. The research process is about the production and deployment of specific divisions. Research must distinguish itself from lay comment and, in its theoretical moments, divide those factors and events that are of importance from those which can be discarded as anomolous. As we have noted, it is the sequentiality of research, especially the differentiation in time between data gathering, data analyzing and theorizing, that sunders social scientific research from lay comment. But how well are these factors differentiated in practice?

The objection from reflexivity

We have seen how vital the sequentiality of the research process is to preserving the status of expert knowledge. But very few nowadays would give wholehearted endorsement to the picture of the research process we have presented. It is not nearly 'reflexive' enough for contemporary tastes (Casey, 2002). The temporal distinction between data gathering and theorizing is particularly vital for distinguishing the expert researcher from the lay commentator. But as the sociological research process has come under increasing scrutiny, it has become apparent that empirical observation is inherently 'theory-laden'. After all, how are we to know the data worth gathering unless we have some preconception of what is worth looking at?

Commentators such as Haraway (1991) and Woolgar (1988a) rediscovered what was also apparent to an earlier generation of scholars (Hanson, 1958; Hampshire, 1959; Schutz, 1967; Gadamer, 1975); as observations are irrevocably theory-laden the operationalizing of the research process becomes habitually short-circuited. This point is in no way novel, nor is it necessarily threatening to the possibility of field research. The objection from reflexivity simply reinforces the view that field research has a long and successful history of confounding data with theory. This is not, in practice, a crisis. Yet it has been treated as a crisis because the principle of sundering data and theory is what has for so long separated expert research findings from lay comment.

With the uttering of the magic word 'reflexivity', then, the spell of expertise appears broken and researchers come to occupy seemingly much the same position that they had allotted to lay commentators. Everyone, without exception, lays perceptions and preconceptions over the world. All views are infected by interests. Reflexivity thus places relativism over the quality of empirical claims. Since research is a reflexive process, it follows that researchers should be reflexive — attuned to recognize that they have preconceptions and are always ready to give a cleansing account of their positions, preconceptions and interests.

But let us return to the quotation from Bonß and Hartmann (1985) earlier. This is in fact extracted from Beck's (1992) *Risk Society*, where he offers a quite different account of reflexivity from that offered by the philosophy of social research, one that is drawn on a far broader analytical canvas. Beck's reflexivity is nothing less than the 'modernisation of modernisation'. He argues that we made ourselves modern by respecting the research process described above; by allowing that its discriminations held good; and by acknowledging that these discriminations let us know what factors and, above all, what points of view (lay comment) it was safe to ignore. The objection from reflexivity, as we have portrayed it, then, is that the modern project of producing 'better' knowledge by discriminating between stages of research has failed because these discriminations cannot reasonably be maintained. Beck's argument, however, is different. He suggests that the success of the modern project has brought about a quite unexpected result — symmetry between expert and lay positions. Ours is an age of uncertainty not because our theories of knowledge have failed, but because there is now *so much* competing expertise.

Expertise, sustained by well-organized research, has been so good at discriminating what/who really matters from what/who does not matter, that it has long been able to portray the undesirable effects of its interventions as 'side' effects. Undesirable consequences of the application of expert knowledge are parcelled up as unintended by-products which, being unintended, should have little significance for the assessment of expert performance. Of course, whether an effect is a 'side' effect depends on whether one is experiencing it or not. While the objection from reflexivity, then, arises in the form of a philosophical debate, at the same time the recipients of such side effects can turn the modern rhetoric of disputing knowledge claims on the experts themselves, through exposing the partiality, subjectivity and interest-driven nature of research and expertise. What is basically a societal change, therefore, driven by distributions of unawareness, has been registered in the social sciences as a quasi-philosophical problem of knowledge, and expressed typically in the objection from reflexivity's epistemological scepticism.

Over the past few years, this objection from reflexivity has turned into positive zeal for rooting out the founding assumptions not only of particular research projects but also of whole traditions. The current 'acceptable' alternative to expert distinction (and the claim of a regular and sequential research process) appears to be *further* expert distinction, this time by the demonstration of skills of epistemological 'excavation'. To embark on the process of attempting to reveal another's implicit assumptions is to allow and to invite a similar scrutiny of one's own. Vertigo and claustrophobia are combined in what quickly becomes an infinite regression (Ashmore, 1989). Beck's analysis makes it clear that this situation within the social sciences is a *reflection* of societal change, not a creative response to it. We are making a great show of surrendering the crown long after the 'mob' has already stormed the palace. We may not notice this too often, but we are also in danger, potentially, of writing ourselves out of a job!

In sociological enquiry, therefore, word has generally got around that everybody speaks from one position or another. Reflexivity has become an element of good manners in presenting research findings, and the storm of scepticism seems to have largely blown itself out. So how are we to proceed? We could fall back on our traditional resources of 'rigour', re-draw the internal boundaries of the research process and reassemble our expertise. This would leave us safe in the knowledge that our colleagues are so tired from raising the standard objection from reflexivity that a nod towards our own partiality will be enough to keep them quiet. If reflexivity named only a problem of 'knowledge' this would be quite satisfactory. But Beck reminds us that it is not just our colleagues we have to respond to — reflexivity also names the *social* problem that arises out of the organized distribution of unawareness that expertise has been an enthusiastic party to. As non-experts have been excluded on the grounds of their ignorance, so the areas of which the expert is ignorant have expanded.

If we intend to respond positively and creatively to the changing fortunes of expertise, then an interminable and indiscriminate brawl of mutual accusation will not help. Yet discussions of research strategy that are broad enough to recognize that expertise is problematic are, all too often, limited to a choice between the re-making of our own boundaries or the insistence that there are no real boundaries at all. It is at this point that ANT's ongoing strategy of ridding itself of its own internal boundaries becomes valuable. ANT's struggle against producing its own vision of the world provides a clue to a research strategy which departs from the expertise form, yet retains a clear sense of the purpose of doing field research.

As we have seen, a relativist disposition towards empirical data, that is to say a refusal to treat data as evidence, reflects a waning of those institutional forms that preserved expertise for researchers. Further, the apparent exhaustion of the modern/postmodern debate in the sphere of research strategy (about the philosophical status of the empirical, with issues of politics and power transformed into gainsaying) appears to have left us with something resembling a consensus. This consensus suggests that it is important to recognize reflexivity and empirical relativism, as long as we do not take it 'too far'. Taking empirical relativism 'too far' results in a knee-jerk scepticism that undermines any rationale for undertaking field research. But what if the terms of the debate and of this current consensus were in fact misconceived all along?

Ontological relativism

By exposing the extant variability of views and interests, recent debate has explored the flexibility of the empirical. Our argument, however, takes us further — to ask whether institutional processes themselves (e.g. the making, unmaking and remaking of boundaries, categories and discriminations) rely on a quite distinct kind of flexibility: an ontological flexibility. If this were the case, an appropriate research strategy would concern itself less with the problem of gaining accurate descriptions of discrete elements and more with investigating the *processes* through which discretion emerges. It would accept, for example, that there is organization and that boundaries and discriminations are at work, but it would ask crucially how such organization is *performed*.

Empirical relativism, then, in the shape of the questioning, in principle, of each and every description, would be taken for granted as a feature of the substantive project under study. For after all, we know it is not just researchers who argue about alternative descriptions. Thus, to research an area would not be to imagine simply that, as an expert, one could ever have the final word, but that one's research strategy would inevitably need to be ontologically relativist. ANT in particular would actively fail to produce its own decisions about what phenomena are to be studied. As it would fail to create its own theoretical discriminations and boundaries, the better then to focus on how organizational forms *emerge*. We must remember that it is ontological relativism that has given ANT its own flexibility. In this ontologically relativist view, the empirical would not be a passive collection of 'raw materials' silently awaiting the researcher's gift of intelligibility, form and voice. Rather, it would be the site of *active processing* — organizational participants, working and re-working not just their various descriptions of organizational form, but organizational form itself.

It would be quite wrong, however, to suggest that the field of organization studies has failed to examine *processes* of organization. But, as Chia (1996b) argues, such processes have most frequently been understood in terms of the interactions of 'entities'. The study of these interactions has required that the existence of such entities be taken for granted. Organizational research often comes ready to analyse organization *in its own terms* and thus habitually lays its ontology across the area of study. Chia (1996b) gives goals, environment and strategy as examples of ontologically referenced entities, with such entities being often treated as if they were the fundamental building blocks of organization. The aspects of organization that are open for study in this view of process are those that relate to the mutual impact and influence of such entities. The success of a bid for expertise can be judged by the degree to which it can impose its ontology on organization. In other words, 'expert' knowledge of organization amounts to an ability to describe organizational processes in terms of the interaction of familiar entities. This is unproblematic as long as we are content with the range of research questions this approach opens up for us.

Arguably, though, viewing process as the impact of ready-made entities on one another imposes unnecessary limits on the range of viable research questions. With regard to goals we can ask, for example: how effectively are the goals being pursued? Is the strategy properly aligned with the goals? And are environmental conditions having an impact on goals and strategy? But once goals are analytically isolated, we *cannot* ask: what comprises goals? Are goals stable? (And if so, how are they made stable over time and across space?) Do goals have the temporal precedence and governing centrality we might expect of them? And how do goals mobilize and become mobilized? For these latter questions are the kind that an *ontologically relativist* research strategy would concern itself with.

The kinds of answer that ANT's research strategy would yield therefore are not those that help compose expertise for the researcher. An ANT research agenda is unlikely to confer the magical powers of the language of instrumentalism on the researcher. Indeed, as we have seen, its purpose is not to tell research users what they should achieve, rather how they are achieving what they are achieving. This is a direct consequence of blankness and ontological relativism.

At this point the objection may be raised that instrumental *magic* is exactly what non-academic research users demand of professional researchers. On this view the neat distinctions wrought between research strategies would appear merely academic. It has not escaped the attention of Colville *et al.* (1999) that organizational practitioners do not want for clearly stated ontological 'prescriptions'. There are many brands of snake oil! Ontological prescriptions are readily delivered by the commercial business publishing sector and by organizations' own planners and strategists. The field of organizational research comes prepacked with commodified expertise. To deploy Bauman's (1987) distinction there are more 'legislators' than 'interpreters'. But where Bauman urges a shift from legislation to interpretation on philosophical and ethical grounds, we would argue that the actual proliferation of legislators urges ontological relativism on academic researchers of organization increasingly as a matter of quality assurance and brand loyalty!

Organizational flexibility

Having outlined the distinctiveness of ANT in terms of its ontological relativism, we can now turn, briefly, to the question of why ANT's characteristic flexibility may be of particular use in studying contemporary organizational form.

Picture the scene. There are pearls on the ocean floor. On one boat, the crew lets down a deep-sea diver encased in a sturdy metal diving suit and fed with air piped from the surface. Protected by his suit, kept right side up by lead boots, he lumbers towards the oyster bed. A boy dives into the sea from a second boat. He wears no protective gear. He swims like a fish. A race for pearls is afoot, a race between an adult, protected from the *environment* by his suit and his back-up team, and a small boy. What the boy loses in protection, he gains in *flexibility*. As the deep-sea diver bears down on the oyster bed, the boy twists past and makes off with the prize.

This fable has been presented by the Cheltenham and Gloucester Building Society in a UK television advertisement for its financial products. It establishes a connection between the building society and the successful boy. It plays on flexible unboundedness, a key trope of contemporary organizational thinking (Arthur and Rousseau, 1995; Askenas *et al.*, 1995).

The fable tells us that when we erect boundaries around ourselves, we think we are protecting ourselves. But boundaries reduce our flexibility. If we lack flexibility, we lack responsiveness to the ocean we swim in, and, thus, we fail. One should not protect oneself from environmental change. The boundary between organization and environment is otiose. It prevents one from responding to environmental change 'just in time'. The fable suggests that certainty of boundaries and fixity of identity are tokens of unawareness. Just when we thought we knew how to be organized, how to divide, categorize and ring-fence, how, thereby to make ourselves 'successful', the world turned. If we are to have successful organizational form *now*, it must emerge through interaction and negotiation, and if we are to respect organizational form as an emergent property of relationships we must allow that form to change at a moment's notice.

The new flexibility, as indexed by this fable, is basically an ideological resolution of an inherent contradiction of modern organizational form, a contradiction that has long been fodder for critical organizational analysis. Designed to reach human ends and to serve human values, rational and bureaucratic organization materializes and reifies human cognitive capacities of discrimination and ordering. The result?

> disembodied, the very forms of our sociality turn against us, and within them there is no place for humane values. The soulful corporation or the compassionate state are, by virtue of the very constitution of these social forms, contradictions in terms.
>
> (Sayer, 1991: 154)

Disembodied, inhuman and soulless, the static, dead hand of organizational form chokes the life out of us. Perversely, our most rational products have been made more real, solid and powerful than what is truly human in us — soul and compassion. If we want to rescue our humanity from the stifling embrace of institutional forms that become *too* solid, it is argued that we should pursue 'embodied' organization, or organization which at least forms boundaries of a kind that remain negotiable. The tradition that criticizes rational organization on the grounds that it is inflexible and deadening, is very strong. It informs injunctions to postmodern playfulness in organizational research (Gergen, 1992) as much as it does Habermas' serious discrimination of system and lifeworld (Habermas, 1998).

But if it is becoming possible to think of organization precisely in terms of liveliness and flexibility, if the critical tradition is now an element of organization theory's own self-perception, how mordant can such critique be? This perhaps 'orthodox' critical view of organizations, with its admirable defence of the living, operates on the basis that there is a detectable ontological discrimination between those parts that are alive and those that are deceased. The 'new' flexibility — unlike earlier, more conservative, variants derived from contingency theory (see Burns and Stalker, 1961; Lawrence and Lorsch, 1967; Pugh and Hickson, 1976) that prescribed *bespoke* socio-technical systems — presents us with 'nothing but life', that is, *universal* prescriptions based on 'boundaryless' or 'seamless' organizational development. Here the more organizations can appear lively the less open to critique they are, a point raised by Kickert (1993) in relation to the autopoietic model of organization (see also Maturana, 1981; Luhmann, 1986). Cheltenham and Gloucester's pearl-diving boy is perhaps emblematic of this new flexibility.

ANT is well known, however, for including *non-humans* in its list of organizational participants (Ashmore *et al.*, 1994; Law and Hassard, 1999; see also Chapter 4). But this is not an example of fudging an otherwise clearly marked ontological boundary. It is an example of ANT's unwillingness to decide the shape of the world on behalf of the domains it examines. It is an example of ANT's 'blank' flexibility. If ANT took recourse simply to an unreflexive or uncritical ontological commitment — that there is no difference between the living and the non-living; that nothing ever divides what is human from what is non-human — then it would perhaps do little more than contradict the critical tradition that relies on detecting and exposing this difference. But, equally, in contemporary circumstances where 'life' is the organizing principle, critique on the grounds of the living/dead distinction is unlikely to thrive.

The research question that would be obscured by a prior ontological distinction between the living and the dead, or by the view that the ideology of flexibility is merely a fiction, therefore, is that of how contemporary organizational flexibility, responsiveness and liveliness, whatever this may consist of, is *achieved*. To answer this question we would need to pay close attention to what boundaries are being created as organizations become flexible, and where, when and for whom these boundaries are being created. These concerns are in no way unique to ANT, but ANT's research strategy, as we have characterized it, may hopefully be useful in addressing them.

Conclusion

In this chapter we have made two related arguments. Concerning the question of *research strategy*, we have argued that ANT's strategic failure to construct expertise by mobilizing analytical ontological categories is an alternative both to the deliberate construction of expertise on the one hand and to the noisy disavowal of our distinctiveness as researchers on the other. Not only is Latour's (1999a) 'sliding' possible, but further, in a context of the proliferation of expertise, it may well be helpful in maintaining the distinctiveness of organizational knowledge.

With regard to *institutional flexibility*, we have argued that contemporary developments in organizational practice have outpaced the traditional grounds of organizational critique, notably regarding the readiness to hand of moral ontological distinctions between human and non-human and living and dead. ANT's ontological relativism allows us to approach contemporary organizations with the question of how the 'liveliness' and 'flexibility' they currently exhibit is realized. Thus, critique need no longer focus discretely on the strategic dormancy of rational institutionalism, or the ideological superficiality of boundaryless organization, but rather on the means by which such organizational arrangements are *achieved*.

ANT's race away from its own boundedness, therefore, contrasts sharply with the race towards boundedness that has characterized much organizational discourse (Lee, 1998). Although it parallels contemporary organizational trends towards 'unboundedness', ANT does not advocate them. In so far as organizations have been flexible in the past, and are becoming newly so, ANT is of value because it is a means of revealing economies of boundedness *and* unboundedness.

10 Rethinking triangulation

This chapter extends the discussion of the potential contribution of postmodern theorizing to the domain of organizational research through a critique and re-presentation of triangulation. The aim is not to dismiss or reject triangulation, but to present a new perspective (or re-view) in an effort to encourage innovative ways of thinking about this increasingly popular research approach in organizational analysis. First, triangulation is defined and discussed through the contrasting lenses of positivism and postpositivism/postmodernism. Then we discuss triangulation as a metaphor and relatively unquestioned principle of 'good' organizational research. In so doing, we consider the concept of triangulation in terms of 'metaphorization', and notably of movement between researcher and subject positions in the research process. In concert with a shift of thinking 'from plane geometry' to 'crystallization and light theory' (Richardson, 1994) we argue for rethinking the lines and angles of triangulation inquiry. In particular, we suggest a shift from the 'triangulation of distance' to a more reflexive consideration of 'researcher stance'. This includes movement across three perspectives: the researcher as a follower of nomothetic lines; the researcher as the taker of an ideographic overview; and the researcher as the finder of a particular angle. Each of these perspectives is outlined and consideration given to associated possibilities and impossibilities. We discuss implications of this analysis in terms of methodological issues of perspective, data capture, reflexivity and metatriangulation.

Triangulation in organizational research

Hailing from navigation, military strategy, and surveying, triangulation is often understood as a method for the fixing of a position (Jick, 1984; Blaikie, 1991, 2000; Neuman, 1994; Ghauri and Gronberg, 2002). For example, Blaikie (1991) discusses the use of triangulation in geodetic surveying, which is the measurement of the positions of widely separated points on the earth's surface. In this context, triangulation is an efficient and precise method for 'location of a point from two others of known distance apart, given the angles of the triangle formed by the three points' (Clark, 1951: 145, cited in Blaikie, 1991: 118).

In social research, the term *triangulation* is used in a less literal sense: it involves the use of multiple methods and measures of an empirical phenomenon in order 'to overcome problems of bias and validity' (Blaikie, 1991: 115, see also Blaikie, 2000: 262–69; Scandura and Williams, 2000). In a widely cited work, Denzin (1978) distinguishes: (a) data triangulation, where data are collected at different times or from different sources; (b) investigator triangulation, where different researchers or evaluators independently collect data on the same phenomenon and compare the results; (c) methodological triangulation, where multiple methods of data collection are used; and (d) theory triangulation, where different theories are used to interpret a set of data. Janesick (1994) adds a fifth type to this list: (e) interdisciplinary triangulation, where the research process is informed not only by a single academic discipline (e.g. psychology), but by one or more other disciplines (e.g. art, sociology, history, dance, architecture, anthropology). And within each type of triangulation there are various sub-types, for example, methodological triangulation can include various combinations of qualitative and quantitative research designs (Creswell, 1994; and for examples see: Meyer, 1982; Sutton and Rafaeli, 1988; Paul, 1996; Currall *et al.*, 1999; Saunders *et al.*, 2001).

Triangulation is typically described through the language of capture and constraint — of fixing, positioning, and confining (Denzin, 1989: 48; see also Murphy, 1989; Smith, 1989; Blaikie, 1991, 2000; Keim, 1993; Grey *et al.*, 1996; Miller, 1997; Ghauri and Gronberg, 2002). For example, Paul (1996) draws on systems theory to suggest that mixed-method triangulation is one way of 'capturing' reality, arguing that 'analysis of complex organizational systems demands requisite variety in data collection methodologies in order to mirror the complexity which they attempt to describe' and that 'leveraging is possible because the strengths of one method often lie in an area of weakness of another method' (Paul, 1996: 136; cf. Fielding and Fielding, 1986: 35; Scandura and Williams, 2000).

Similarly, Jick argues that triangulation 'can be something other than scaling, reliability and convergent validation. It can also capture a more complete, holistic, and contextual portrayal of the unit(s) under study' (Jick, 1984: 365). Eisenhardt describes triangulation of methods both as an aid to data 'capture' and to 'stronger substantiation of constructs and hypotheses' (Eisenhardt, 1995: 73). And somewhat over-extending the metaphor perhaps, Miles and Huberman suggest that triangulation is 'a way to get to the finding in the first place — by seeing or hearing multiple instances of it from different sources by using different methods and by squaring the finding with others it needs to be squared with' (Miles and Huberman, 1994: 267).

The implicit assumption in much of the social science literature on triangulation, therefore, is of developing a more effective method for the capturing and fixing of social phenomena in order to realize a more accurate analysis and explanation. For our area of organization studies, the concomitant phenomenal perspective is of organizations as 'concrete, stable and identifiable entities with distinctive boundaries that can be described and analyzed, using appropriate research methodologies' (Chia, 1996a: 143). By extension it can be argued that, in keeping with this 'dominant assumption in traditional representational thinking' (Chia, 1996a: 143) of the 'modernist search for a determinate, fixable empirical entity' (Keenoy, 1999: 17) the object of organizational research traditionally lies inside the neatly aligned boundary of an enclosing metaphorical triangle. Once checked from more than one angle (Macdonald and Tipton, 1996) and 'secured' (Denzin, 1989: 39) inside a stable boundary, the subject/object can be more closely examined. The argument is simply that after 'squaring' (Miles and Huberman, 1994) the triangle, we can presumably capture its centre.

The positivist view of triangulation

This emphasis on stabilization and capture derives from positivism (Platt, 1996). In terms of epistemology, or 'the relationship between the knower or would-be-knower and what can be known' (Guba and Lincoln, 1994: 108), positivism is dualist and objectivist and assumes: (a) 'objective' reality can be captured; (b) the observer can be separated from the observed; (c) observations and generalizations are free from situational and temporal constraints, that is, they are universally generalizable; (d) causality is linear, and there are no causes without effects, no effects without causes; and (e) inquiry is value free (Denzin, 1989: 24; cf. Bryman, 1988; Blaikie, 1993, 2000; Chia, 1996a, 1997; McKelvey, 1997, 2003).

Under such positivist assumptions, knowledge is 'hard, real and capable of being transmitted in tangible form' (Burrell and Morgan, 1979: 1), and a 'correspondence is posited between sensory experiences and the objects of those experiences, and between constant conjunctions of such objects of experience (events) and causal laws' (Blaikie, 1991: 120). Accordingly, convergent findings can allow greater researcher confidence in the reliability and/or validity of results, whereas divergence can lead to greater definition and theoretical elaboration as the researcher attempts to 'piece together many pieces of a complex puzzle into a coherent whole' (Jick, 1984: 369, cf. Campbell and Fiske, 1959; Fielding and Fielding, 1986; Blaikie, 2000; Silverman, 2001). Although there may be problems in achieving such convergence because of difficulties in replication, lack of focus on or alignment with the research question, or varying sensitivities among research instruments (Jick, 1984), such 'problems' with triangulation lie with its operationalization as a research strategy rather than with its epistemology (cf. Blaikie, 1991, 2000; Silverman, 2001). Thus, if reality is capable of being captured, the positivist question is: how can we best grasp it? How can we picture it?

Postmodernism and postpositivism

In addition to such methodological concerns from within a positivist framework, it is also important to consider ontological and epistemological concerns from without. In organizational studies, as in other disciplines, positivist assumptions have been the subject of much debate. For example, Donaldson's (1985, 1994, 1995, 1996a, 1996b, 2003) support for positivist organization theory has met with considerable opposition, even sarcasm and derision (see, for example, *Organization Studies* 1988; Marsden, 1993; Reed, 1993; Clegg, 1994; Knights and Morgan, 1994; Hassard and Kelemen, 2002; Case, 2003; Czarniawska, 2003). At its most strident this suggests that, under positivism, the inquirer's voice is that of the 'disinterested scientist' (Guba and Lincoln, 1994), privileged at the expense of that of the subject, who has been neglected, mutilated or even pronounced dead (Burrell, 1996, 1998; Clegg and Hardy, 1996; Casey, 2002;). From this perspective, triangulation is perhaps not only stabilization or silencing but also strangulation.

Since such a proposition can be quite confronting, it invites closer analysis. In a helpful guide, Guba and Lincoln (1994) distinguish between positivist, postpositivist and postmodernist inquiry, grouping postmodernism and poststructuralism within 'critical theory' (cf. Alvesson and Deetz, 1996). The nature of reality, or ontology, assumed by positivism is realism, where 'an apprehendable reality is assumed to exist, driven by immutable natural laws and mechanisms' (Alvesson and Deetz, 1996: 109; cf. Tsoukas, 1989; Blaikie, 1991; Marsden, 1993; see also Chia, 1997; Hancock and Tyler, 2002). In contrast, postpositivism assumes that this 'reality' is only 'imperfectly and probabilistically apprehendable' (Alvesson and Deetz, 1996: 109). And critical theory, founded on the idealist tradition of critique, suggests that a once plastic reality has become inappropriately shaped and reified over time. Although positivism and postpositivism are, to greater and lesser degrees, dualist/objectivist in that they assume detachment between the knower and what can be known, critical theory adopts a more transactional and subjectivist epistemology where 'the investigator and the investigated object are assumed to be interactively linked, with the values of the investigator … inevitably influencing the inquiry' (Alvesson and Deetz, 1996: 110).

In terms of research methodology, and, in particular, possibilities for triangulation, these differences have important implications. Under the positivist assumptions discussed above, 'research can, in principle, converge on the "true" state of affairs' (Guba and Lincoln, 1994: 109). Under postpositivism, emphasis is placed on falsifying (rather than verifying) hypotheses. Under critical theory, this is not possible, for here 'the transactional nature of inquiry requires a dialogue between the investigator and the subjects of that inquiry' (Guba and Lincoln, 1994: 110). Whereas the aim of positivist and postpositivist inquiry is explanation, prediction and control, the aim of critical theory is critique and emancipation (cf. Willmott, 1997). Under positivism and postpositivism, knowledge will accumulate by accretion. Under critical theory, triangulation becomes not only more difficult to accomplish but more problematic as the emphasis is on revision rather than accumulation of findings (Guba and Lincoln, 1994).

Thus, Guba and Lincoln view postpositivism as a variant of the 'received' positivist position (see also Blaikie, 1991: 24–28; 2000: 262–70). Under postpositivism, triangulation of the sort envisaged by Denzin is possible and indeed necessary as 'claims about reality must be subjected to the widest possible critical examination' (Guba and Lincoln, 1994: 110). However, where a transactional and subjectivist epistemology is adopted, triangulation becomes more difficult:

> convergence may mean that consensus exists on how reality is viewed, or that a common reality is shared, while a lack of convergence may reflect legitimate and different views of reality, or the habituation of different social worlds. Such differences cannot be used to attribute bias to any method.
>
> (Blaikie, 1991: 123)

This difficulty stems partly from different assumptions about research epistemology. For example, Burrell and Morgan (1979) suggest that a positivist epistemology is aligned with *nomothetic* research methodology, in which research is based 'upon systematic protocol and technique' (Burrell and Morgan, 1979: 6). In contrast, more subjectivist approaches to social science align with *ideographic* methodology, which 'stresses the importance of letting one's subject unfold its nature and characteristics during the process of investigation' (Burrell and Morgan, 1979: 6), and they are, therefore, more fluid in process (cf. Tsoukas, 1989; Butler, 1997). Thus, Denzin (1989), drawing on Allport (1942), suggests that nomothetic studies 'seek abstract generalizations about phenomenon [*sic*] and often offer nonhistorical explanations', whereas ideographic research 'assumes that each individual case is unique' and 'that every interactional text is ... shaped by the individuals who create it' (Denzin, 1989: 20; see also Luthans and Davis, 1982; Bryman, 1988; Oswick *et al.*, 1996; Daniels and Johnson, 2002). Similarly, an *etic* analysis is based on a researcher's imposed conceptual frame of reference, whereas an *emic* analysis aims to understand the participants' frame of reference (Fielding and Fielding, 1986; Denzin, 1994; Morris *et al.*, 1999). An emic analysis is marked by researchers 'moving closer to the territory they study ... by minimizing the use of such artificial distancing mechanisms as analytic labels, abstract hypotheses, and preformulated research strategies' (Van Maanen, 1979: 520).

In this re-view, we wish to broaden the definition of postpositivist research adopted by Guba and Lincoln, for our interest lies more in the distinctions between positivism and postmodernism, and in postmodernism as *post*positivist (cf. McKelvey, 1997, 2003). Under postmodernism, the separation of researcher and subject is no longer assumed, reality is mediated rather than objective, and language constitutes or 'censors' rather than reflects or describes anymore essential, central mental processes (Cooper, 1989: 482). Indeed, postmodernism 'is directed against a "picture theory" of language in which physical properties of the world are considered fixed while language can be adjusted to meet the needs of their description' (Hassard, 1994: 313; see also Gergen and Thatchenkery, 1996). Rather than attempting to capture 'the impression of a pregivenness in the object of analysis' (Chia, 1995: 589), postmodernism attempts 'resuscitation' (Clegg and Hardy, 1996). Further, if the living subject is no longer a concrete object, its representation, capture, and transmission become more difficult, regardless of whether quantitative or qualitative methods are attempted (see Chia, 1996a: 33–35, 67; and also Stablein, 1996; Casey, 2002).

Under postmodernism, where 'the proper understanding of a solution can only be got from seeing how the problem was structured in the first place', the concern is more with 'problemizing' than finding answers (Cooper and Burrell, 1988: 102):

> Postmodern thinking … implies according primacy to reality as a processual, heterogeneous and emergent configuration of relations. It also implies that we may not take established social categories such as "individuals" and "organizations" as already given and "out there". Instead, these taken-for-granted categories need to be explored and explained.
>
> (Chia, 1995: 594)

Metaphorization

Incorporation of the work of Derrida within organizational studies has helped to articulate this processual emphasis through introduction of the term *metaphorization*. Rather than meaning being a 'fixed presence' (Cooper, 1989: 488), metaphorization keeps oppositions 'in motion' (Linstead, 1993: 69), in process. Metaphorization:

> keeps process from degrading into structure. Derrida does this by reminding us that there is a perpetual double movement *within* the opposition so that the positively-valued term (e.g., "civilization") is defined only by contrast to the negatively-valued second term (e.g., "barbarism") which continually threatens the former's sovereignty.
>
> (Cooper, 1989: 483, emphasis in original)

With regard to research on organizational change, for example, the emphasis moves from metaphors as representations of change (as movement across time or space) to the 'ceaseless moving' or continual undecidability of meaning (Cooper and Burrell, 1988; Cooper, 1989; cf. Hassard, 1993a, 1993b; Linstead, 1993; Ford and Ford, 1994; Hopfl, 1994; Chia, 1996a, 1996c; Palmer and Dunford, 1996; Lee and Hassard, 1999; Casey, 2002). Whereas metaphors of change might include references, for example, to driving forces (Lewin, 1951), waves (Morgan, 1988), or white water (Vaill, 1991), the instability of *metaphorization* is of a different nature, questioning the constitution of oppositions such as change/stability and readiness/resistance (Wolfram Cox, 1997).

In the context of organizational research methods, the concern shifts to oppositions such as author/subject, theory/data, qualitative/quantitative, and, once again, individual/organization (cf. Kilduff and Mehra, 1997; see also contributions to Westwood and Clegg, 2003). This shift reflects an 'almost permanent state of science's questioning of its own rules and its search for instabilities and the unknown that seems to characterize the postmodern scientific scene' (Kallinikos, 1997: 123; see also Kritzman, 1988). Thus, postmodern thinking adopts logics of exposure and de-ossification (Chia, 1996c, 2003). In the following section we attempt to apply such logic to the technology of triangulation.

Postpositivist triangulation: some possibilities and impossibilities

Chia (1996c: 132) suggests that 'the metaphorization of metaphors helps cultivate our aesthetic sensitivities and enables us to open up new and previously unthought possibilities for consideration'. Before commencing a search for such possibilities, let us consider further triangulation as a metaphor. In its most literal sense (cf. Tsoukas, 1991), the triangle is an enclosing shape; three lines meet to cover an enclosed space. In the more figural sense employed by Denzin, triangulation is a means of representation based on the logic that we can move closer to obtaining a 'true' picture if we take multiple measurements, using multiple methods, or at multiple levels of analysis (e.g. Gersick, 1991; Lewis and Grimes, 1999). Despite the caution that consensus is a 'horizon that is never reached' (Lyotard, 1984: 61), the temptation is to 'put it all together', to 'impose a logic on events' (Parker, 1992: 3), and to forget the messiness of the process of so doing (Wolfram Cox, 1997; cf. Isabella, 1990). While 'the understanding of organization is inseparable from the organization of understanding' (Jeffcut, 1994: 244), organizing is often presented as an 'accomplished phenomenon' rather than as a 'precarious local orchestration' (Chia, 1995: 584) or 'culturally defined patterns of social abstraction' (Chia, 2003: 109).

If we accept that postmodern organizational analysis replaces the 'factual' with the 'representational' (Hassard and Holliday, 1998) it is worthwhile to consider not only the triangulation of *distance* but also the *distance* of triangulation, that is, not only triangulation of *distance* to the 'true' subject, but the reflexive *stance* of the researcher (Hassard, 1993a; Palmer and Dunford, 1996; Butler, 1997; Hardy and Clegg, 1997; Kilduff and Mehra, 1997; Calás and Smircich, 1999; Alvesson and Sköldberg, 2000). In doing so, the focus is not only on the metaphorical space within the enclosing triangle, but also on 'the micro-practices involved in making true' (Chia, 1996a: 129); how and by whom it is drawn or, as noted above, structured in the first place. It is, therefore, important to direct attention not only to the output of empirical studies but also to what has been termed 'ultra-empirical' or 'upstream' ordering and organizing (Chia, 1995, 1996a), and to the dilemmas, inclusions and exclusions of the research process as a social and relational act (cf. Case, 2003; see also Gergen, 1992; Schwandt, 1994).

Accompanying such recognition of the research author's stance is a demystification of the researcher's authority. Rather than profess to being privileged, masterful assimilators of insightful research findings, authors are now only tentative interpreters embedded within and dependent on a particular social context (see Kilduff, 1993; Chia, 1996a: 97; Gergen and Thatchenkery, 1996; Baack and Prasch, 1997; Calás and Smircich, 1999: 653; Casey, 2002). Rather than attempt to generalize from limited findings to a whole picture, such authors can be more playful and tentative with the parts, coming in at them from different perspectives and combining and re-combining them to form new possibilities, but always within the particular traditions and limitations of their referent communities (Hardy *et al.*, 2001). As Weick (1999: 802) has suggested 'there seem to be growing pressures on theorists to … see just how situated and constructed their universals are and how few voices their situated assertions incorporate'.

In terms of triangulation, it is perhaps timely to rethink the lines and angles of inquiry. We suggest that a shift from the *triangulation of distance* to a more reflexive consideration of *researcher stance* can include movement across three perspectives: the researcher as a follower of nomothetic lines; the researcher as the taker of an ideographic overview; and the researcher as the finder of a particular angle. We now outline these perspectives on triangulation and consider each in terms of both its possibilities and impossibilities (see Figure 10.1). In doing so, we take heed of Richardson's call for a shift in thinking from that of plane geometry to that of crystallization and light theory, for:

> the central image for "validity" for postmodernist texts is not the triangle — a rigid, fixed, two-dimensional object. Rather, the central image is the crystal, which combines symmetry and substance in an infinite variety of shapes, substances, transmutations, multidimensionalities, and angles of approach.

Following nomothetic lines:
Convergence and divergence in the search for patterns
– Possibilities for refraction and holography
– The problem of capture:
◆ instability and slippage

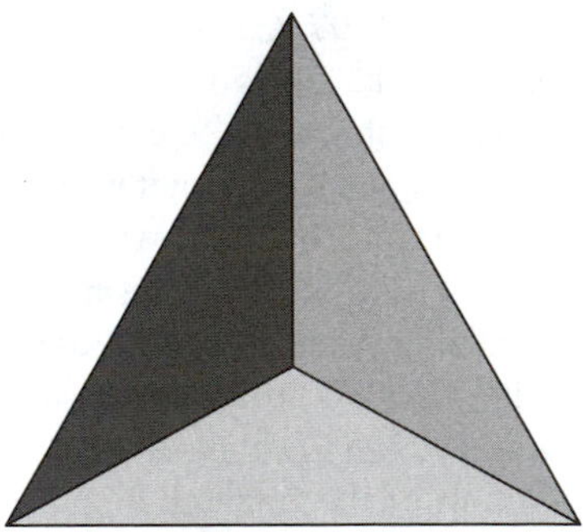

Taking an ideographic overview:
– Possibility
◆ getting closer to the participant/s' point of view
– The problem of perspective:
◆ is moving back moving away?
◆ is the wholeness an illusion of (di)stance?

Finding an angle:
Choosing an appreciative stance
– Some possibilities:
◆ pragmatism
◆ organization development
– The problem of (en)closure
◆ a partial picture

Figure 10.1 Stances for triangulation: possibilities and impossibilities

> Crystals grow, change, alter, but are not amorphous ... What we see depends on our angle of repose.
>
> (Richardson, 1994: 522)

I Following nomothetic lines: refraction, holography and the problem of capture in the search for convergent patterns

In planning an approach to interpreting data gathered using multiple methods and across multiple levels of analysis, the first 'cut' is often to search for patterns based on theoretical propositions (Diesing, 1971; Yin, 1994). For example, based on the systematic testing of a series of hypotheses (developed from a review of the research literature), interview and questionnaire data can be analyzed for recurrent patterns across different sources of information. Whether undertaken via the use of qualitative or quantitative techniques, such approaches can be understood as strategies of convergence and divergence. The process would start, for example, with convergences at one data point before attempts to *refract* or 'spread out' to other data points in the search of associated patterns of similarity and difference, before ultimately generalizing and predicting the likelihood of similar patterns in a wider population (cf. Taber, 1991; Gioia *et al.*, 1994; Yin, 1994; Covaleski *et al.*, 1998).

As part of this search the researcher might attempt, for example, to test for between-group differences: Did those who 'fell' at particular levels of an independent variable also fall at particular levels on other, dependent measures, and at levels distinct from those of other groups? Or, starting from a different position, one could attempt to predict group membership based solely on knowledge of patterns on dependent measures. Or, third, the researcher might ask whether those whose data could be 'split' to show contrasting patterns on one set of variables were also likely to form analytically separable clusters on others.

Further convergence could be found through identification of *holographic typical cases* that best describe the data set through a model of best fit and/or through a detailed qualitative description of an individual or situation, supplemented by ample quotations and detailed contextual information. In either form, this kind of representation assumes that careful examination of a subset of variables or data can help us to see the 'whole picture'; that 'we can find pictures of the whole contained within the parts, if only we can find different ways of looking at the parts' (Smith and Simmons, 1983: 390; cf. Diesing, 1971; Morgan, 1986).

While both approaches draw on the imagery of light, a signal difference between them is that a holographic approach is a virtual, three-dimensional image, whereas refraction is two-dimensional in nature. As such, the latter is less able to represent a 'whole' (assuming that such representation is possible). Keenoy's (1999: 9) description of the relational nature of holograms as 'projected images which, as we shift our visual field in relation to them, appear to have contours, depth, and in some cases, movement' is particularly relevant to our consideration of researcher stance. Keenoy describes holograms as comprised of both technical and social processes, for:

> the hologram itself, the virtual reality, is a static phenomenon while the holographic *illusions* of depth, contour, shade, shape and, sometimes, movement are entirely dependent on the relationship between the observer and the observed: they only come into being in the process of interaction.
>
> (Keenoy, 1999: 10 — emphasis in original)

Like Richardson's (1994) analysis with respect to crystals, Keenoy argues that 'holograms underline the point that what we see … varies according to where we, quite literally, stand' (Keenoy, 1999: 11).

An advantage of holographic thinking in relation to research is that it relaxes the representational and linear assumptions implicit in traditional triangulation. No longer is the object or phenomenon to be captured a discrete, fixed and unmediated entity. No longer is the identity of the space being represented or refracted of linear and symmetrical proportion: an elegant two-dimensional triangle or three-dimensional prism-like tetrahedron of unblemished surfaces and uniform density (cf. Burrell, 1998: 138, 150). Instead, 'the hologram provides a metaphor which depicts "social reality" as a multi-dimensional, multi-causal, mutually implicated and constantly changing facticity' (Keenoy, 1999: 11).

Thus, although the surfaces, lines and points of a metaphorical prism have stability, the field being 'captured' may not. Indeed, attempts to impose order through the more two-dimensional imagery of operationalizable, refractable 'dimensions' (Bryman, 1988: 23) may seem like attempts to 'formalize the unformalizable' with the associated danger not only of failing to capture the whole but of anaesthetizing the 'informal substrata of human life' (Cooper and Burrell, 1988: 109, 110).

Even so, it is worth remembering that the holographic image is only ever virtual and thus always beyond the viewer's reach. Despite its sophistication (and despite the conflation of the terms *virtual* and *reality* in science fiction and film), the hologram is only ever a representation, and its apparent nearness may be illusory. Thus while representations are 'a means of enabling us to bring the remote, obdurate and intractable to hand', this nearness belies the difficulty that 'the very act of representing … distances the event from the representer' (Chia, 1996a: 131).

In addition, there may be instability not only in the relations being described but also in the data collection process, which can be affected by participants' non-compliance and personal agendas (e.g. Wolfram Cox, 1997). Although data collection procedures may *appear* systematic and linear when presented in published form, that form may be abbreviated (Bryman, 1988: 19, 21) (or polished for a journal's readership) so that it ' "hides" or "deflects" inconsistencies and contradictions behind a wall of rhetorical and textual practices' (Chia, 1996a: 218). Thus rather than stability there may be slippage, with the result that one path or line of investigation does not necessarily join neatly with another. Indeed the pattern codes typical of qualitative research studies may reflect a 'map' more than a (uniform) prism (Miles and Huberman, 1994; Van Maanen, 1979) and the interplay of data sources and perspectives is often nonlinear (Neuman, 1994) and more iterative than refractive.

In summary, following nomothetic lines in the search for patterns offers possibilities for refraction and holography, but also presents impossibilities in that we cannot capture the whole where there is slippage and iteration over time. Even the relaxed assumptions of representing research as spatial holography do not address this fourth, temporal dimension. Even if they could, Keenoy suggests that modernist, representationist assumptions do not acknowledge that human beings project as well as perceive 'what we take to be "social reality"' (Keenoy, 1999: 17). Since 'the observer is implicated in the observed' (Keenoy, 1999: 11), there is no clean line between the capturer and captured. Yet again, the hologram is close but ungraspable.

II Taking an ideographic overview: possibilities for diffraction and the problem of perspective

Although it is perhaps comforting to look for typifications, the life of a research study often comes from experiencing difficulties in such classification. To return to an earlier metaphor, if both the content and process of a study are fluid rather than firm, are there other possibilities for triangulation? Perhaps a second option is to stand back from the data and to look for patterns and typifications not from nomothetic, researcher-generated classifications based on research questions derived from literature reviews, but from a multidimensional scaling analysis or, using qualitative techniques, from a content analysis of metaphors and other tropes used by participants (Oswick and Grant, 1996).

Bryman (1988), for example, cites an observation and interview study of disorder in classrooms and on football terraces. Deploying both methods, the analysis of episodes in both contexts revealed that disorder was only 'apparent', belying 'a very distinct and orderly system of roles, rules and shared meanings' (Marsh *et al.*, 1978: 97, cited in Bryman, 1988: 61). This study of what is in effect the organization of disorganization (cf. Cooper, 1986) is typical of what Harré (1974, 1979, 1986; Harré and Secord, 1972) has termed an ethogenic approach: 'It is the task of ethogenics to elucidate the underlying structures of such episodes by investigating the meanings actors bring to the constituent acts' (Bryman, 1988: 60). Such a shift from the researcher's categories to those of the participants can be seen as an effort to maintain the interpretations and experiences of the informants 'in the foreground' (Gioia *et al.*, 1994). However, efforts to bring the viewer closer to a representation of the 'real picture' may still be fraught with difficulty. Alvesson (1999), for example, suggests that in any presentation of interview data, interview statements are limited in their efforts to reflect either an objective reality or an experienced subjectivity. Instead interviewees are affected by context and by 'the available cultural scripts about how one should normally express oneself on particular topics' (Alvesson, 1999: 4; see also Alvesson, 2003a).

While the possibility of taking an ideographic overview is certainly an alternative stance (and a different way of viewing data) further questions can be raised regarding whether such 'stepping back' allows the researcher to get closer to the data or, indeed, further away (cf. Van Maanen, 1979; Smith and Simmons, 1983). It can be argued that stepping back is like looking through a diffraction grating in an effort to see a light pattern that is not otherwise visible. Such regression may be more like 'looking over', or trying to 'play the god trick' when 'the quest for a "God's eye view", a disembodied and disembedded timeless perspective that can know the world by transcending it, is no longer readily accepted' (Usher *et al.*, 1997: 210; see also Jacques, 1992).

Thus research that appears to be 'inquiry from within', characterized by researcher involvement and attempts to understand local realities, may still in many ways resemble the researcher detachment of 'inquiry from without' (Evered and Louis, 1981), which uses *a priori* categories characteristic of the following of nomothetic lines (see also Bryman, 1988: 96–97). This is a problem of perspective, for the wholeness that the researcher is trying to see may be, instead, an illusion of distance. Once again, the 'inside/outside' distinction is a boundary that, on closer scrutiny, offers only an illusion of order and separability, and of 'closing off' or containing the play of meaning (cf. Cooper, 1986; with reference to Derrida, 1978: 279).

III Finding an angle: choosing an appreciative stance, and the problem of (en)closure

Is there a third angle? If attempts to see the whole pose difficulties, perhaps one option is for the researcher not only to enter the picture but to choose to adopt a *partial* view, accepting that: 'The only criteria for judging a theory is [*sic*] whether we feel it lends itself to patterns of social life that we like or dislike; whether we feel that it has positive or negative consequences' (Parker, 1992: 8 with reference to Gergen, 1989).

One possibility is to take an 'appreciative' stance in the sense of positively valuing 'what is best about a human system' (Barrett, 1995; see also Cooperrider and Srivastva, 1987; Ludema *et al.*, 1997) and to recognize the affirmative potential of research input into organizational analysis beyond the *status quo*. This pragmatic possibility derives from Vickers' (1968) proposition that, in a wider sense, appreciation of a situation or setting involves readiness for action. Rather than being saccharine, empty or even anaesthetizing, such an analysis may well prove generative and restorative (Gergen, 1982; Gergen and Thatchenkery, 1996) within a logic of attraction rather than one of opposition, contradiction or replacement (Ford and Ford, 1994).

What can such a partial view offer? Perhaps it allows for a new way of thinking about the stance of the researcher, for instead of considering triangulation only as an approach to closure or capture (of the whole) it can be seen as an opening or angling. Here difficulties with corroboration, inconsistency and conflict across data sources (Miles and Huberman, 1994) are no longer 'problems of enclosure' locatable in the project methodology or in the researcher, but simply reflect the 'intense struggle' of the process (Weick, 1995b) and the impossibilities of the task of 'fitting everything into' the triangle as a container (cf. Cooper, 1989).

Golembiewski (1998) has reviewed both the conceptual and empirical research on appreciative inquiry (AI), a form of social constructionism that can perhaps illustrate this third approach — one described by Gergen and Thatchenkery (1996: 368) as 'particularly promising'. Citing Leibler (see 1997: 31–32), Golembiewski (1998: 6–7) states that AI follows five general principles: (a) image and action are linked; (b) organizations move in the direction of the questions they ask; (c) all organizations have things to appreciatively build on: they 'all … have something about their past to value'; (d) no organization is fixed or immutable; and (e) a, or *the*, leadership task involves building appreciative skills. Derived from the field of organization development, AI assumes that organizational research or diagnosis is also an act of intervention (see, for example, Schein, 1988; cf. Golembiewski, 1998: 6, 22–23). Unlike traditional action research, based on problem-solving and return to the *status quo*, appreciative inquiry is instead founded on affirmation of and improvement beyond best practice, and is, therefore, claimed to be generative and innovative (Cooperrider and Srivastva, 1987; Golembiewski, 1998; French and Bell, 1999). In contrast to mainstream, 'comprehensive' approaches to organizational development, AI's 'conceptual reach' is neither 'far-reaching nor firm' (Golembiewski, 1998: 20). Instead it is more of a 'one legged stool' (ibid: 20), a 'narrow niche player' (ibid: 32). Unlike the normative generic technologies of organization development, AI finds use in situations where, for example, there is urgent need 'to mobilize … assemblages of agreement' (ibid: 39).

It can be argued, therefore, that as it is never possible to be neutral and dispassionate in attempts to enclose the whole, perhaps we should abandon attempts to do so (see Yardley, 1987; Hermans, 1991; Bartunek, 1994). We should instead resist closure (Linstead, 1993) and be open to (rather than foreclose) alternatives (Jeffcutt, 1994). We should display increased sensitivity to the context as well as the contents of any framing process (cf. MacLachlan and Reid, 1994). With respect to AI, Golembiewski suggests the need to elaborate rather than remove its 'value posture' (1998: 42). He notes, however, that this elaboration should not involve the negation of empirical research into AI, for the rejection of 'value-neutral and positivist empirical theory' should not entail a rejection of empirical research and 'poses no clearly insuperable obstacle' to the creation of 'goal-based, empirical theory' (Golembiewski, 1998: 40; see also Wicks and Freeman, 1998).

Once again, this calls for research that is 'different', allowing us to consider rather than ignore the stance of the researcher, and to advocate and generate new social possibilities through research (Gergen and Thatchenkery, 1996; Jacques, 1997). While AI may represent the romantic extreme for such research there are, of course, more intermediate positions. For example, Seale (1999: 470) describes subtle realism (Hammersley, 1992, 1995) as 'maintaining a view of language as both constructing new worlds and as referring to a reality outside the text'. Seale suggests that this is one of several approaches to research that take 'the view that, although we always perceive the world from a particular viewpoint, the world acts back on us to constrain the points of view that are possible' (1999: 470).

Triangulation, dualism and metatriangulation

If the logic of triangulation is to be revised, there is a need for less dualistic thinking — signally for less separation of observer and observed. The reflexive consideration of the researcher stance considered here aims to introduce a non-dualist revisiting of the assumptions of triangulation in which the researcher and researched are mutually defined. In this analysis, emphasis shifts from observation and stabilization to an appreciation of organizing and ordering practices and of the very situated and precarious nature of the organizational research endeavour (cf. Chia, 1996a: 16, 209).

Instead of looking for 'problems' *in* triangulation, we should perhaps think more of 'problemizing' (Cooper and Burrell, 1988: 101), that is, of thought *about* triangulation. We should recognize that meaning is constantly slipping beyond our grasp and can never be lodged in one term (Hassard, 1994) — or one stance. Rather than being enervating or anti-empirical, reflexive postpositivist research allows for 'ultra-empiricism' (Chia, 1995: 587). Rather than exemplifying replication in the sense of the search for conceptual closure in normal science (Chia, 1996a: 97), future postpositivist research reports might, rather like this one, adopt a style of representation or illustration (cf. Wolfram Cox, 1997).

However, this style raises some further concerns. First, Hardy and Clegg (1997) have suggested that postmodern concerns with reflexivity can be criticized for an overemphasis on the dilemmas of authorship. Indeed, the possibilities and impossibilities presented here are presented from the researcher's point of view, and, it can be argued, retain the author/subject outside/inside dichotomies and hierarchies of triangulation rather than, as was the intent, emphasizing the process and mutual constitution of observer and observed (cf. Knights, 1997: 3). Second, while the critique of dualism is evident in much postmodern writing, it is noteworthy that 'writers are likely to replicate the distinctions and assumptions that they criticize' (Kilduff, 1993: 29; see also Knights, 1997) and that this analysis may have retained the Cartesian dualism of 'the notion of the scientific "observer" as a privileged mediator of objects and their representations' (Chia, 1996a: 39; see also Baack and Prasch, 1997; Law and Hassard, 1999). This irony may well be associated with the use of light imagery, visual perception, and the 'dominance of the I' as spectator (Burrell, 1998: 139). Perhaps it is also because triangulation is so associated with the language of visual observation that this paper is itself an example of looking *at* triangulation rather than grappling *with* it, of optocentric observation rather than immersion (cf. Linstead, 1996; Burrell, 1998), and of crystal rather than craft.

A third point is that while this discussion has been limited to triangulation in organizational research methods, it is also relevant to the larger issue of metatriangulation in organization theory, which is used 'for exploring complex phenomena from disparate theoretical and epistemological perspectives' (Lewis and Grimes, 1999: 685). In particular, *metatheorizing* helps theorists to 'explore patterns that span conflicting understandings' in search of common ground (Lewis and Grimes, 1999: 675, with reference to Grimes and Rood, 1995). Lewis and Grimes (1999) compare metatriangulation with Denzin's depiction of theoretical triangulation defined earlier:

> Denzin advocated deductively testing opposing views (views that differ yet are grounded within *common* paradigmatic assumptions) to determine which is the "truth". In contrast, metatriangulation requires applying – with fidelity – multiple paradigms to explore their disparity and interplay and, thereby, arrive at an enlarged and enlightened understanding of the phenomena of interest, as well as the paradigms employed.
>
> (Lewis and Grimes, 1999: 676, emphasis in original)

The language of metatriangulation supplements the visual (e.g. the lens, the view) with the topological, with references, for example, to theoretical maps, paradigm bridging, and transition zones (Gioia and Pitré, 1989; Lewis and Grimes, 1999). This has the consequence of returning us to issues of representation and distance in triangulation, but in three rather than in two dimensions, and at a higher level of abstraction. Chia (1996a: 79) has commented on such 'meta-theoretical preoccupations', notably concerning 'the search for a higher vantage point from which commentaries about the field of study can be legitimately defended without being haunted by the question of reflexivity'. Chia suggests that 'no amount of methodology … will ever bring "representation" closer to "reality"' (1996a: 90) and that searching for or assembling an ultimate truth or an enlightened understanding leads to an ever-expanding 'hall of mirrors' (see also Lewis and Grimes, 1999: 687).

The challenges of postmodernity call, instead, for a more humble *dis*assembly, for taking the time to reconsider the taken-for-granted, and for thinking about organizational research as an aesthetic as well as a technical exercise (Silverman, 1997; see also Neuman, 1994; Booth, 1995; Golden-Biddle and Locke, 1997). This particular re-presentation of triangulation is but one illustration of the potentials and dilemmas of such an effort. Others may wish to explore further the areas of organizational research design and technique, ethics, and report writing as these also invite the unseating of conventional assumptions (Gergen and Thatchenkery, 1996), the breaking of prevailing consensus (Kallinikos, 1997), and the problematizing of what appears as self-evident (Chia, 1996a).

Conclusion

This chapter has extended discussion of postmodern thinking in organizational theory by re-presenting the concept of triangulation in organizational research. The aim is not to dismiss or reject triangulation, or to call for more of it (Scandura and Williams, 2000), but to present a new perspective in an effort to encourage innovative ways of thinking about this highly valued research tenet (cf. Seale, 1999). In our analysis, triangulation was initially defined through the contrasting lenses of positivism and postpositivism/postmodernism and assessed as a metaphor and taken-for-granted principle of 'good' methodology. The concept was then 're-presented' in terms of 'metaphorization', notably of movement between researcher-subject positions. Noting Richardson's (1994) call for a shift in thinking from 'plane geometry' to 'crystallization and light theory', we have argued for rethinking the lines and angles of inquiry in triangulation. We have suggested in particular that a shift from the 'triangulation of distance' to a more reflexive consideration of 'researcher stance' can include movement across three perspectives: the researcher as a follower of nomothetic lines; the researcher as the taker of an ideographic overview; and the researcher as the finder of a particular angle. Each of these perspectives on triangulation was outlined in terms of associated 'possibilities' and 'impossibilities'. Implications of this re-presentation were discussed in terms of perspective, data capture, reflexivity and metatriangulation. Overall the reflexive consideration of researcher stance considered here attempted, for good or ill, to introduce a less 'dualist' revisiting of the assumptions of triangulation, one in which the researcher and researched are mutually defined. This involves a shift from observation and stabilization to an appreciation of organizing and ordering practices, and thus of the very situated and precarious nature of the organizational research endeavour.

11 Critical retrospective research

This final chapter on alternative methodology explores the issue of 'critical retrospective research'. In their introduction to critical management research, Alvesson and Deetz (2000) argue that much of mainstream management research is built on modernist science, which itself is founded on the Enlightenment promise for an 'autonomous subject progressively emancipated by knowledge acquired through scientific methods' (Alvesson and Deetz, 2000: 13). In contrast to a past defined by authority and traditional values, the eighteenth-century Enlightenment represented the rise of reason and modernist science, which:

> proclaimed a transparent language (freed from the baggage of traditional ideology) and representational truth, a positivity and optimism in acquisition of cumulative understanding which would lead to the progressive enhancement of the quality of life. The Enlightenment's enemies were darkness, tradition, ideology, ignorance, and positional authority.
>
> (Alvesson and Deetz, 2000: 13; see also Cooper and Burrell, 1988)

Within the associated grand narratives of progress and emancipation (cf. Lyotard, 1984), the past was displaced and 'the traditional was marginalized and placed off in the private realm' (Alvesson and Deetz, 2000: 14). Citing Schaffer (1989), Alvesson and Deetz (2000) even suggest that modern philosophy of science overcompensated for the fear of authority, rhetoric and ideology by producing its own ideology manifested in scientific procedures such as hypothesis testing.

In both its interests and practices, modernism, therefore, looks to the future rather than to the past, for its emphasis rests on hope, prediction and control for a better future. In contrast to the dignity of the present and hope for such a future, the past is marginalized, romanticized, oversimplified as kitsch, or overcomplicated as pandemonium (cf. Burrell, 1997). Within this context, it is perhaps not surprising that social science methods for researching the past receive less attention than methods that assist us in understanding the present or predicting the future.

In an effort to redress this imbalance, this chapter makes a case for the greater application of retrospective methods in organizational research. The chapter identifies four positions on retrospective research — Controlling the Past, Interpreting the Past, Reconstructing/Revising the Past, and Representing the Past – and discusses the methodological assumptions of each. From this analysis, representative arguments are illustrated and variants of the positions described. Thereafter, the various positions are summarized and comparisons between them made in order to provide a classification of methodological similarities and differences. Finally, implications from this comparative analysis are drawn in terms relevant to the practice of retrospective research in organization studies.

Four positions on retrospective research

Controlling the past

This first position assumes that there was an objective truth in the past and that any 'difficulties' in uncovering or capturing such truth lie with the efficacy of present research methods and accounting processes. In terms of epistemology, or 'the relationship between the knower or would-be-knower and what can be known' (Guba and Lincoln, 1994: 108), such assumptions derive from positivism. Both dualist and objectivist, positivism assumes that: (a) 'objective' reality can be captured; (b) the observer can be separated from the observed; (c) observations and generalizations are free from situational and temporal constraints, that is, they are universally generalizable; (d) causality is linear, and there are no causes without effects, no effects without causes; and (e) inquiry is value free (Denzin, 1989: 24; cf. Bryman, 1988; Blaikie, 1993; Chia, 1996b, 1997; McKelvey, 1997; Williams, 2000; Brewerton and Millward, 2002).

In qualitative positivist research, problems in accessing the past are typified by 'pitfalls in retrospective accounts' (Golden, 1992: 849). These occur due to faulty memories, oversimplifications and rationalizations, subconscious attempts to maintain self-esteem due to needs for acceptance, achievement and security, and social desirability. In addition, recall problems are caused by inaccessibility and by hindsight bias, which has been defined by Azar (2000) as the way the memory of judgements changes when we learn the outcome of an event (see also Fischhoff, 1975). As March and Sutton point out:

> Performance information itself colors subjective memories, perceptions, and weightings of possible causes of performance. Informants exist in a world in which organizational performance is important … As a result, retrospective reports of independent variables may be less influenced by memory rather than by a reconstruction that connects standard story lines with contemporaneous awareness of performance results.
>
> (March and Sutton, 1999: 345)

For example, work by Louie *et al.* (2000) reported that the memory of judgements by MBA students playing a market simulation game was affected by knowledge of team performance. Azar (2000) suggests that we may become more confident of our judgements in retrospect than we were at the time, giving the example of a physician's confidence in a diagnosis being affected by knowledge of the outcome of the case. In addition, if we are told of an outcome and then asked to reconstruct the events that led to that outcome, the reconstruction will be affected by what is known even if we try to ignore the outcome (Azar, 2000). Also, people are concerned with reproducing response patterns that seem appropriate to the accuracy expected for a task (Winman and Juslin, 1999).

Interest here lies not only in understanding the nature and functions of such faults, but also in reducing the potential for the epistemological space between the real and the known. For this position, the nature of reality, or ontology, is one of realism, where 'an apprehendable reality is assumed to exist, driven by immutable natural laws and mechanisms' (Alvesson and Deetz, 1996: 109; cf. Tsoukas, 1989; Blaikie, 1991; Marsden, 1993; see also Chia, 1997). While the distinctions between positivism and realism have been well articulated by these and other authors, Chia (1996b: 51) argues that 'both positivism and epistemological realism are fully committed to the view that theories are serious attempts to accurately mirror and represent the real world as it exists out there. It is this representationalist injunction which unites positivistic and realist science'.

Accordingly, particular remedies have been devised in order to control for the impact of judgement processes on accounts of the past. The issue is how not to bias recall and how to minimize the potential for such bias to affect/infect the present and, potentially, the future. In retrospective qualitative organizational studies, efforts to reduce 'errors' (Golden, 1992: 855) include the use of free rather than forced reports, multiple knowledgeable informants per firm, a focus on simple facts and concrete events, avoiding discussions of the distant past, ensuring confidentiality, minimizing inconvenience and following 'guidelines generally associated with proper retrospective data collection' (Miller *et al.*, 1997: 201).

For example, in an influential paper Golden (1992) discussed the use of these efforts as part of his concern with the accuracy of chief executive officers' retrospective accounts of past strategy. Such key informants may have difficulty in recalling the past due to 'inappropriate rationalizations, oversimplifications, faulty *post hoc* attributions, and simple lapses of memory' (Miller *et al.*, 1997: 189). In addition, 'key informants may try to present a socially desirable image of themselves or their firms' (ibid: 190). While Golden's study 'underscores the value of a healthy dose of scepticism in the study design stage, and ultimately, in the interpretation of retrospective data' (Golden, 1992: 857), Miller *et al.* (1997) were more optimistic. They suggested that if such guidelines are followed, 'scholars could be truly comfortable with the idea that retrospective reports are not fiction' (1997: 201). In response, Golden later maintained his call for researchers to be critical of retrospective data but argued that '*if* significant efforts are made to minimise retrospective biases and error *and* these data can be validated, retrospective data may well provide unique access to past organizational events' (Golden, 1997: 1251 — emphasis in original).

Measurement issues are also important in retrospective quantitative research designs. For example, in experimental studies, a retrospective pretest-posttest control group design has been developed for assessment of training interventions through self-report measures (Sprangers, 1988). This design controls for the effect of a response shift that occurs when training affects participants' understanding or internal standard of measurement for the dimension under consideration. If training affects this understanding, the self-report data will otherwise be confounded by the response shift and trainers may fail to document the benefits of their training (Sprangers, 1988; see also Sprangers, 1989).

Similar concerns have been noted with respect to collective learning. For example, Busby (1999) investigated postdesign reviews as a mechanism for learning from collective experience and reviewed the argument that retrospective reviews can promote double loop learning. In addition to problems with hindsight bias, Busby pointed out that there are limits to the extent to which retrospective reviews can examine judgements that have not been made with conscious attention or access behaviour that is 'instinctive, automated and unavailable to conscious processes' (Busby, 1999: 110). In summary, Busby (1999: 111, with reference to March *et al.*, 1991) argues that:

> people's recall tends to exaggerate the consistency of experience with their prior conceptions; they often fail to notice incorrect predictions (or interpret them as measurement errors) and remember as being real data that are consistent with mental models that are in fact missing.

In historical research there are similar concerns with accuracy of access to the past. For example, and with respect to the work of Frederick Taylor, Wrege and Hodgetts (2000: 1290) have expressed concern that 'what the typical management reader "knows" about what happened at Bethlehem Iron a century ago is more fiction than fact'. They caution against the acceptance of published sources, commenting that:

> The reason for the continued acceptance of Taylor's observations largely lies in the persistent reliance of management scholars on published sources (usually those appearing in management publications) rather than on original documents prepared at the time of the actual events Taylor described. Unfortunately, for the majority of the readers of management publications, the printed word has an aura of authenticity that is seldom questioned, and original documents are neglected.
>
> (Wrege and Hodgetts, 2000: 1283; see also DiMaggio, 1995 for a similar argument with respect to the reading of theory)

Wrege and Hodgetts hope that such neglect will not continue, arguing that 'in the new millennium, managers will have to increasingly focus on data collection and analysis and fight the tendency to accept anecdotes and hearsay as accurate' (2000: 1290). Thus, accuracy is paramount, and the task of both the researcher and reader is to maintain a critical stance so as not to be duped into receiving a less-than-objective view of the world.

In summary, from this position, retrospective research is potentially flawed research that is at best avoided and at worst controlled through careful attention to method and measures, depending on the nature of the research design. The various forms of control, such as experimental control in quantitative designs, or limitation to recent, concrete events, and use of multiple informants in qualitative interview surveys are employed to improve the validity and reliability of the research and to reduce the many sources of potential interference that affect the potential of the research to mirror (or at least access) a past reality. Under such assumptions, retrospective research is only employed on a qualified and even apologetic basis. For example, in their study of changes in employee perceptions of psychological contracts, De Meuse *et al.* (2001) wrote:

> To track employee perceptions of the psychological contract over 50 years in a truly longitudinal fashion would have been virtually impossible. Consequently, a retrospective methodology was utilized in this study. The authors recognize that there are problems associated with this approach … Despite justifiable concerns about the accuracy of retrospective designs, this study supports the contention of researchers who assert that these designs can be useful in identifying patterns indicative of dynamic processes …
>
> De Meuse *et al.* (2001: 113–14)

Such qualification can be contrasted with the greater affirmation of retrospective research that occurs from the other three positions, and these are now examined.

Interpreting the past

Under this position, the emphasis is not on obtaining a clear picture of a past reality, but on the present interpretation of past reality. Whether or not that interpretation has ties with any actual past is immaterial from this position, which is sympathetic to the idea that present reality is socially constructed (Berger and Luckmann, 1966) and that the consequences of such construction can have material effects (Thomas, 1937). For example, and with reference to ethnomethodology, Weick argued that 'to talk about sensemaking is to talk about reality as an ongoing accomplishment that takes form when people make retrospective sense of the situations in which they find themselves and their creations' (Weick, 1995a: 15). Initially, such sense-making is an equivocal process due to elapsed experience making 'many different kinds of sense' (Weick, 1995a: 27), and it only becomes less tentative at a later stage of interpretation. Weick's interest lies in the firming up of this sense-making, and he suggests that such firming up has a particular functionality:

> If people want to complete their projects, if effort and motivation make a difference in completing those projects, and if the environment is malleable,

> then a reading of past indeterminacy that favors order and oversimplifies causality … may make for more effective action, even if it is lousy history.
>
> (Weick, 1995a: 28–29)

It is here that Weick distinguishes his emphasis from work on hindsight bias, arguing that discussions of this bias 'tend to emphasize how much the backward glance leaves out and the problems that this can create' (Weick, 1995a: 28). Based on the relatively short time between act and reflection and an argument that 'people are mindful only of a handful of projects at a time' (Weick, 1995a: 29), Weick argues that distortions due to hindsight bias are unlikely to be substantial in everyday life. However, his interest is more in how making sense of the past is important for present action and future decision-making, and he comments that 'students of sensemaking find forecasting, contingency planning, strategic planning and other magical probes into the future wasteful and misleading if they are decoupled from reflective action and history' (Weick, 1995a: 30). It is not that such activities are uninteresting, but that they need to be more broadly conceived: 'Strategists take credit for their foresight when they are actually trading on their hindsight. A well-developed capability for hindsight is neither a dramatic accomplishment, nor especially rare, which is probably why strategists shun that depiction of their contribution' (Weick, 1995a: 78).

Weick's retrospection is, therefore, a pragmatic, normative retrospection rather than one that is purely interpretive (cf. Burrell and Morgan, 1979; Deetz, 1996). It is one centred more in the present than in the past, and his critique is not of inadequate access to the past but of inadequate representation of the present. His calls for greater appreciation of the past (see, for example, Weick, 2001: 462) aim to improve the accuracy of that representation and it is in this emphasis on accuracy that Weick's position can be seen as not all that different from the position of controlling the past discussed above. Both emphasize accuracy, but while the first position is concerned with an accurate past, this second is concerned with an accurate (and more humble) present in which 'people know what they have done only after they do it' (Weick, 2001: 462; cf. Schutz, 1967).

There are also several variants of this second position. As noted above, more interpretive studies may be, arguably, distinguishable from the functionalism of Weick's argument and focus solely on the interpretation of a past situation or event (see, for example, Isabella, 1990; Wolfram Cox, 1997). More social constructionist positions are concerned not with individual constructions of the past but with how those constructions develop in interaction and with generative potential for new futures (see, for example, Cooperrider and Srivastva, 1987; Gergen and Thatchenkery, 1996; Gergen, 2001). More critical retrospective studies may draw attention to or disrupt prevailing discourses of the past or historicize and politicize present order, pointing to potential for future action, emancipation, or transformative redefinition (see, for example, Deetz, 1996; Alvesson and Deetz, 2000). For example, much critical management work is informed by Habermas' emancipatory interest, 'which aims at stimulating self-reflection in personal and social life in order to free man from the restrictions and repressions of the established order and its ideologies' (Alvesson, 1991: 216). Here the past informs the present, and research assumes a historical realism, where a once plastic reality has become inappropriately shaped and reified over time (Guba and Lincoln, 1994). Thus, in critical studies the fuller picture that emerges is more disturbing than more 'accurate', directing attention to issues such as mystification and colonization (see Alvesson and Willmott, 1996), and highlighting material or psychic disadvantage or defense (cf. Casey, 1999; Brown and Starkey, 2000).

While the differences among and within these variants both deserve and have received much fuller attention than is possible here (see, for example, Chia, 1996b; Alvesson and Deetz, 2000; Alvesson and Sköldberg, 2000), the third position presents a further shift in emphasis that is also the subject of current attention in social research.

Reconstructing/revising the past

Our third position is in some ways like the first in that it assumes that the past and the present are discrete. Rather than attempting to gain access to the past from the present, or to understand how constructions of the past affect the future, the emphasis here is on *why* particular causal links are made between the past and the present and on individual cognitive processes in making causal explanations. In the case of retrospective research it is attribution theories that provide the clearest exemplars of this position, and some of the major works from this tradition are now discussed.

Martinko and Thompson (1998) reviewed Kelley's (1973) attributional cause model that describes how different types of information affect social attribution processes. Under this well-known model, it is suggested that the cause of behaviour can be judged to come from an internal/person, external/situation or stimulus source depending on the information available about the event. Three information variables that determine the attribution of causality are consensus (whether or not the same behaviour is exhibited by others in the same situation), consistency (whether the behaviour is usual or unusual for this person in this situation) and distinctiveness (whether or not this person also exhibits this behaviour in other situations). Martinko and Thomson (1998) extend this analysis through a synthesis of Kelley's model with the achievement-motivation model of Weiner *et al.* (1971) in terms of the locus of causality (internal or external), stability (whether or not the cause of the outcome changes over time) and global or specific attributions (the degree to which the cause of an outcome is generalizable across situations).

In contrast to such complicating of causality (see also Blount and Janicik, 2001), Hewstone and Agoustinos (1998) have instead extended the unit of analysis for attribution theory. They argued that 'attribution theory is predominantly a North American theoretical perspective which seeks to understand the processes by which people attribute causes to their own behaviour and to the behaviour of others' (Hewstone and Agoustinos, 1998: 60). They reviewed major works on attribution theory and drew attention to Weiner's (1985) examination of whether 'the extent and nature of attributional activity that the research suggests is an artefact of the reactive methodologies used in attribution research' (Hewstone and Agoustinos, 1998: 62). As there have been few attribution studies in natural contexts, such as conversation or in the print media, Hewstone and Agoustinos (1998) suggest that in such settings it is important to examine the social and collective nature of explanations. As they argue, their aim is 'to make clear that attributions or lay explanations are not only the outcome of individual cognitive processes but are also linked to social and cultural representations' (Hewstone and Agoustinos, 1998: 76). They draw on social representation theory as a relevant basis for this extension of attribution theory in an effort to 'reveal pre-existing knowledge structures and expectations which people use to filter and process incoming information' (Hewstone and Agoustinos, 1998: 63).

In general, issues of whether or not causal explanations are 'accurate' and how they alter future understanding are neither as central nor as interesting to researchers taking this position as why the explanations are formed in the first place. However, as in the previous cases, there are variants of this third position and these variants overlap with the two previous ones. For example, Bell-Dolan and Anderson (1999) examine the consequences of inaccurate attributions, distinguishing between proximal consequences (thoughts, emotions, behaviours) and distal consequences (academic achievement, depression, anxiety, relationship satisfaction and aggression). They also examine implications for clinical intervention, concluding that 'although wildly inaccurate attributions (and attributional styles) are certainly maladaptive in the long run, it is less clear that this positive relation between accuracy and adaptiveness holds true at less extreme levels of inaccuracy' (Bell-Dolan and Anderson, 1999: 58). Similarly, Cannon (1999) was concerned with the current implications of attributions for past experiences, examining memories of failure experiences and finding that these memories triggered strong emotion reactions that affected sense-making and distorted current reasoning.

In contrast, Harvey and Weary (1981: 6) suggested that by using attribution processes to understand workplace violence, participants attempt to find an 'inference about why [violence] occurred'. Thus, knowledge of attribution processes may assist both in understanding a particularly difficult past and in functioning in the present. Similarly, storytelling work examines not only causal attributions for the past events but narratives of how the past is told. For example, telling retrospective accounts of organizational atrocities attributed to others may provide the storyteller with additional time and experience to 'reconstruct a story' (Charmaz, 1999: 372). While such stories may be anxiety provoking and hard to hear (Frank, 1995), their telling may allow the expression of a mix of emotions in an effort to deal with a process of change (Bromley *et al.*, 1979).

In summary, attention to attributional processes has been extended from the individual to the social arena, and from accounts of particular events to full sequential narratives. In organizational research narrative methods have gained increasing prominence (Boje, 2001; cf. Czarniawska, 1998), demonstrating not only the importance of different narrative genres for accounting for the past (e.g. Jeffcutt, 1994; Barry and Elmes, 1997) but also the variety of narrative methods now available to researchers. It is important to note that the growth of interest in such methods extends not only from attempts to create a fuller understanding of attribution processes but also from a questioning of the very nature of research and of the configuration of temporal relations in the first place. Such questioning informs the fourth position identified in this chapter, for this final position concerns representing, or re-presenting, the past.

Representing the past

Our first three positions attempt to recall the past more accurately, to make sense of it, or to examine causal links between the past and the present. In all three, the present exists independently of the past. At issue are the nature of temporal recall, understanding and evaluation. In contrast, the fourth position does not assume that the present is ontologically independent of the past, or that there is schematic time. Under such assumptions, time is often presented as one-dimensional, and it has been argued that 'the notion of a single, unitary form of time which is objective, absolute, homogeneous, linear, evenly flowing, measurable, readily divisible and independent of events' is 'massively inhibiting' (Clark, 1990: 143; see also Hassard, 2002). For Burrell (1992), such linearity is associated with:

> notions of progress, where what is contemporary and fashionable is claimed to represent a 'higher' level of development (as well as a newer one) than that which has preceded it. This assumption of linear progress rests heavily on an optimistic view of the Enlightenment and a belief that rationalistic management of change is possible.
>
> (Burrell, 1992: 168)

In contrast, and with reference to organizational contexts, for example, Clark (1990: 141) calls for recognition that 'all corporations require and possess a plurality of chronological codes', some focusing on time as unfolding and regular, others holding more heterogeneous conceptions of time where interpretations of pace and duration are socially constructed and affected by events of local cultural importance (see also Hassard, 1989, 2001; and Ancona *et al.*, 2001). Further, and from a contextualist stance, there are not merely different chronological codes but an interpenetration of the past and the future, for 'an event is never what is immediately available but also includes its contiguous past and present' (Tsoukas, 1994: 767).

It is this stance that informs the fourth position, for when the very definition of past-present-future is problematized, facts themselves may vary over time (Gergen, 1973) as there is no stable knowledge outside of the representation of that knowledge (see Calás and Smircich, 1999). This argument differs from that of Weick presented above, for Weick's concerns are epistemological rather than ontological. Weick argues that our knowing of the present is affected by our knowing of the past but does not go so far as to suggest that the past, present and future are discrete, real phenomena.

Importantly, when the semblance of realism is no longer attainable or valued, retrospective research shifts from the status of poor science or poor history to art, craft or fiction. The researcher is no longer a 'disinterested scientist' (Guba and Lincoln, 1994), analytical excavator or historian, but writer, storyteller and editor 'embedded in a social context and in relation to others' (Calás and Smircich, 1999: 653). For example, in their discussion of strategy as fiction, Barry and Elmes (1997) argued that strategy is something created or made up rather than something that is fake. Thus, their interest is not in the distinction between the fake and the real, but in the construction of the real or at least the taken-for-granted (cf. Latour, 1987). As noted above, narrative methods are not 'just stories' but legitimate means for representing, accounting for and constituting past, present, and the play of their characters, events, interconnections and fragmentations (see Boje, 2001).

Within narrative, the past may affect the present to various degrees depending on genre (see also Jeffcutt, 1994). For example, Roemer (1995) pays particular attention to the deterministic role of the past in tragic narratives and argues that here the plot embodies the past:

> Since plot preexists the action, we can think of it as embodying the past. Like time and process, the past constitutes necessity, for we can neither escape nor undo it. We *are* the past ... In story, the plot is the past and our attempt to escape it is the action. Paradoxically, though the figures cannot escape it, their effort to do so is mandated *by* the past.
>
> (Roemer, 1995: 53 — emphasis in original)

Overall, where there is no assumption of transcendent truth, the variability among research genres becomes more than an array of different methods for data capture in the positivist sense. Retrospective research methods do not merely assist in the investigation of a past reality but constitute the very nature of that reality from the position of the researcher. As an objective stance is no longer possible, questions of interest concern not error, construction or attribution but reflexivity in the sense of 'the ability to be critical or suspicious of our own intellectual assumptions' (Hassard, 1993a: 12, with reference to Lawson, 1985):

> Method is thus not primarily a matter of "data management" or the mechanics and logistics of data production/processing, but is a reflexive activity where empirical material calls for careful interpretation – a process in which the theoretical, political and ethical issues are central.
>
> (Alvesson and Deetz, 2000: 5)

For example, Macbeth (2001) has argued that reflexivity has become a central topic in contemporary discussions of qualitative research and that positional reflexivity involves the researcher in efforts to examine how pace, biography, and delineations of self and other combine to shape the nature of the research endeavour. The extent to which this reflexivity takes place is dependent more upon the researcher than the method. For example, Hall and Callery (2001) discuss various interpretations of grounded theory method, arguing that while some claim that grounded theory incorporates reflexivity, others treat interview and participant observation data as if they mirror informants' realities. For others, even the extent to which reflexivity is possible is under question if one recognizes that there can be no unmediated truth and that 'no privileged position exists from which analysis might arbitrate' (Hardy and Clegg, 1997: S5).

Thus there is also variety within this fourth position on retrospective research, and like each of the other three, it deserves fuller explication. In an effort to assist such endeavours, a short summary of each position is now presented to allow comparison of their similarities and differences.

Comparative analysis

In Table 11.1, each of our four positions on retrospective research is described and compared in terms of its method, ontology, epistemology, exemplars, variants and potential contribution. While Controlling the Past, Interpreting the Past and Reconstructing the Past all exhibit realist ontologies; Representing the Past differs in that it takes an anti-realist stance. It also adopts a constructionist epistemology that differs from the social constructionism of the second position on Interpreting the Past. As noted above, there is a distinct difference between the two, for Interpreting the Past is based on the assumption that constructions of the past inform a fuller understanding of the present, and that such understanding can be of assistance in determining a better future. The past may well exist as real, even though its construction may vary depending on interpretive or sense-making processes. In contrast, the fourth position, Representing the Past, is anti-realist in both its ontology and epistemology, and has no progressive intent. Unlike the first position, its proponents would not view retrospective research as something to be avoided, but such research would be of interest only for local illustration of the idea of questioning the taken-for-granted in research methods.

It is the second and third positions, namely, Interpreting the Past and Reconstructing/Revising the Past in which retrospective research is not only of interest but also of central importance. In both, this importance derives from the value of interpretations and explanations of the past. In Reconstructing/Revising the Past, such interpretations have instrumental value for managing the present, while in Interpreting the Past that value relates to the future and may be emancipatory or even generative (cf. Gergen and Thatchenkery, 1996). While the more interpretive variants of the second position are informed by what Habermas called a practical interest, 'concerned with the understanding of the historical and traditional context of human life' (Alvesson, 1991: 216), the emphasis on management across most of the second and third positions adopts instead a technical interest, 'which aims to find laws or law-like relationships, through which processes can be manipulated and controlled' (Alvesson, 1991: 216).

Table 11.1 Comparison of positions on retrospective research

Position	*Method*	*Ontology*	*Epistemology*	*Exemplars*	*Variants*	*Potential contribution of retrospective research*
1. Controlling the past	Attempts to maximize accurate recall or to reveal potential sources of error or bias	Realist	Positivist	Studies of hindsight bias (e.g. Fischhoff, 1975)	Degree of emphasis on control of research design, measures and methods to improve validity and reliability	Marginal; best avoided
2. Interpreting the past	Understanding of the present is informed by the construction of past reality	Historical realism	Interpretive	Sensemaking (e.g. Weick, 1995a)	Interpretive; social constructionist; critical	Necessary; valued for better futures
3. Reconstructing/ revising the past	Causal explanations linking past and present	Realism	Mixed: positivist; interpretive	Attribution theory (e.g. Kelley, 1973)	Social representations; narrative accounts; some overlap with positions 1 and 2	Necessary; valued for a more manageable present
4. Representing the past	Problematization of time and research on time	Anti-realist	Constructionist	Fragmented narrative methodologies (e.g. Boje, 2001)	Possibility and nature of reflexivity	Of interest for illustration of questioning of the taken-for-granted

Conclusions

This chapter has examined an area of management and organizational research — retrospective research — generally considered of marginal relevance to mainstream professional practice. Retrospective research receives relatively little attention in either the professional research journals or methodology textbooks. This chapter has attempted to fill the void by developing a taxonomic classification of the use of retrospective research. The aim has been to provide a focus for the future employment of retrospective methods in organizational analysis.

In so doing, we have identified, described and analyzed four positions on retrospective research: Controlling the Past, in which attempts are made to maximize accurate recall or to reveal potential sources of error or bias; Interpreting the Past, in which understanding of the present is informed by the construction of past reality; Reconstructing or Revising the Past, in which causal explanations link the past and the present; and Representing the Past, which involves the problematization of time and research on time. These positions have been compared in terms of method, ontology, epistemology, exemplars, variants and potential contribution. This comparative analysis has attempted to draw out some of the main methodological implications for the practice of retrospective research in organizational analysis.

Of course, there are many limitations to this analysis. First, and as with any typology or list of classifications, this one includes 'tacit messages' such as the message that positions those not on this list as less critical than those on it (cf. Weick, 1995b: 388). For example, it is largely dependent on a review of qualitative research and may exclude or fudge the subtlety of positions within or outside what has been termed Controlling the Past. Second, it is informed largely by studies within the traditions of organizational behaviour, organization and management theory, and social psychology and will undoubtedly gain from the inclusion of work from other disciplines. Third, and with reference to its inclusions rather than exclusions, each of the four positions includes several variants. As such, the classificatory system that is used here is, of necessity, tentative rather than exhaustive.

Within these limits, however, we feel the chapter makes several contributions. It takes seriously an area of research methods that tends to be marginalized and regarded as relatively unimportant, if not second rate, by mainstream management researchers. This is done with the aim of stimulating others to take an interest in retrospective research, and to adopt and develop retrospective research practices in line with their particular ontological and epistemological assumptions. For those who already do retrospective research, the chapter provides a starting point for further debate and refinement of the categories proposed here. For example, it identifies some unlikely paradigmatic bedfellows within the second category of Interpreting the Past, grouping interpretive, social constructionist and critical retrospective studies in terms of a common interest in the creation of better futures (cf. Alvesson and Deetz, 2000). No doubt, many will find this alignment unusual, if not provocative. In addition, the separation of generative postmodern work (e.g. Cooperrider and Srivastva, 1987; Gergen and Thatchenkery, 1996; Gergen, 2001) into this second category and away from the fourth classification, Representing the Past, may also invoke further discussion. The distinction has been made due to the normative intent of such work, which is distinct from the problematization emphasis of the fourth category.

More generally, it is hoped that this chapter will encourage further interest in the micropractices of other research methods that occupy a marginal or at least non-traditional place in mainstream management and organization studies. While narrative methods have been gaining ground (e.g. Boje, 2001; Czarniawska, 1998), and discursive and rhetorical studies have attracted considerable attention (e.g. Abrahamson, 1997; Kieser, 1997; Grant *et al.*, 1998; Jackson, 1999), aesthetic endeavours are perhaps still borderline (e.g. Gagliardi, 1996; Strati, 1999; Linstead and Höpfl, 2000) and worthy of further review and development. The challenge is for that development to be done with care.

12 Concluding remarks

An agenda for future alternative organization studies

We end the book by presenting a summary of the ontological, epistemological and methodological tenets of our version of alternative organizational analysis. This chapter also examines the issue of thinking reflexively and argues that reflexive methodology is a key process in the development of alternative management and organization studies. Finally, we discuss an agenda for alternative organizational studies in the years to come.

The tenets of alternative organization studies

There is a plethora of ways to go about being 'alternative' in organization and management studies. Our approach stresses ontological fluidity and indeterminacy, epistemological reflexivity and the centrality of pluralist methodologies to the research process.

Fluidity and indeterminacy

Alternative organization studies show an acute interest in processes rather than outcomes, in verbs rather than nouns (Cooper, 1986). As such, they view organizational reality as constantly in the making, on its way to be constituted but not quite achieved yet. Researchers call attention to the fluid and slippery nature of the processes that go into the making of social and organizational reality. Organizations are no longer seen as collections of stable and static entities (people, material resources, ideologies and so on) but as shifting networks in a permanent state of flux and transformation (see for example, Chapters 4 and 8). Our version of alternative organization studies posits the end of the strong, stable, coherent and unified subject. Chapter 5 highlights the fluidity of identity construction. Here gender is not seen as a static category, something that is just brought to organizations; gender is performed, reproduced and, occasionally, transgressed in organizations. Therefore, researchers need to become accustomed to the indeterminacy of organizational and individual identities as any attempt to close them off or contain them is highly problematic.

Epistemological reflexivity

Alternative organization studies question the neutrality of scientific language by drawing attention to the rhetorical nature of scientific facts and the political processes by which certain accounts become established as legitimate at a particular point in time and within a particular context. In so doing, the role of reflexivity in refining researchers' sensitivity to differences and enhancing their ability to tolerate ambiguity and paradox, is highlighted. Social theory and concepts are regarded as perspectivist narratives arising from, justifying and reproducing hegemonic relations and identities of specific socio-cultural relations. If the project of modernist science is built upon the myth of the heroic social scientist who, armed with objective procedures and methods of research, proceeds to discover the 'truth', alternative organization studies view social science as *emerging* from the workings of heterogeneous networks of humans, materials, ideologies and traditions that come together at a particular point in time within a particular context (see Chapters 9 and 10).

Methodological pluralism

Alternative organization studies celebrate methodological pluralism. The social world is seen as complex, multifaceted and contradictory and, therefore, no single point of view can ever take in the whole scene. In order to recapture as much as possible of the social world, researchers have to change position, mental gear and frames of analysis. The myth of paradigm incommensurability is challenged in favour of multiparadigmatic representations (see Chapters 1 and 2), which offer 'insights into the characteristic contradictions and tensions embodied in contemporary organizations' (Reed, 1985: 201). Alternative organization studies researchers are invited to apply whatever combinations of research methods they deem useful and urged not to regard the research process as a timid adventure (Kilduff and Mehra, 1997). At the heart of this methodological pluralism lies a reflexive mode of thinking and being.

Reflexivity as a central methodology for critical/alternative methodology

Of growing importance since the early 1990s (e.g. Hassard, 1993b), reflexivity has become an obligatory passage point in organization studies (Hardy *et al.*, 2001). As a consequence, being sufficiently reflexive (e.g. Cunliffe, 2003: 991) has to a large extent replaced being sufficiently objective as a criterion for distinguishing worthy organizational research. Indeed, reflexive organizational metatheory has now achieved 'Handbook' status (Tsoukas and Knudsen, 2003). Advocating the need for reflexivity in organizational research has become a fashionable focus for the critical/alternative text (see, for example, Alvesson and Sköldberg, 2000; Monin, 2004). So how is this book different? Throughout the chapters, we have argued implicitly or explicitly that reflexivity is central to our alternative agenda.

Before we set out our vision for reflexive alternative organizational research, we highlight some of the controversies surrounding the concept of reflexivity.

While the roots of this concept have been traced back to Socrates and the associated 'know thyself' practices of ancient Greece, one of the first social scientists to put reflexivity on a pedestal was Gouldner (1970). In a nutshell, reflexivity is a way of problematizing what we know and how we know it, by revealing some of the assumptions on which knowledge is based, for example, the author's background, or theoretical standpoint, as well as the social and political relations in which these are located and cannot be transcended easily (Foucault, 1980; Wray-Bliss, 2002). Drawing on Heidegger (1966), Cunliffe (Cunliffe, 2003; Cunliffe and Jun, 2005) has argued that reflexivity involves emphasis on questioning, unsettling and opening rather than on categorization, complacency and closure. Accordingly, reflexivity remains a concept fraught with ambiguity (Johnson and Duberley, 2003) and any attempt to provide a widely accepted definition or a definitive position on how to pursue reflexivity remains a chimera.

There are numerous conceptualizations of reflexivity. Lynch (2000) has identified six genres: mechanical, substantive, methodological, meta-theoretical, interpretative and ethnomethodological, each of them with sub-genres. Thus, reflexivity has been defined, *inter alia*, as: a habitual response to stimulus, the property of feedback systems, a hall of mirrors, the organizing principle of late modernity, a property of intersubjective relations, self-knowledge, an aid to correct bias, communal or individual self-reflection, an existential engagement with marginalized standpoints, the questioning of taken-for-granted reality, a device of sociological exegesis, the problematization of representation and objectification, and the everyday property of networks of individuals, practices and interactions.

A cursory glance at the literature on reflexivity suggests that there are as many critics as supporters of the concept (Booth, 2000). For the supporters, reflexivity is something to be cherished and strongly pursued (Chia, 1996b; Weick, 1999). For the critics, reflexivity is a 'monster: the abyss, the spectre, the infinite regress' (Ashmore, 1989: 234) for they bemoan the self-referentiality of the social sciences and the textual character of social reality (Woolgar, 1988a).

Even supporters of reflexivity warn of the dangers lurking behind its promising facade: Karl Weick suggested that reflexivity for its own sake, as an end rather than a means, could have narcissistic consequences to the point where the author becomes obsessed with her own voice and forgets about those of others (Antonacopolou and Tsoukas, 2002). Lynch (2000), in turn, argues that it is important to question the premises and assumptions of any form of reflexivity rather than merely representing it as a source of authenticity for the writing of social text (see also Hardy *et al.*, 2001).

One needs to understand how different versions (genres) of reflexivity come about, how they coexist with each other and to what extent one can assess and judge a particular version of reflexivity outside the paradigmatic assumptions that allows its creation in the first place (Johnson and Duberley, 2003). We argued in Chapters 1 and 2 that paradigmatic assumptions shape our communities of practice.

However, certain forms of reflexivity downplay, or more likely, ignore, the role of paradigmatic assumptions in shaping scholarly practice. Researchers merely question whether they have rigorously applied appropriate techniques to get closer to the 'truth' or to capture meaning within a certain context.

This mechanistic form of reflexivity is dangerous for, 'it is only by constantly re-examining and questioning the foundational assumptions of various theories and practices that the discipline can avoid becoming trapped within a limited range of conceptual possibilities' (Brocklesby, 1997: 192).

In a more advanced form of reflexivity, researchers learn to identify their own and others' viewpoints, scrutinizing their underpinnings and influence on research (Flood and Romm, 1997). The view is taken that we can never expand our understandings unless we constantly examine our own assumptions in light of insights made available by other paradigms. As Chapter 2 suggested, multiparadigm research extends this thinking by encouraging researchers to travel across paradigms to appreciate different languages and methodologies (Holland, 1999). At this level, research appears as a continuous process of self-discovery, and reflexivity arises out of experimentation with new research practices.

Holland (1999) takes this notion further suggesting that a form of intense reflexivity should not be bound by paradigmatic constraints. This form transcends personal and political concerns, as researchers explore intricate differences in identity between researchers, the subjects of research and the audiences for the text (Herts, 1997).

This is not to say that reflexivity is the ultimate goal, as it may, if taken to its extreme, encourage the formation of 'navel-gazing' scholarly communities, which could become excessively introspective and egotistical. Given such precautions, however, one of the greatest values of reflexivity is the potential for personal learning and for opening new doors for cognition. As Weick (2002) suggests, perception and conception are the two sides of the reflective coin, hence an embodied reflexivity is key to a more nuanced comprehension of ourselves and our social surroundings. His version of 'disciplined reflexivity' bridges reflexivity 'lived forward' with one which is understood backward (see Chapters 6 and 11).

An agenda for future alternative organization studies

We conclude with a programmatic agenda for the future of alternative organization studies.

How to avoid orthodoxy

In order to retain their liveliness and usefulness, alternative organization studies must constantly challenge their own assumptions and search for novel forms of inquiry. Such novel forms of inquiry have to be empirically grounded for organizational reality cannot be considered in a purely conceptual manner: it needs to be subject to both theoretical and empirical criticism (Strinati, 1993). Esping-Andersen (2000) advocates intentional and purposeful empiricism, for if there is a microcosm in the making one cannot identify it by trying abstractly to imagine a hidden Gestalt. A far better strategy is to examine empirically what is happening in organizations and report it in a reflexive and useful way to wider audiences. The important thing is that 'the alternative' does not become complacent: in order to keep reviving organization studies, 'the alternative' has to continue to disrupt, re-inscribe and re-think the world of organizations, consistent with the notion that reflexivity demands a 'turning back' or unsettling of representation (Lawson, 1985; Parker, 2001; Cunliffe, 2003).

Embodied rationality

For the alternative organization studies researcher, rationality must remain embodied in order to be able to cope effectively with the perennial indeterminancy and contingency with which humans have to struggle in organizations. To think means to experience the world in one way or another and not accounting for this experience means escaping into abstract and useless theory. Experience means not only turning to what had happened in the past but more importantly, accounting for our visceral and embodied response to the immediate context. Extending Pollner's (1991) notion of questioning of 'the natural' through radical reflexivity, the suggestion that we need to 'go further than questioning the truth claims of others, to question how we as researchers (and practitioners) also make truth claims and construct meaning' (Cunliffe, 2003: 985) allows consideration of an embodied rationality that demands attention not only to why and how we respond but also to how our situated, physical presence, monstrous or otherwise (Thanem, 2006), is itself worthy of analysis.

Emancipation

Researchers acting from an alternative standpoint should view practical action as crucial by getting out of the ivory tower to attend to the needs of marginalized groups in organizations and society. This is not to say that those subjects in a more visible position (e.g. managers) are to be ignored entirely: rather they need to be inscribed with new faculties and placed in a more equal relation to the marginal subjects. In other words, it is not enough to study workers, women, blacks, etc.; one has to study and eventually affect their relation with managers, men, and whites, respectively. Some critical researchers take an anti-managerialist stance, suggesting that providing managers with tools for understanding the concerns of the marginalized others would in fact re-enforce managers' centrality and dominance (Nord and Jermier, 1992). This stance, however, preserves the ivory tower of the organizational researcher who is not interested in stepping down to engage with the immediate, the contingent and the local. Our agenda emphasizes the importance of pragmatic action and the central role of the reflexive practitioner/manager in transforming organizations in more democratic workplaces. The role of alternative social science is to adapt successfully to contingencies and exigencies of experience and help processes of emancipation unfold.

Within the Critical Management Studies arena, such efforts are at the centre of debate about whether an emancipatory agenda is consistent with relativist epistemology and ontology (see Fournier and Grey, 2000). Rather than 'settling' such debate, either through the modified, limited concept of 'micro-emancipation' (Alvesson and Willmott, 1992a; Parker, 1995) or through the re-location of critical management studies within critical realism rather than postmodernism, our interest lies more in how emancipation (and we could add resistance) has remained a site for debate and disturbance permeating organizational studies despite attempts from many sides to write it out of analysis.

Eclectic methodologies

The alternative researcher must remain comfortable with indeterminate truth values in the attempt to handle situational indeterminacy. Fuzziness, multiple realities, paradox and ambiguity can be accommodated via an eclectic bricolage of methods. Critical/alternative forms of inquiry encourage playfulness in the service of inquiry, not simply for its own sake. This is a sort of playfulness of the mind that allows one to think of a subject in all sorts of strange ways. Some critics view playfulness as a passive, reactionary position, one of letting the world go by like a play/carnival that has been scripted before and in which the ending never changes. Others view playfulness as a thinly disguised façade that spares post-structuralist theory the embarrassment of revealing its atheoretical impression and meaningless nature (Huyssen, 1984). We, however, strongly disagree with them. For us, playfulness is an active project, one which seeks not only to gather insights into the world but also to change it for the better by interrogating and disrupting modernist logic.

In the spirit of reflexivity as a turning back, we have revisited both the highly valued tenet of triangulation (Chapter 10) and the problematic nature of retrospective research (Chapter 11) in ways that, we hope, encourage the reader to interrogate rather than dismiss or adopt without question notions such as objectivity (cf. Haraway, 1988; Holland, 1999) or functionalism (Chapter 7). More generally, we have drawn in several places on Irigaray's notions of fluidity (Chapters 3 and 5) and on the slipperiness of actor-network theory with its mix of ontological relativism and epistemological realism (Chapters 4 and 9) and encourage further analysis that is less tidy and more *dis*organized, breaking up further the much-valued consistency of ontology, epistemology and research methodology (Burrell and Morgan, 1979; cf. Johnson and Duberley, 2003). While Burrell (1996) has long warned against the anatomization of organizational knowledge, we note with some concern that reflexivity has itself become the subject of categorization (Holland, 1999; Johnson and Duberley, 2003), as have arts-based approaches to organizational analysis (Taylor and Hansen, 2005). In disorganizing such attempts, we suggest more deliberate attention to what falls outside neat categorizations, and particularly, in the spirit of Cooper, to the placement of boundaries. In Chapter 7 we extend Cooper's application of linguistic deconstruction to the disorganization of material form and encourage others to take such arguments further, (re)surfacing the aesthetic as well as political and ethical domains of organization using eclectic methodologies.

The centrality of ethics

Alternative researchers have a moral responsibility in presenting knowledge that has consequences for future applications. Drawing on Chia (1996b), Cunliffe and Jun (2005: 228) have argued that critical reflexivity, the questioning and complicating of our thinking and experience, involves not only the examination of taken-for-granted assumptions but also examination of 'who may be excluded or marginalized by policy and practice, and the responsibility for ethical action at the organizational and societal levels'. The research endeavour should be towards knowledge that makes a positive difference and contributes to enlightened practice. Theories cannot be neutral for they have ethical and political implications. A critical/alternative position counsels tolerance to ambiguity and calls for personal responsibility on the part of the researchers. Personal effort in one's immediate community of practice is more important than following universal codes of ethics, for every moral situation is a unique situation.

We end by paraphrasing Dening, for whom being a reflexive writer means having a 'heightened sense of experience in our utterances', making a 'conscious effort to join the conversation around us', believing that 'all narrations are to somebody as well as of something', and finally embarking seriously on 'an effort to regain the moral force of writing' (1996: 26). Perhaps, this is an ambitious agenda but we cannot see a future for organization studies unless such challenges become central to our research efforts.

Notes

2 Organizational knowledge: production and consumption

1 Guba and Lincoln (1994) suggest that paradigms are predicated on the interaction of three types of assumptions: *ontological* — concerning the nature of reality; *epistemological* — concerning the process of knowing; and *methodological* — concerning the research techniques and strategies available to researchers.

2 While for some authors the notion of paradigm incommensurability is 'crucial', as it raises 'fundamental questions about the reality of phenomena under investigation' (McKinley and Mone, 1998: 639), for others, the concept may be 'one of the greatest intellectual myths of the 20th century' (Donaldson, 1998: 269).

3 In the field of cultural production, for example, Bourdieu (1993) accounts similarly for not only the product of science itself but also the producers of symbolic goods, their position in the field, publishers (as intermediates between producers and consumers) and consumers of symbolic goods.

4 Whilst tactics of consumption are never fixed, they are nevertheless spatially constrained. However, researchers can temporarily transform knowledge into something quite different from that originally intended. In so doing, they may take the opportunity to resist normative practices, albeit that such a 'victory' will only be cadmean, for such researchers do not possess a knowledge space of their own, being constrained by the limits of traditional knowledge production.

5 The so-called hard sciences, however, would possibly refuse to acknowledge this fact in order to maintain cultural hegemony (see, for example, Astley and Zammuto, 1992; Mauws and Phillips, 1995; Lyotard, 1997).

6 Lyotard derives his use of the concept of agonistics largely from Nietzsche's (1974) *Homer's Conquest*. In the process he outlines how it is also 'the basis of Heraclitus's ontology and of the Sophists' dialectic, not to mention the early tragedians. A good part of Aristotle's reflections in the *Topics* and the *Sophistici Elenchi* is devoted to it' (Lyotard, 1997: 88).

7 For Lyotard it is important that little narratives do not in fact seek 'mutual encroachment' via linkages constructed with ideological ends in view.

8 However as Schultz and Hatch (1996: 530) argue, 'regardless of whether organizational researchers acknowledge paradigmatic assumptions, they make and use them when they develop and apply theory'.

9 This integrationist argument has both intellectual and political dimensions. According to Donaldson (1998) the integration of paradigms is an achievable task, although 'there are real difficulties as to whether scholars will reach agreement' (1998: 267). In his view, in North America new paradigmatic views are intertwined with a drive for intellectual novelty and the personal career advancement that this may promote. In contrast,

in Europe he feels paradigm debate is viewed as the means to continue the tradition of radical critique.

10 It could be argued that much research published in leading journals in management studies and organizational analysis is of this nature. This is perhaps not surprising given that potential contributors to the *Academy of Management Review* (AMR), for example, are informed that 'the management and organization theory contributions present in AMR are grounded in the "normal science disciplines" of economics, psychology, sociology, or social psychology' (Information for Contributors). The Notice to Contributors of the *Administrative Science Quarterly* suggests similarly that the aim of the journal is to 'build a coherent, cumulative body of knowledge'. In so doing, the journal has traditionally welcomed research of a consensual kind. A seeming concern for 'coherence' in knowledge is emphasized also in the Notice for Contributors of a leading UK journal, the *Journal of Management Studies*, which states 'our ultimate criterion for a paper's acceptability is that an informed reader is likely to learn something new from it that contributes to the development of coherent bodies of knowledge'.

11 Some leading journals in management and organization studies regularly publish research which challenges dominant discourses. For example, *Organization* and the *Journal of Management Inquiry* aim to promote 'dialogue and innovation in studies of organization' (*Organization*, Aims and Scope) and 'alternative modes of expression as play, fiction, speeches, movies, new events, and scholarly work outside the common boundaries of the field' (*Journal of Management Inquiry*, Submission Guidelines). These journals are replete with postmodernist and feminist critiques of management, work and organization.

3 Escaping the confines of organization theory

1 At face value, however, the various radical perspectives do appear to possess a common commitment to social theories of the political left, and thus opposition to the managerialist pedagogy of functionalist organization theory. A commitment to political change is indeed basic to radical theory. The primary purpose of, for example, radical structuralism is to clarify the status of late capitalism. Knowledge gained is to be used in the interests of the 'exploited social majority', because radical theory 'should always have discontinuous revolutionary change of such societies as [its] ultimate political goal' (Burrell, 1980: 90).

2 In appropriating Derrida's work in this way, we note that considerable violence has been inflicted, as his concern is with a disruption of the Platonic notion of mimesis — as revealed truth — whereas our own is the hegemony of intertextual representation.

3 For organization theory, the conceptual imagery of systems orthodoxy is rendered from functionalist social theory. Through this association many of the criticisms made against functionalism also hold for systems theory.

4 Fundamental to the ethics of a responsibility to otherness is a sympathetic following of the texts of those who are themselves the 'other'. This is necessary so as to explore the oppression of the other while respecting the integrity of political discourses from the margins. To terrorize the conventions of orthodox organization theory, we will appropriate the gestures of Irigaray's mimicry through which she retrieves the feminine other.

5 Fluidity and identity

1 It is worth noting that in philosophical communities some feminist scholars perceive the postmodern movement as representing the 'voices of the powerful' (Harstok, in Mumby, 1996), and being concerned with philosophy and epistemology rather than

wider social and political issues. Flax (1990: 183), however, is committed to political engagement/rejuvenation and believes: 'Our lives and alliances belong to those who seek to decentre the world further' (1990: 183). This is not to suggest, however, that modernist feminism exists in opposition to postmodernist feminism — rather that postmodernist feminism engages/represents 'multiple voices' on issues of meaning, power and identity.

2 We are not pinpointing Calás and Smircich as theorists who have ignored a particular scholar but as representative of organization studies which has tended to ignore Irigaray's work.

3 Her doctoral thesis 'Speculum de'autre femme' in 1974 led to immediate expulsion from Lacan's Ecole Freudienne at Vicennes. Ever since she has held what might be called a marginal position within French academia, and especially within psychoanalytic fields. She has claimed that one does not go unpunished by the fathers!

4 The word speculum derives from the original Latin meaning of mirror — *specere* — to look. It also refers to an instrument for dilating cavities of the human body for inspection. The construction of her book strives to enact a speculum-like structure. By starting with Freud and ending with Plato, Irigaray reverses the normal historical order in an action which resembles that of the concave mirror which is the speculum that gynaecologists use to inspect the cavities of the female body. She states 'turned horizontally into relation to the face, the concavity will make it seem as if it is turned upside down' (1985a: 183).

5 Moi (1985) suggests that Irigaray undertakes one of the most insightful deconstructive analyses of Plato but does not make it explicitly clear she is following Derrida. Moi, like other feminist literary critics, uses the terms textual critique and deconstruction interchangeably. Whitford states that she is obviously indebted to Derrida but is categorical that her sole aim was not in itself deconstruction since she rested on wanting to create transformative capacity for feminism (see Whitford, 1991: 122–135). In *To Speak is Never Neutral* (2002) Irigaray reveals her debt to structural linguistics and deconstruction showing that Derrida has undoubtedly influenced her work. However, this collection of essays, based on her early work on schizophrenia, is chiefly concerned with linguistic theory rather than feminist philosophy.

6 The 'other' of the other woman is the secondary title of *Speculum* and should be read as a noun. Irigaray wishes to show how the 'other' is in fact not neutral, neither grammatically or semantically (Irigaray, 1995).

7 Schor (1994: 57–67) acknowledges her indebtedness to Gallop (1988) whose early work on the ' "I" body politics' urges us to beware of too literal a reading of Irigaray's anatomy.

8 Fuss too is convincing when she states there is no 'essence to essentialism ... essence as irreducible has been constructed to be irreducible' (1996: 93). Reviving John Locke's binary oppositions she distinguishes between kinds of essentialism — *real* and *nominal*. Real essence corresponds to Aristotelian understanding and is unchanging, whereas nominal essence signifies a linguistic convenience.

9 This, of course, supports accounts of subjectivity as advocated by Benhabib (1995) who argues that a subject position is constituted through an individual having the capacity to exercise choice. In contrast, Butler argues that the doer is constituted by the deed that is engaged in 'reiterative and citational practices by which discourse produces the effects that it names' (1993: 2). Hence subjectivity is constituted by the *effect* on the subject, and not the *capacity* of the subject.

10 Irigaray's mimetic strategy is most convincing when she points out Freud's failure to locate the facts of female specificity which Freud could not see because of his male lens (see 1985a: 29–40).

11 Butler acknowledges this strategy and posits that the 'feminine is unthematizable, the non-figurable' (1993: 48). For Butler, the only criticism is where is the feminine then?

This is exactly the point, as we will go on to show. Whitford also acknowledges this lack of feminine follow-through, since what is required is engagement with *two sexes*, incorporating a new female symbolic, one that makes 'fertile' male and female readings 'both at once' (Whitford, 1991: 22–25). We would argue that what Irigaray does is to show the philosophical conditions which *disavow* the feminine and in this sense 'Irigaray is not enough; she cannot alone fulfil our needs' (Whitford, 1991: 5), but she has brought into existence the unthought and unsymbolized and has at least started an important feminist journey.

12 Whitford notes that the terminology of men/women; masculine/feminine etc. and its translation from French to English is not always so clear and exclaims 'I throw my hands up in despair' (1991: 8). Like her, we hope that in interrogating Irigaray's use of the word feminine our arguments are clear enough and that the reader will forgive the occasional ambiguity.

Bibliography

Abrahamson, E. (1997) 'The emergence and prevalence of employee management rhetorics: The effects of long waves, labor unions, and turnover 1875–1992', *Academy of Management Journal*, 40: 491–533.

Adeney, E. (1996) 'The invisible reconstruction of the Victorian metropolitan hospital system', *Journal of Law and Medicine*, 4: 267–275.

Adorno, T. (1984) *Aesthetic Theory*, trans. C. Lenhardt. London: Routledge and Kegan Paul.

Adorno, T. (1997) *Aesthetic Theory*, trans. Robert Hullot-Kentor. Minneapolis: Minnesota University Press.

Alberti, L. B. (1957) 'On architecture', in E. G. Holt (ed.), *A Documentary History of Art*, vol. 1, revised edition, 218–243. New York: Doubleday Anchor.

Allport, G. (1942) *The Use of Personal Documents in Psychological Research*. New York: Social Science Research Council.

Alvesson, M. (1991) 'Organizational symbolism and ideology', *Journal of Management Studies*, 30: 515–552.

Alvesson, M. (1999) *Beyond neo-positivists, romantics and localists — A reflexive approach to interviews in organization research*. Working Paper 3, Department of Business Administration, School of Economics and Management, Lund University, Sweden.

Alvesson, M. (2003a) 'Beyond neopositivists, romantics, and localists: a reflexive approach to interviews in organizational research', *Academy of Management Review*, 28: 13–33.

Alvesson, M. (2003b) *Studying Management Critically*. London: Sage.

Alvesson, M. and Deetz, S. (1996) 'Critical theory and postmodernism approaches to organizational studies', in S. R. Clegg, C. Hardy and W. R. Nord (eds), *Handbook of Organization Studies*, 191–217. London: Sage.

Alvesson, M. and Deetz, S. (2000) *Doing Critical Management Research*. London: Sage.

Alvesson, M. and Sköldberg, K. (2000) *Reflexive Methodology: New Vistas for Qualitative Research*. London: Sage.

Alvesson, M. and Willmott, H. (1992a) 'On the idea of emancipation in management and organization studies', *Academy of Management Review*, 17/3: 432–464.

Alvesson, M. and Willmott, H. (eds) (1992b) *Critical Management Studies*. London: Sage.

Alvesson, M. and Willmott, H. (1996) *Making Sense of Management: A Critical Introduction*. London: Sage.

Ancona, D. G., Okhuysen, G. A. and Perlow, L. A. (2001) 'Taking time to integrate temporal research', *Academy of Management Review*, 26: 512–529.

Antonacopolou, E. and Tsoukas, H. (2002) 'Time and reflexivity in organization studies: an introduction', *Organization Studies*, 23 (6): 857–862.

Arthur, M. and Rousseau, D. (1995) *The Boundaryless Career*. New York: Oxford University Press.

Asendorf, C. (1999) 'The Bauhaus and the world of technology — work on industrial culture', in J. Fiedler and P. Feierabend (eds), *Bauhaus*, 160–171. Cologne: Konemann.

Ashmore, M. (1989) *The Reflexive Thesis: Writing the Sociology of Scientific Knowledge*. Chicago: Chicago University Press.

Ashmore, M., Woolfitt, R. and Harding, S. (1994) 'Humans and others, agents and things', *American Behavioral Scientist*, 37 (6): 733–740.

Askenas, R., Ulrich, D., Jick, T. and Kerr, S. (1995) *The Boundaryless Organisation*. San Fransisco CA: Jossey Bass.

Astley, W. G. (1985) 'Administrative science as socially constructed truth', *Administrative Science Quarterly*, 30: 497–513.

Astley, W. G. and Zammuto, R. F. (1992) 'Organization science, managers and language games', *Organization Science*, 3 (4): 443–460.

Atkin, I. and Hassard, J. (1996) 'Liberation from within: organizational implications of Irigaray's concept of "residue"', in D. Boje, R. Gephart Jnr and T. Joseph (eds), *Postmodern Management and Organization Theory*. Thousand Oaks: Sage.

Atkinson, J. (1984) 'Manpower strategies for flexible organizations', *Personnel Management*, August: 28–31.

Atkinson, P., Coffey, A. J., Delamont, S., Lofland, J. and Lofland, L. H. (2001) *Handbook of Ethnography*. London: Sage.

Atler, C. and Hage, J. (1993) *Organizations Working Together*. Newbury Park, CA: Sage.

Azar, B. (2000) 'Blinded by hindsight', *Monitor on Psychology*, 31: 28–29.

Baack, D. and Prasch, T. (1997) 'The death of the subject and the life of the organization: Implications of new approaches to subjectivity for organizational analysis', *Journal of Management Inquiry*, 6: 131–141.

Bakhtin, M. M. (1981) *The Dialogic Imagination: Four Essays,* translated by C. Emerson and M. Holquist, edited by M. Holquist. Austin: Texas University Press.

Barley, S. and Kunda, G. (2004) *Gurus, Hired Guns, and Warm Bodies: Itinerant Experts in a Knowledge Economy*. New Jersey: Princeton University Press.

Barrett, F. (1995) 'Creating appreciative learning cultures', *Organizational Dynamics*, 24: 36–49.

Barringer, B. R. and Harrison, J. S. (2000) 'Walking a tightrope: creating value through interorganizational relationships', *Journal of Management*, 26: 367–403.

Barry, D. and Elmes, M. (1997) 'Strategy retold: Toward a narrative view of strategic discourse', *Academy of Management Review*, 22: 429–452.

Bartky, S. (1997) 'Foucault, femininity and the modernization of patriarchal power', in Conboy, K., Medina, N. and Stanbury, S. (eds), *Writing on the Body*. New York: Columbia University Press.

Bartunek, J. M. (1994) 'Wanted: a more participative role for research participants', *Organization*, 1: 39–43.

Bauman, Z. (1987) *Legislators and Interpreters: On Modernity, Postmodernity and Intellectuals*. Cambridge: Polity.

Bauman, Z. (1993) *Postmodernist Ethics*. Oxford: Blackwell.

Bauman, Z. (1995) *Life in Fragments: Essays in Postmodern Morality*. Oxford: Blackwell.

Bauman, Z. (1998) *Work, Consumerism and the New Poor*. Buckingham: Open University Press.

Bazzoli, G. J., Miller, R. H. and Burns, L. R. (2000) 'Capitated contracting roles and relationships in healthcare', *Journal of Healthcare Management*, 45: 170–188.

Beck, U. (1992) *Risk Society: Towards a New Modernity*. London: Sage.

Bell-Dolan, D. and Anderson, C. A. (1999) 'Attributional processes: an integration of social and clinical psychology', in R. M. Kowalski and M. R. Learey (eds), *The Social Psychology of Emotional and Behavioural Problems: Interfaces of Social and Clinical Psychology*, 37–67. Washington, DC: American Psychological Association.

Benhabib, S. (1995) 'Feminism and postmodernism', in Benhabib, S., Butler, J., Cornell, D. and Fraser, N. (eds), *Feminist Contentions, A Philosophical Exchange*. New York: Routledge.

Benson, J. K. (1977a) 'Organizations: a dialectical view', *Administrative Science Quarterly*, 18/1: 3–16.

Benson, J. K. (1977b) 'Innovation and crisis in organizational analysis', *Sociological Quarterly*, 18/4: 229–249.

Berger, P. and Luckmann, T. (1966) *The Social Construction of Reality*. New York: Anchor Books.

Bernstein, B. (1990) *Class, Codes, and Control. Vol. 4: The Structuring of Pedagogic Discourse*. London: Routledge.

Bernstein, J. M. (1997) 'Why rescue semblance? Metaphysical experience and the possibility of ethics', in T. Huhn and L. Zuidervaart (eds), *The Semblance of Subjectivity: Essays in Adorno's Aesthetic Theory*, 177–212. Cambridge, MA and London: The MIT Press.

Best, E. (1922) 'The Maori division of time', *Dominion Museum Monograph*, 4.

Best, S. and Kellner, D. (1991) *Postmodern Theory*. New York: The Guilford Press.

Beynon, H., Grimshaw, D., Rubery, J. and Ward, K. (2002) *Managing Employment Change: The New Realities of Work*. Oxford: Oxford University Press.

Bijker, W. E. (1993) 'Do not despair: there is life after constructivism', *Science, Technology and Human Values*, 18 (1): 113–138.

Black, R. (1964) *Old and New Australian Aboriginal Art*. Sydney: Angus and Robertson.

Blaikie, N. (1991) 'A critique of the use of triangulation in social research', *Quality and Quantity*, 25: 115–136.

Blaikie, N. (1993) *Approaches to Social Inquiry*. Cambridge: Polity Press.

Blaikie, N. (2000) *Designing Social Research*. London: Polity.

Bloomfield, B., Coombs, R., Cooper, D. and Rea, D. (1992) 'Machines and manoeuvres: responsibility accounting and the construction of hospital information systems', *Accounting, Management and Information Technology*, 2 (4): 197–219.

Bloomfield, B. and Danieli, A. (1995) 'The role of management consultants in the development of information technology: the indissoluble nature of socio-political and technical skills', *Journal of Management Studies*, 32 (1): 23–46.

Bloomfield, B. and McLean, C. (1996) 'Madness and organization: informed management and empowerment', in W. Orlikowski, G. Walsham, M. Jones and J. DeGross (eds), *Information Technology and Changes in Organizational Work*. London: Chapman and Hall.

Bloomfield, B. and Vurdubakis, T. (1994) 'Re-presenting technology: IT consultancy reports as textual reality constructions', *Sociology*, 28 (2): 455–477.

Bloomfield, B. and Vurdubakis, T. (1999) 'The outer limits: monsters, actor networks and the writing of displacement', *Organization*, 6 (4): 625–648.

Blount, S. and Janicik, G. A. (2001) 'When plans change: examining how people evaluate timing changes in work organizations', *Academy of Management Review*, 26: 566–585.

Bluedorn, A. C., Johnson, R. A., Cartwright, D. K. and Barringer, B. R. (1994) 'The interface and convergence of the strategic management and organizational environment domains', *Journal of Management*, 20: 201–262.

Boje, D. (1995) 'Stories of the storytelling organization: a postmodern analysis of Disney as Tamara-land', *Academy of Management Journal*, 38: 997–1035.

Boje, D. M. (2001) *Narrative Methods for Organizational and Communication Research*. London: Sage.

Boland, R. and Schultze, U. (1996) 'From work to activity: technology and the narrative of progress', in W. Orlikowski, G. Walsham, M. Jones and J. DeGross (eds), *Information Technology and Changes in Organizational Work*. London: Chapman and Hall.

Bonß, W. and Hartmann, H. (1985) 'Konstruierte gesellschaft, rationale deutung. zum wirklichkeitscharakter soziologischer diskurse', in W. Bonß and H. Hartmann (eds), *Entzauberte Wissenschaft. Zur Relitavität und Geltung soziologischer Forschung*. Special Issue 3 of Soziale Welt. Göttingen.

Booth, C. (2000) 'The problems and possibilities of reflexivity in strategy', *Electronic Journal of Radical Organization Theory*, 4/1.

Booth, W. C. (1995) *The Craft of Research*. Chicago: University of Chicago Press.

Bourdieu, P. (1990) *The Logic of Practice*. Cambridge: Polity Press

Bourdieu, P. (1993) *The Field of Cultural Production*. Cambridge: Polity Press.

Bowers, J. (1992) 'The politics of formalism', in M. Lea (ed.), *Contexts of Computer-Mediated Communication*. Hemel Hempsted: Harvester Wheatsheaf.

Bowker, G. and Star, L. (1999) *Sorting Things Out: Classification and Its Consequences*. Cambridge, Mass: MIT Press.

Bowker, G., Timmermans, S. and Star, L. (1996) 'Infrastructure and organizational transformation: classifying nurses' Work', in W. Orlikowski, G. Walsham, M. Jones and J. DeGross (eds), *Information Technology and Changes in Organizational Work*. London: Chapman and Hall.

Braidotti, R. (1994) 'Of bugs and women: Irigaray and Deleuze on the becoming woman', in Whitford, M. (ed.), *Engaging with Irigaray*. New York, Columbia University Press.

Braithwaite, J., Vining, R. F. and Lazarus, L. (1994) 'The boundaryless hospital', *Australia and New Zealand Journal of Medicine*, 24: 565–571.

Braverman, H. (1974) *Labor and Monopoly Capital: The Degradation of Work in the Twentieth Century*. New York, London: Monthly Review Press.

Brewerton, P. and Millward, L. (2002) *Organizational Research Methods*. London: Sage.

Brewis, J. and Linstead, S. (1998) 'Time after time', *Human Relations*, 7 (2): 232–248.

Brocklesby, J. (1997) 'Becoming multimethodology-literate: an assessment of the cognitive difficulties of working across paradigms', in J. Mingers and A. Gill (eds), *Multimethodology: the Theory and Practice of Combining Management Science Methodologies*, 189–216. Chichester: Wiley.

Bromley, D., Shupe, A. and Ventimiglia, J. (1979) 'Atrocity tales, the Unification Church and the social construction of evil', *Journal of Communication*, 29: 42–53.

Brown, A. D. and Starkey, K. (2000) 'Organizational identity and learning: a psychodynamic perspective', *Academy of Management Review*, 25: 102–120.

Brunsson, N. and Sahlin-Andersson, K. (2000) 'Constructing organizations: the example of public sector reform', *Organization Studies*, 21: 721–746.

Bryman, A. (1988) *Quantity and Quality in Social Research*. London and New York: Routledge.

Bubner, R. (1997) 'Concerning the central idea of Adorno's philosophy', in T. Huhn and L. Zuidervaart (eds), *The Semblance of Subjectivity: Essays in Adorno's Aesthetic Theory*, 147–175. Cambridge, MA and London: The MIT Press.

Burawoy, M. (1979) *Manufacturing Consent*. Chicago: University of Chicago Press.

Burawoy, M. (2001) 'Manufacturing the global', *Ethnography*, 2 (2): 147–159.

Bürger, P. (1984) *Theory of the Avant-garde* (trans. Michael Shaw, foreward by Jochen Schulte-Sass). Minneapolis: University of Minnesota Press.

Burke, C. (1994) 'Irigaray through the looking glass', in Whitford, M. (eds), *Engaging with Irigaray*. New York, Columbia University Press.

Burns, T. and Stalker, G. (1961) *The Management of Innovation*. London: Tavistock.

Burrell, G. (1980) 'Radical organization theory', in D. Dunkerley and G. Salaman (eds), *The International Yearbook of Organization, 1979*. London: Routledge and Kegan.

Burrell, G. (1988) 'Modernism, postmodernism and organization studies 2: The contribution of Micheal Foucault', *Organization Studies*, 9 (2): 221–235.

Burrell, G. (1992) 'Back to the future: time and organization', in M. Reed and M. Hughes (eds), *Rethinking Organization: New Directions in Organization Theory and Analysis*, 165–183. London: Sage.

Burrell, G. (1996) 'Normal science, paradigms, metaphors, discourses and genealogies of analysis', in S. R. Clegg, C. Hardy and W. R. Nord (eds), *Handbook of Organization Studies*, 642–658. London: Sage.

Burrell, G. (1997) *Pandemonium: Towards a Retro-Organization Theory*. London: Sage.

Burrell, G. (1998) 'Linearity, control and death', in D. Grant, T. Keenoy and C. Oswick (eds), *Discourse and Organization*, 134–151. London: Sage.

Burrell, G. (2003) 'The future of organization theory: prospects and limitations', in H. Tsoukas and K. Knudsen (eds), *Oxford Handbook of Organization Theory*. Oxford: Oxford University Press.

Burrell, G. and Morgan, G. (1979) *Sociological Paradigms and Organizational Analysis: Elements of the Sociology of Corporate Life*. Portsmouth, NH: Heinemann.

Busby, J. S. (1999) 'The effectiveness of collective retrospection as a mechanism of organizational learning', *The Journal of Applied Behavioral Science*, 35 (1): 109–129.

Butler, J. (1990) *Gender Trouble*. New York: Routledge.

Butler, J. (1993) *Bodies That Matter*. New York: Routledge.

Butler, J. (1995) 'Contingent foundations', in Benhabib, S., Butler, J., Cornell, D. and Fraser, N. (eds), *Feminist Contentions, A Philosophical Exchange*. New York: Routledge.

Butler, R. (1997) 'Stories and experiments in social inquiry', *Organization Studies*, 18: 927–948.

Buttery, E., Fulop, L. and Buttery, A. (1999) 'Networks and interorganizational relations', in L. Fulop and S. Linstead (eds), *Management: A Critical Text*. South Yarra: Macmillan Education Australia.

Button, G. (1993) 'The curious case of the vanishing technology', in G. Button (ed.), *Technology in Working Order: Studies of Work, Interaction and Technology*. London: Routledge.

Calás, M. and Smircich, L. (1991) 'Voicing seduction to silence leadership', *Organisation Studies*, 12 (4): 571–601.

Calás, M. and Smircich, L. (1992a) 'Using the "F" word, feminist theories and the social consequences of organisational research', in Mills, A. and Tancred, P. (eds), *Gendering Organisational Analysis*. London: Sage.

Calás, M. and Smircich, L. (1992b) 'Rewriting gender into organisational theorising: directions from feminist perspectives', in Reed, M. and Hughes, M. (eds), *Rethinking Organisation: New Directions into Organisational Theory and Analysis*. London: Sage.

Calás, M. and Smircich, L. (1994) 'From the woman's point of view, feminist approaches to organisation studies', in Clegg, S., Hardy, C. and Nord, W. (eds.), *Handbook of Organisation Studies*. London: Sage.

Calás, M. and Smircich, L. (1999) 'Past-postmodernism? Reflections and tentative directions', *Academy of Management Review*, 24 (4): 649–671.

Callon, M. (1986) 'Some elements of a sociology of translation: domestication of the scallops and fishermen of St. Brieuc Bay', in Law, J. (ed.), *Power, Action and Belief: A New Sociology of Knowledge*?, 196–233. London: Routledge.

Callon, M. (ed.) (1998) *The Laws of the Markets*. Oxford: Blackwell.

Callon, M. (1999) 'Actor-network theory — the market test', in J. Law and J. Hassard (eds), *Actor Network Theory and After*. Oxford: Blackwell.

Callon, M. and Latour, M. (1992) 'Don't throw the baby out with the bath school', in A. Pickering (ed.), *Science as Practice and Culture*. Chicago: University of Chicago Press.

Callon, M. and Latour, B. (1995) 'Agency and the hybrid collectif', *South Atlantic Quarterly*, 94 (2): 481–507.

Callon, M. and Law, J. (1997) 'L'irruption des non-humans dans les sciences humaines: quelques lecons tirees de la sociologie des sciences et des techniques', in B. Reynaud (ed.), *Les Limites de la Rationalite: Vol 2, Les Figures du Collectif*. Paris: La Decouverte.

Callon, M., Law, J. and Rip, A. (1986) *Mapping the Dynamics of Science and Technology: Sociology of Science in the Real World*. London: Macmillan.

Cameron, D. (1998) 'Gender and language gender, language and discourse: a review essay', *Signs*, 23 (4): 945–979.

Campbell, D. T. and Fiske, D. W. (1959) 'Convergent and discriminant validity by the multi-trait, multi-method matrix', *Psychological Bulletin*, 56: 81–105.

Cannon, D. R. (1999) 'Cause or control? The temporal dimension in failure sensemaking', *Journal of Applied Behavioral Science*, 35: 416–438.

Carroll, D. (1987) *Paraesthetics: Foucault, Lyotard, Derrida*. New York and London: Methuen.

Case, P. (2003) 'From objectivity to subjectivity: pursuing subjective authenticity in organizational research', in R. Westwood and S. Clegg (eds), *Debating Organization: Point-Counterpoint in Organization Theory*, 156–181. Oxford: Blackwell.

Casey, C. (1995) *Work, Self and Society: After Industrialism*. London: Routledge.

Casey, C. (1999) '"Come join our family": discipline and integration in corporate organizational culture', *Human Relations*, 52: 155–178.

Casey, C. (2002) *Critical Analysis of Organizations*. London: Sage.

Castel, R. (1991) 'From dangerousness to risk', in G. Burchell, C. Gordon and P. Miller (eds), *The Foucault Effect: Studies in Governmentality*, 281–298. Hemel Hempstead: Harvester Wheatsheaf.

Castells, M. (1996) *The Rise of the Network Society*. Oxford: Blackwell.

Cavendish, R. (1982) *Women on the Line*. London: Routledge and Kegan Paul.

Charmaz, K. (1999) 'Stories of suffering: subjective tales and research narratives', *Qualitative Health Research*, 9: 362–382.

Chia, R. (1995) 'From modern to postmodern organizational analysis', *Organization Studies*, 16: 579–604.

Chia, R. (1996a) 'The problem of reflexivity in organisational research: towards a postmodern science of organisation', *Organisation*, 3 (1): 31–59.

Chia, R. (1996b) *Organizational Analysis as Deconstructive Practice*. Berlin and New York: Walter de Gruter.

Chia, R. (1996c) 'Metaphor and metaphorization in organizational analysis: thinking beyond the unthinkable', in D. Grand and C. Oswick (eds), *Metaphor and Organisations,* 127–145. London: Sage.

Chia, R. (1997) 'Essai: thirty years on: from organizational structures to the organization of thought', *Organization Studies*, 18: 685–707.

Chia, R. (ed.) (1998) *Organized Worlds*. London: Routledge.

Chia, R. (2003) 'Ontology: organization as world-building', in R. Westwood and S. Clegg (eds), *Debating Organization: Point-Counterpoint in Organization Theory*, 98–114. Oxford: Blackwell.

Clark, D. (1951) *Plane and Geodetic Surveying for Engineers,* Vol. 1 (4th ed. revised and enlarged by J. Glendenning). London: Constable.

Clark, P. (1982) 'A review of the theories of time and structure for organisational sociology', Working Paper No. 248, Management Centre, University of Aston, UK.

Clark, P. (1990) 'Chronological codes and organizational analysis', in J. Hassard and D. Pym (eds), *The Theory and Philosophy of Organizations*, 137–163. London and New York: Routledge.

Clark, P., Hantrais, L., Hassard, J., Linhart, D. and Starkey, L. (1984) 'The porous day and temps chois', Paper presented at the Labour Process Conference, Aston University, U.K.

Clark, P. A. (1978) 'Temporal innovations and time structuring in large organizations', in J. T. Fraser, N. Lawrence and D. Park (eds), *The Study of Time*, Vol. 3. New York: Springer-Verlag. (1982) 'A Review of the theories of time and structure for organisational sociology', Working paper no. 248, Management Centre, University of Aston.

Clark, T. (1998) 'A Whiteheadian chaosmos: Process philosophy from a Deleuzean perspective', *Process Studies*, 28 (3–4): 179–194.

Clark, T. and Fincham, R. (2002) *Critical Consulting: New Perspectives on the Management Advice Industry*. London: Routledge.

Clark, T. and Salaman, G. (1996) 'The management guru as organizational witchdoctor', *Organization*, 3 (2): 85–107.

Clark. T. and Salaman, G. (1998) 'Telling tales: management gurus' narratives and the construction of managerial identity', *Journal of Management Studies*, 35 (2): 137–161.

Clegg, S. (1979) *The Theory of Power in Organizations*. London: Routledge and Kegan Paul.

Clegg, S. (1990) *Modern Organizations: Organization Studies in the Postmodern World*. London: Sage.

Clegg, S. (1994) 'Power and institutions in the theory of organizations', in J. Hassard and M. Parker (eds), *Towards a New Theory of Organizations*, 24–49. London and New York: Routledge.

Clegg, S. and Dunkerley, S. (1980) *Organizations, Class and Control*. London: Routledge and Kegan Paul.

Clegg, S. R. and Hardy, C. (1996) 'Conclusion: representations', in S. R. Clegg, C. Hardy and W. R. Nord (eds), *Handbook of Organization Studies*, 676–708. London: Sage.

Codrington, R. H. (1891) *The Melanesians*. Oxford: Clarendon Press.

Cole, S. (1983) 'The hierarchy of sciences', *American Journal of Sociology*, 89: 111–139.

Collins, H. and Yearley, S. (1992) 'Epistemological chicken', in Pickering, A. (ed.), *Science, Practice and Culture.* Chicago: University of Chicago Press.

Collins, M. (1987) *Towards Post-Modernism: Design Since 1851*. London: British Museum Press.

Colville, I., Waterman, R. and Weick, K. (1999) 'Organizing and the search for excellence', *Organization*, 6 (1): 129–148.

Commonwealth of Australia (1993) 'Goals and targets for Australia's health in the year 2000 and beyond', Report prepared for the Commonwealth Department of Health, Housing and Community Services by D. Nutbeam, M. Wise, A. Bauman, E. Harris and S. Leeder, Department of Public Health, University of Sydney, Canberra, Australian Government Publishing Service.

Cooper, R. (1983) 'The other: a model of human structuring', in G. Morgan (ed.), *Beyond Method*. Beverley Hills: Sage.

Cooper, R. (1986) 'Organization/disorganization', *Social Science Information*, 25 (2): 299–335.

Cooper, R. (1989) 'Modernism, postmodernism and organizational analysis 3: the contribution of Jacques Derrida', *Organization Studies*, 10 (4): 479–502.

Cooper, R. (1990) 'Organization/disorganization', in J. Hassard and D. Pym (eds), *The Theory and Philosophy of Organizations: Critical Issues and New Perspectives*. London: Routledge.

Cooper, R. (1998) 'Assemblage notes', in Chia, R. C. H. (eds), *Organized Worlds — Explorations in Technology and Organization* with Robert Cooper. London: Routledge.

Cooper, R. (2005) 'Relationality', *Organization Studies*, 26 (11): 1689–1710.

Cooper, R. and Burrell, G. (1988) 'Modernism, postmodernism and organizational analysis: An introduction', *Organization Studies*, 9 (1): 91–112.

Cooper, R. and Law, J. (1995) 'Organization: distal and proximal views', *Research in the Sociology of Organizations*, 13: 237–274.

Cooperrider, D. and Srivastva, S. (1987) 'Appreciative inquiry in organizational life', *Research in Organizational Change and Development*, 1: 129–169.

Covaleski, M. A., Dirsmith, M. W., Heian, J. B. and Samuel, S. (1998) 'The calculated and the avowed: techniques of discipline and struggles over identity in Big Six public accounting firms', *Administrative Science Quarterly*, 43: 293–327.

Covaleski, M. A., Dirsmith, M. W. and Michelman, J. E. (1993) 'An institutional theory perspective on the DRG framework, case-mix accounting systems and health-care organizations', *Accounting, Organizations and Society*, 18 (1): 65–80.

Creswell, J. W. (1994) *Research Design — Qualitative and Quantitative Approaches*. Thousand Oaks, CA: Sage.

Cunliffe, A. L. (2003) 'Reflexive inquiry in organizational research: questions and possibilities', *Human Relations*, 56/8: 983–1003.

Cunliffe, A. L. and Jun, J. S. (2005) 'The need for reflexivity in public administration', *Administration and Society*, 37/2: 225–242.

Currall, S. C., Hammer, T. H., Baggett, L. S. and Doniger, G. M. (1999) 'Combining qualitative and quantitative methodologies to study group processes: an illustrative study of a corporate board of directors', *Organizational Research Methods*, 2: 5–36.

Czarniawska, B. (1997) *Narrating the Organization*. Chicago: The University of Chicago Press.

Czarniawska, B. (1998) *A Narrative Approach to Organization Studies*. Thousand Oaks, CA: Sage.

Czarniawska, B. (2003) 'Social constructionism and organization studies', in R. Westwood and S. Clegg (eds), *Debating Organization: Point-Counterpoint in Organization Theory*, 128–140. Oxford: Blackwell.

Daniels, K. and Johnson, J. (2002) 'On trees and triviality traps: locating the debate on the contribution of cognitive mapping to organizational research', *Organization Studies*, 23: 73–81.

de Certeau, M. (1984) *The Practice of Everyday Life*. California: University of California Press.

Deetz, S. (1996) 'Describing differences in approaches to organization science: rethinking Burrell and Morgan and their legacy', *Organization Science*, 7 (2): 191–207.

de Laet, M. and Mol, A. (2000) 'The Zimbabwe bush pump: mechanics of a fluid Technology', *Social Studies of Science*, 30 (2): 225–263.

Delbridge, R. (1998) *Life on the Line in Contemporary Manufacturing*. Oxford: Oxford University Press.

Delbridge, R. (2000) *Life on the Line*. Berlin: Walter de Gruyter.

Deleuze, G. (1994) *Difference and Repetition*. London: Athlone.

De Meuse, K. P., Bergmann, T. J. and Lester, S. W. (2001) 'An investigation of the relational component of the psychological contract across time, generation, and employment status', *Journal of Managerial Issues*, 13: 102–118.

Dening, G. (1996) *Performances*. Chicago: University of Chicago Press.

Denzin, N. (1978) *The Research Act: A Theoretical Introduction to Sociological Methods* (2nd ed.). New York: McGraw-Hill.

Denzin, N. (1989) *Interpretive Interactionism*. Newbury Park, CA: Sage.

Denzin, N. (1994) 'The art and politics of interpretation', in N. K. Denzin and Y. S. Lincoln (eds), *Handbook of Qualitative Research*, 500–515. Thousand Oaks: Sage.

Derrida, J. (1978) *Writing and Difference*. London: Routledge and Kegan Paul.

Derrida, J. (1981a) *Positions*, translated by Bass, A. London: Athlone Press.

Derrida, J. (1981b) *Dissemination*. London: The Athlone Press.

Derrida, J. (1983) 'The principles of reason: the university in the eyes of its pupils', *Diacritics*, 19/3: 3–20.

Derrida, J. (1992) *Acts of Literature*, in Attridge, D. (ed.). London: Routledge.

Diesing, P. (1971) *Patterns of Discovery in the Social Sciences*. Chicago, IL: Aldine Atherton.

DiMaggio, P. J. (1995) 'Comments on "What theory is not"', *Administrative Science Quarterly*, 40: 391–397.

Ditton, J. (1979) 'Baking time', *Sociological Review*, 27: 157–167.

Donaldson, L. (1985) *In Defence of Organization Theory: A Reply to the Critics*. Cambridge, UK: Cambridge University Press.

Donaldson, L. (1994) 'The liberal revolution and organization theory', in J. Hassard and M. Parker (eds), *Towards a New Theory of Organizations*, 190–208. London and New York: Routledge.

Donaldson, L. (1995) *American Anti-Management Theories of Organization: A Critique of Paradigm Proliferation*. Cambridge: Cambridge University Press.

Donaldson, L. (1996a) *For Positivist Organization Theory: Proving the Hard Core*. London: Sage.

Donaldson, L. (1996b) 'The normal science of contingency theory', in S. R. Clegg, C. Hardy and W. R. Nord (eds), *Handbook of Organization Studies*, 57–76. London: Sage.

Donaldson, L. (1998) 'The myth of paradigm incommensurability in management studies: comments by an integrationist', *Organization*, 5 (2): 267–272.

Donaldson, L. (2003) 'Position statement on positivism', in R. Westwood and S. Clegg (eds), *Debating Organization: Point-Counterpoint in Organization Theory*, 116–127. Oxford: Blackwell.

Duckett, S. J. (1994) *Reform of Public Hospital Funding in Victoria.* Australian Studies in Health Services Management, No. 77, Sydney, Australia, School of Health Services Management, University of New South Wales.

Duckett, S. J. (2000a) *Ministerial review of Health Care Networks*, Interim report, Melbourne, Victoria, Australia, Victorian Government Department of Human Services, February.

Duckett, S. J. (2000b) *Ministerial Review of Health Care Networks*, Final report, Melbourne, Victoria, Australia, Victorian Government Department of Human Services, May.

Dudley, K. (1994) *The End of the Line*. Chicago: University of Chicago Press.

Durkheim, E. (1915) *The Elementary Forms of the Religious Life*. London: George Allen and Unwin.

Earley, P. C. and Singh, H. (1995) 'International and intercultural management research: what's next?' *Academy of Management Review*, 38 (2): 327–340.

Eco, U. (1984) *The Name of the Rose*. London: Picador.

Edgell, S., Hetherington, K. and Warde, A. (1996) *Consumption Matters*. Oxford: Blackwell Publishers/The Sociological Review.

Eisenhardt, K. (1995) 'Building theories from case study research', in G. P. Huber and A. H. Van de Ven (eds), *Longitudinal Research Methods: Studying Processes of Organizational Change*, 65–90. Thousand Oaks, CA: Sage.

Eliade, M. (1959) *Cosmos and History: The Myth of the Eternal Return*. New York: Harper and Row.

Elliott, R. (1996) 'Discourse analysis: exploring action, function and conflict in social texts', *Marketing Intelligence and Planning*, 14: 65–68.

Ely, R. J. and Meyerson, D. E. (2000) 'Theories of gender in organizations: A new approach to organizational analysis and change', Working Paper, *Centre for Gender in Organizations*, Simmons School of Management, Boston.

Enthoven, A. (1985) *Reflections on the Management of the National Health Service: an American looks at incentives to efficiency in health services management in the UK*, Nuffield Provincial Hospitals Trust, London.

Enthoven, A. (1993) 'The history and principles of managed competition', *Health Affairs*, 12 (Suppl.): 24–48.

Ermarth, E. (1992) *Sequel to History: Post-modernism and the Crisis of Representational Time.* Princeton, NJ: Princeton University Press.

Esping-Andersen, G. (2000) 'Two societies, one sociology, and no theory', *British Journal of Sociology*, 51/1: 59–77.

Etzioni, A. (1961) *A Comparative Analysis of Complex Organizations*. New York: Free Press.

Evans-Pritchard, E. E. (1940) *The Nuer*. Oxford: Oxford University Press.

Evered, R. and Louis, M. R. (1981) 'Alternative perspectives in the organizational sciences: "Inquiry from the inside" and "inquiry from the outside" ', *Academy of Management Review*, 6: 385–395.

Fabian, F. H. (2000) 'Keeping the tension: pressures to keep the controversy in the management discipline', *Academy of Management Review*, 25 (2): 350–371.

Fabian, J. (1983) *Time and the Other: How Anthropology Makes its Object*. New York: Columbia University Press.

Fairclough, N. (1992) *Critical Discourse Analysis: The Critical Study of Language.* London and New York: Longman.

Fairclough, N. (1996) *Language and Power*. Harlow: Addison Wesley Longman.

Feyerabend, P. (1970) *Against Method*. Minnesota Studies in the Philosophy of Science. Minnesota: University of Minnesota Press.

Fielding, N. G. and Fielding, J. L. (1986) *Linking Data: Qualitative and Quantitative Methods in Social Research*. Beverley Hills, CA: Sage.

Fischhoff, B. (1975) 'Hindsight not equal to foresight: the effect of outcome knowledge on judgment under uncertainty', *Journal of Experimental Psychology: Human Perception and Performance*, 1: 288–299.

Flax, J. (1990) *Thinking Fragments: Postmodernism, Feminism and Psychoanalysis*. Oxford: University of California Press.

Fleischmann, A. (1924) 'Economic living' *Neue Frauerkleidung und Frauenkultur* (supplement), Karlsruher.

Flick, U. (2003) *An Introduction to Qualitative Research*. London: Sage.

Flood, R. and Romm, N. (1997) 'From metatheory to "multimethodology" ', in J. Mingers and A. Gills (eds), *Multimethodology*, 291–322. New York: John Wiley and Sons.

Fondas, N. (1997) 'Feminisation unveiled, management qualities in contemporary writings', *Academy of Management Review*, 22 (1): 257–282.

Ford, J. D. (1998) 'Organizational change as shifting conversations', *Academy of Management Proceedings*, Organization Development and Change, C1: C7, San Diego.

Ford, J. D. and Ford, L. W. (1994) 'Logics of identity, contradiction, and attraction in change', *Academy of Management Review*, 19: 756–785.

Ford, J. D. and Ford, L. W. (1995) 'The role of conversations in producing intentional change in organizations', *Academy of Management Review*, 20: 541–570.

Forster, N. (1994) 'The analysis of company documentation', in C. Cassell and G. Symon (eds), *Qualitative Methods in Organizational Research*, 147–166. London, Sage.

Foucault, M. (1977) *Discipline and Punish: the Birth of the Prison*. Harmondsworth: Penguin.

Foucault, M. (1980) *Power/Knowledge*. New York: Pantheon.

Foucault, M. (1988) 'The ethic of care for the self as a practice of freedom', in J. Brenauer and D. Rasmussen (eds), *The Final Foucault*. Cambridge, MA: MIT Press.

Foucault, M. (1989) *Resumé des cours*. Paris: Juillard.

Foucault, M. (1991a) 'Governmentality', in G. Burchell, C. Gordon and P. Miller (eds), *The Foucault Effect: Studies in Governmentality: with two lectures by and an interview with Michel Foucault*, 87–104. Chicago: University of Chicago Press.

Foucault, M. (1991b) 'Politics and the study of discourse', in G. Burchell, C. Gordon and P. Miller (eds.), *The Foucault Effect: Studies in Governmentality: With Two Lectures By and an Interview With Michel Foucault*, 53–72. Chicago: University of Chicago Press.

Fournier, V. (2002) 'Fleshing out gender: Crafting identity on women's bodies', *Body and Society*, 8 (2): 55–77.

Fournier, V. and Grey, C. (2000) 'At the critical moment: conditions and prospects for critical management studies', *Human Relations*, 53/1: 7–32.

Frank, A. (1995) *The Wounded Storyteller: Body, Illness and Ethics*. Chicago: The University of Chicago Press.

Fraser, N. (1995) 'Pragmatism, feminism and the linguistic turn', in Benhabib, S., Butler, J., Cornell, D. and Fraser, N. (eds), *Feminist Contentions, A Philosophical Exchange*. New York: Routledge.

French, W. L. and Bell, C. H. Jr. (1999) *Organization Development: Behavioral Science Interventions for Organization Improvement* (6th ed.). Upper Saddle River, NJ: Prentice Hall.

Friedrichs, R. (1970) *A Sociology of Sociology*. New York: Free Press.

Fujimura, J. (1992) 'Crafting science: standardized packages, boundary objects and translation', in A. Pickering (ed.), *Science, Practice and Culture.* Chicago: University of Chicago Press.

Fuller, P. (1989) 'Aesthetics after modernism', in P. Abbs (ed.), *The Symbolic Order: A Contemporary Reader on the Arts Debate*, 126–142. London: The Falmer Press.

Fuller, S. (1999) 'Why Science Studies Have Never Been Critical of Science', *Philosophy of Social Sciences*, 30 (1): 5–32.

Fuss, D. (1996) 'Essentially speaking: feminism, nature and difference', in Eagleton, M. (ed.), *Feminist Literary Theory: A Reader*. Oxford: Blackwell.

Gadamer, H. (1975) *Truth and Method*. London: Sheed and Ward.

Gagliardi, P. (1996) 'Exploring the aesthetic side of organizational life', in S. R. Clegg, C. Hardy and W. R. Nord (eds), *Handbook of Organization Studies*, 565–580. London: Sage.

Gale, R. (ed.) (1968) *The Philosophy of Time: A Collection of Essays*. Sussex: Harvester.

Gallop, J. (1988) *Thinking Through the Body*. New York: Columbia University Press.

Gamble, J., Morris, J. and Wilkinson, B. (2004) 'Mass production is alive and well: the future of work and organization in East Asia', *International Journal of Human Resource Management*, 15: 397–409.

Gearing, E. (1958) 'The structural poses of the 18th century Cherokee villages', *American Anthropologist*, 60: 1148–1157.

Gephart, R. P. (1993) 'The textual approach: Risk and blame in disaster sensemaking', *Academy of Management Journal*, 36: 1465–1514.

Gergen, K. J. (1973) 'Social psychology as history', *Journal of Personality and Social Psychology*, 26: 309–320.

Gergen, K. J. (1982) *Toward Transformation in Social Knowledge.* New York, NY: Springer-Verlag.

Gergen, K. J. (1989) 'Organisational theory in the postmodern era', Paper presented at the Rethinking Organization conference, University of Lancaster, United Kingdom.

Gergen, K. (1992) 'Organization theory in the postmodern era', in M. Reed and M. Hughes (eds), *Rethinking Organization: New Directions in Organization Theory and Analysis*, 207–226. London: Sage.

Gergen, K. J. (2001) 'Psychological science in a postmodern context', *American Psychologist*, 56: 803–813.

Gergen, K. J. and Thatchenkery, T. J. (1996) 'Organization science as social construction: Postmodern potential', *Journal of Applied Behavioral Science*, 32: 356–377.

Gersick, C. G. (1991) 'Revolutionary change theories: A multilevel exploration of the punctuated equilibrium paradigm', *Academy of Management Review*, 16: 10–36.

Ghauri, P. and Gronberg, K. (2002) *Research Methods in Business Studies* (2nd ed.). London: Prentice Hall.

Gherardi, S. (1995) *Gender, Symbolism and Organizational Cultures.* London: Sage.

Gherardi, S. and Nicolini, D. (2000) 'To transfer is to transform: the circulation of safety knowledge', *Organization*, 7 (2): 329–348.

Giddens, A. (1984) *The Constitution of Society: Outline of the Theory of Structuration*. Berkeley: University of California Press.

Giddens, A. (1990) *The Consequences of Modernity*. Cambridge: Polity Press.

Giddens, A. (1991) *Modernity and Self-Identity*. Cambridge: Polity Press.

Gill, R. (1995) 'Relativism, reflexivity and politics: Interrogating discourse analysis from a feminist perspective', in Wilkinson, S. and Kitzinger, C. (eds), *Feminism and Discourse*. London: Sage.

Gioia, D. and Pitre, E. (1989) 'Multi-paradigm Perspectives on Theory Building', *Academy of Management Review*, 5 (4): 584–602.

Gioia, D. and Pitre, E. (1990) 'Multiparadigm perspectives on theory building', *Academy of Management Review*, 15 (4): 584–602.

Gioia, D., Thomas, J., Clark, S. and Chittipeddi, K. (1994) 'Symbolism and strategic change in academia: The dynamics of sensemaking and influence', *Organization Science*, 5: 363–383.

Gioscia, V. (1972) 'On social time', in H. Yaker, H. Osmond and F. Cheek (eds), *The Future of Time*. New York: Anchor Books.

Glaser, B. G. and Strauss, A. (1965) 'Temporal aspects of dying', *American Journal of Sociology*, 71: 48–59.

Goffman, E. (1974) *Frame Analysis*. Cambridge, MA: Harvard University Press.

Golden, B. R. (1992) 'The past is the past — or is it? The use of retrospective accounts as indicators of past strategy', *Academy of Management Journal*, 35: 848–860.

Golden, B. R. (1997) 'Further remarks on retrospective accounts in organizational and strategic management research', *Academy of Management Journal*, 40: 1243–1252.

Golden-Biddle, K. and Locke, K. D. (1997) *Composing Qualitative Research*. Thousand Oaks, CA: Sage.

Goldman, P. and Van Houten, D. (1977) 'Managerial strategies and the worker', *Sociological Quarterly*, 18 (1): 108–125.

Golembiewski, R. T. (1998) 'Appreciating appreciative inquiry: Diagnosis and perspectives on how to do better', *Research in Organizational Change and Development*, 11, 1–45.

Gomart, E. and Hennion, A. (1999) 'A sociology of attachment: music amateurs, drug users', in J. Law and J. Hassard (eds), *Actor Network Theory and After*. Oxford: Blackwell.

Gordon, C. (1991) 'Government rationality: an introduction', in G. Burchell, C. Gordon and P. Miller (eds), *The Foucault Effect: Studies in Governmentality*. Chicago: University of Chicago Press.

Gordon, C. and P. Miller (eds) (1991) *The Foucault Effect: Studies in Governmentality*, 1–51. Chicago: University of Chicago Press.

Gouldner, A. (1970) *The Coming Crisis of Western Sociology*. London: Heinemann.

Government response. *Ministerial review of Health Care Networks* (2000) Melbourne, Victoria, State Government of Victoria, May.

Graham, R. J. (1981) 'The perception of time in consumer research', *Journal of Consumer Research*, 7: 335–342.

Graham, F. (2003) *Inside the Japanese Company*. London: RoutledgeCurzon.

Graham, F. (2005) *A Japanese Company in Crisis: Ideology, Strategy and Narrative*. London: Routledge Curzon.

Grant, D., Keenoy, T. and Oswick, C. (1998) 'Introduction: Organizational discourse: Of diversity, dichotomy and multi-disciplinarity', in D. Grant, T. Keenoy and C. Oswick (eds), *Discourse and Organization*, 1–13. London: Sage.

Grazia, S. de (1972) 'Time and work', in H. Yaker, H. Osmond and F. Cheek (eds), *The Future of Time*. New York: Anchor Books.

Grazia, S. de (1974) *Of Time, Work and Leisure*. New York: Anchor Books.

Green, F. (2001) 'It's been a hard day's night: The concentration and intensification of work in late twentieth-century Britain', *British Journal of Industrial Relations*, 1 (39): 53–80.

Greenberg, C. (1996) 'Bauhaus: A look back at the future', *Art and Antiques*, October, 66–73.

Grey, C. (2004) 'Reinventing business schools: the contribution of critical management education', *Academy of Management Learning and Education*, 3 (2): 178–186.

Grey, C., Knights, D. and Willmott, H. (1996) 'Is a critical pedagogy of management possible?', in R. French and C. Grey (eds), *Rethinking Management Education*, 94–110. London: Sage.

Grimes, A. J. and Rood, D. L. (1995) 'Beyond objectivism and relativism: Descriptive epistemologies', in J. P. Jones III, W. Natter and T. R. Scharzki (eds), *Objectivity and its Other*, 161–178. New York: Guildford.

Grint, K. (1991) *The Sociology of Work*. Cambridge: Polity.

Grint, K. (1998) *The Sociology of Work*. Cambridge: Polity.

Grint, K. and Woolgar, S. (1997) *The Machine at Work*. Cambridge: Polity.

Gropius, W. (1919) *Bauhaus Manifesto*. Staatliches Bauhaus: Weimar.

Guba, E. and Lincoln, Y. (1994) 'Competing paradigms in qualitative research', in N. K. Denzin and Y. S. Lincoln (eds), *Handbook of Qualitative Research*, 105–117. Thousand Oaks: Sage.

Gurdon, P. T. R. (1914) *The Khasis*. London: Royal Anthropological Institute (Reprinted 1981 by Cosmos Publications, New Delhi).

Gurvitch, G. (1964) *The Spectrum of Social Time*. Dordrecht: D. Reidel.

Habermas, J. (1998) *On the Pragmatics of Communication*. London: Polity.

Habers, H. and Koenis, S. (1996) 'The political eggs of the chicken debate', *EASST Review*, 15 (1): 9–15.

Halford, S. and Leonard, P. (2001) *Gender, Power and Organizations*. London: Palgrave.

Hall, W. and Callery, P. (2001) 'Enhancing the rigor of grounded theory: Incorporating reflexivity and relationality', *Qualitative Health Research*, 11: 257–273.

Hammersley, M. (1992) *What's Wrong with Ethnography*? London: Routledge.

Hammersley, M. (1995) *The Politics of Social Research*. London: Sage.

Hampshire, S. (1959) *Thought and Action*. London: Chatto and Windus.

Hancock, P. (2005) 'Uncovering the semiotic in organizational aesthetics', *Organization: The Interdisciplinary Journal of Organization, Theory and Society*, 12 (1): 29–60.

Hancock, P. and Tyler, M. (2002) *Work, Postmodernism and Organisation: A Critical Introduction*. London: Sage.

Hansen, A. and Mouritsen, J. (1999) 'Managerial technology and netted networks. competitiveness in action: The work of translating performance in a high-tech firm', *Organization*, 6 (3): 451–472.

Hansen, C. J. (1995) 'Writing the project team: Authority and intertextuality in a corporate setting', *Journal of Business Communication*, 32: 103–122.

Hansen, M. B. (1997) 'Mass culture as hieroglyphic writing: Adorno, Derrida, Kracauer', in Max Pensky (ed.), *The Actuality of Adorno*, 83–111. Albany, NY: State University of New York Press.

Hanson, N. (1958) *Patterns of Discovery*. Cambridge University Press: Cambridge.

Haraway, D. (1988) 'Situated knowledges: The science question in feminism and the privilege of partial perspective', *Feminist Studies*, 14: 75–99.

Haraway, D. (1989) *Primate Visions: Gender, Race and Nature in the World of Modern Science*. New York: Routledge.

Haraway, D. (1991) *Simians, Cyborgs and Women: The Reinvention of Nature*. London: Free Association Books.

Haraway, D. (1997) Modest Witness@SecondMillennium.FemaleMan_Meets_Oncomouse™: Feminism and Technoscience. New York and London: Routledge.

Harding, J. M. (1997) *Adorno and 'A Writing of the Ruins'*. Albany, NY: State University of New York Press.

Hardy, C. (2001) 'Researching organisational discourse', *International Studies in Management and Organisation*, 31 (3): 25–47.

Hardy, C. and Clegg, S. (1997) 'Relativity without relativism: Reflexivity in post-paradigm organization studies', *British Journal of Management*, 8 (Special Issue), S5–S17.

Hardy, C. and Phillips, N. (1999) 'No joking matter: Discursive struggle in the Canadian refugee system', *Organization Studies*, 20: 1–24.

Hardy, C., Phillips, N. and Clegg, S. (2001) 'Reflexivity in organization and management studies: A study of the production of the research "subject"', *Human Relations*, 54: 3–32.

Hardy, C., Phillips, N. and Lawrence, T. B. (1998) 'Distinguishing between trust and power in interorganizational relations: Forms and façades of trust', in C. Lane and R. Bachman (eds), *Trust Within and Between Organizations*, 64–87. Oxford, UK: Oxford University Press.

Harré, R. (1974) 'Blueprint for a new science', in N. Armistead (ed.), *Reconstructing Social Psychology*, 240–259. Harmondsworth: Penguin.

Harré, R. (1979) *Social Being*. Oxford: Basil Blackwell.

Harré, R. (1986) 'Ethogenics', in R. Harré and R. Lamb (eds), *The Dictionary Of Personality and Social Psychology*, 102–105. Oxford: Basil Blackwell.

Harré, R. and Secord, P. F. (1972) *The Explanation of Social Behaviour*. Oxford: Basil Blackwell.

Harrison, C. (1991) *Essays on Art and Language*. Oxford: Blackwell.

Harvey, D. (1989) *The Condition of Postmodernity*. Oxford: Blackwell.

Harvey, D. F. and Brown, D. R. (1996) *An Experiential Approach to Organization Development* (5th ed.). Upper Saddle River, NJ: Prentice-Hall.

Harvey, J. and Weary, G. (1981) *Perspectives of Attributional Processes*. Iowa: Wm. C. Brown Company.

Hassard, J. (1985) *Multiple Paradigms and Organizational Research: An Analysis of Work Behaviour in the Fire Service*. Unpublished doctoral dissertation, University of Aston, UK.

Hassard, J. (1988) 'Overcoming hermeticism in organization theory: an alternative to paradigm incommensurability', *Human Relations*, 41 (3): 247–259.

Hassard, J. (1989) 'Toward a qualitative paradigm for working time', *International Social Science Journal*, 119: 93–104.

Hassard, J. (1990) 'Introduction', in J. Hassard (ed.), *The Sociology of Time*. London: Macmillan.

Hassard, J. (1991) 'Multiple paradigms and organizational analysis: a case study', *Organization Studies*, 12 (2): 279–299.

Hassard, J. (1993a) 'Postmodernism and organizational analysis: An overview', in J. Hassard and M. Parker (eds), *Postmodernism and Organizations*. London: Sage.

Hassard, J. (1993b) *Sociology and Organization Theory: Positivism, Paradigms and Postmodernity*. Cambridge: Cambridge University Press.

Hassard, J. (1994) Postmodern organizational analysis: Towards a conceptual framework, *Journal of Management Studies*, 31 (3): 303–324.

Hassard, J. (1996) *Sociology and Organization Theory*. Cambridge: Cambridge University Press.

Hassard, J. (2001) 'Commodification, construction and compression: A review of time metaphors in organisational analysis', *International Journal of Management Reviews*, 3: 131–140.

Hassard, J. (2002) 'Organizational time: Modern, symbolic and postmodern reflections', *Organisation Studies*, 23: 885–892.

Hassard, J. and Holliday, R. (eds) (1998) *Organisation/Representation: Work and Organisations in Popular Culture*. London: Sage.

Hassard, J., Holliday, R. and Willmott, H. (eds) (2000) *Body and Organization*. London: Sage.

Hassard, J. and Kelemen, M. (2002) 'Production and consumption in organizational knowledge: The case of the paradigms debate', *Organization: the Interdisciplinary Journal of Organization, Theory and Society*, 9 (2): 331–356.

Hassard, J., Law, J. and Lee, N. (1999) 'Introduction: actor-network theory and managerialism', *Organization*, 6 (3): 387–391.

Hassard, J. and Parker, M. (eds) (1993) *Postmodernism and Organizations*. London: Sage.

Hatch, M.-J. (1993) 'The dynamics of organizational culture', *Academy of Management Review*, 18 (4): 657–693.

Hatch, M.-J. (1999) *Organization Theory*. Oxford: Oxford University Press.

Hearn, J. (2000) 'On the complexity of feminist intervention in organizations', *Organization*, 7 (4): 609–624.

Heath, L. R. (1956) *The Concept of Time*. Chicago: University of Chicago Press.

Heidegger, M. (1966) *Discourse on Thinking: a Translation of gelassenheit* by J. M. Anderson and E. H. Freund. New York: Harper and Row.

Hermans, H. J. M. (1991) 'The person as co-investigator in self-research: valuation theory', *European Journal of Personality*, 5: 217–234.

Herts, R. (ed.) (1997) *Reflexivity and Voice*. Thousand Oak and London: Sage.

Hewstone, M. and Agoustinos, M. (1998) 'Social attributions and social representations', in U. Flick (ed.), *The Psychology of the Social*, 60–76. New York, NY: Cambridge University Press.

Hindess, B. (1996) *Discourses of Power: From Hobbes to Foucault*. Oxford: Blackwell.

Hine, C. (1995) 'Representations of information technology in disciplinary development: disappearing plants and invisible networks', *Science, Technology and Human Values*, 20 (1): 65–85.

Hirsch, E. and Olsen, G. A. (1995) 'Je-Luce Irigaray: A meeting with Luce Irigaray', *Hypatia*, 10 (2): 93–114.

Hochman, E. S. (1997) *Bauhaus: Crucible of Modernism*. New York: Fromm International.

Hodson, T. C. (1908) *The Meitheis*. London: Unwin.

Holland, R. (1999) 'Reflexivity', *Human Relations*, 52/4: 463–484.

Holliday, R. and Hassard, J. (eds) (2001) *Contested Bodies*. London: Routledge.

Hopfl, H. (1994) 'The paradoxical gravity of planned organizational change', *Journal of Organizational Change Management*, 7: 20–31.

Horowitz, G. M. (1997) 'Art history and autonomy', in T. Huhn and L. Zuidervaart (eds), *The Semblance of Subjectivity: Essays in Adorno's Aesthetic Theory*, 177–212. Cambridge, MA and London: The MIT Press.

Hospital services report (2000) Melbourne, Victoria, Australia, Department of Human Services, June quarter.

Howard, J. (1996) *Art Nouveau: International and National Styles in Europe*. Manchester and New York: Manchester University Press.

Hubert, H. (1905) 'Etude sommaire de la representation du temps dans la religion et la magie', *Annuaire de l'Ecole Pratique des Hautes Etudes*, 1–39.

Hubert, H. and Mauss, M. (1909) *Mélanges d'Histoire des Religions*. Paris: Alcan.

Hughes, E. C. (1971) *The Sociological Eye*. New York: Aldine.

Huhn, T. (1997) 'Kant, Adorno, and the social opacity of the aesthetic', in T. Huhn and L. Zuidervaart (eds), *The Semblance of Subjectivity: Essays in Adorno's Aesthetic Theory*, 238–257. Cambridge, MA and London: The MIT Press.

Huhn, T. and Zuidervaart, L. (eds) *The Semblance of Subjectivity: Essays in Adorno's Aesthetic Theory*, 29–53. Cambridge, MA and London: The MIT Press.

Hull, R. (1999) 'Actor network and conduct: the discipline and practices of knowledge management', *Organization*, 6 (3): 405–428.

Huyssen, A. (1984) 'Mapping the postmodern', *New German Critique*, 33: 5–52.

Introna, L. and Whitley, E. (1997) 'Against method-*ism*: Exploring the limits of method', *Information, Technology and People*, 10 (1): 31–45.

Introna, L. and Whitley, E. (1997) 'Imagine: Thought experiments in information systems research', in A. Lee, J. Liebenau and J. De Gross (eds), *Information Systems and Qualitative Research*. London: Chapman and Hall.

Ioannou, N. (1997/1998) 'Collaboration in glass', *Craft Arts International*, 41: 61.

Irigaray, L. (1985a) *Speculum of the Other Woman*, translation by C. Porter and C. Burke. Ithaca: Cornell University Press.

Irigaray, L. (1985b) *This Sex Which is Not One*, translation by G. Gill. Ithaca: Cornell University Press.

Irigaray, L. (1991a) *Philosophy in the Feminine*, M. Whitford (ed.). Oxford: Basil Blackwell.

Irigaray, L. (1991b) 'The power of discourse and the subordination of the feminine', *The Irigaray Reader*, M. Whitford (ed.). Oxford: Blackwell.

Irigaray, L. (1993a) *Je, Tu, Nous, Towards a Culture of Difference*, translation by A. Martin. London: Routledge.

Irigaray, L. (1993b) *Sexes and Genealogies*. New York: Columbia University Press.

Irigaray, L. (1993c) *An Ethics of Sexual Difference*, translation by C. Burke and G. Gill. Ithaca: Cornell University Press.

Irigaray L. (1995) 'The question of the other', *Yale French Studies*, 20 (87): 7–19.

Irigaray, L. (2000) *To be Two*, translated by M. M. Rhodes and M. F. Cocito-Monoc. London: Athlone Press.

Irigaray, L. (2002) *To Speak is Never Neutral*. London: Continuum Press.

Isabella, L. A. (1990) 'Evolving interpretations as change unfolds: How managers construe key organizational events', *Academy of Management Journal*, 33: 7–41.

Isambert, F.-A. (1979) 'Henri Hubert et la sociologie du temps', *Revue Française de Sociologie*, 20: 183–204.

Jackson, B. G. (1999) 'The goose that laid the golden egg?: A rhetorical critique of Stephen Covey and the effectiveness movement', *Journal of Management Studies*, 36: 353–377.

Jackson, N. and Carter, P. (1991) 'In defence of paradigm commensurability', *Organization Studies*, 12 (1): 109–127.

Jackson, S. (1999) 'Feminist sociology and sociological feminist: Recovering the social in feminist thought', *Sociological Research Online*, 4 (3), 1–17.

Jacques, R. (1992) 'Critique and theory building: Producing knowledge "from the kitchen"', *Academy of Management Review*, 17: 582–606.

Jacques, R. (1997) 'Classic review: The empire strikes out: Lyotard's postmodern condition and the need for a "necrology of knowledge"', *Organization*, 4: 130–142.

Jaffee, D. (2001) *Organization Theory: Tension and Change*. New York: McGraw Hill.

Janesick, V. (1994) 'The dance of qualitative research design: Metaphor, methodolatry, and meaning', in N. K. Denzin and Y. S. Lincoln (eds), *Handbook of Qualitative Research*, 209–219. Thousand Oaks: Sage.

Jaques, E. (1982) *The Form of Time*. London: Heinemann.

Jay, M. (1997) 'Mimesis and mimetology: Adorno and Lacoue-Labarthe', in T. Huhn and L. Zuidervaart (eds), *The Semblance of Subjectivity: Essays in Adorno's Aesthetic Theory*. Cambridge: MIT Press.

Jeffcutt, P. (1994) 'The interpretation of organization: A contemporary analysis and critique', *Journal of Management Studies*, 31: 225–250.

Jensen, C. and Lauritsen, P. (2005) 'Qualitative research as partial connection', *Qualitative Research*, 5 (1): 59–77.

Jick, T. D. (1984) 'Mixing qualitative and quantitative methods: Triangulation in action', in J. S. Bateman and T. R. Ferris (eds), *Methods And Analysis in Organisational Research*, 364–372. Reston: Reston Publishing.

Johnson, P. and Duberley, J. (2003) 'Reflexivity in management research', *Journal of Management Studies*, 40/5: 1279–1303.

Jones, C., Hesterly, W. S. and Borgatti, S. P. (1997), 'A general theory of network governance: Exchange conditions and social mechanisms', *Academy of Management Review*, 22: 911–945.

Jones, C. and O'Doherty, D. (eds) (2005) *Manifestos for the Business School of Tomorrow*. London: Dvarlin.

Jones, C. and Munro, R. (eds) (2005) *Contemporary Organization Theory*. Oxford: Blackwell.

Jones, G., McLean, C. and Quattrone, P. (2004) 'Spacing and timing', *Organization*, 11 (6): 723–741.

Jones, T. M. (1995) 'Instrumental stakeholder theory: A synthesis of ethics and economics', *Academy of Management Review*, 20: 404–437.

Julkunnen, R. A. (1977) 'A contribution to the categories of social time and the economies of time', *Acta Sociologica*, 20: 5–24.

Kaghan, W. and Phillips, N. (1998) 'Building the Tower of Babel: communities of practice and paradigmatic pluralism in organization studies', *Organization*, 5 (2): 191–215.

Kallinikos, J. (1997) 'Classic review: Science, knowledge and society: The Postmodern Condition revisited', *Organization*, 4: 114–129.

Kamata, S. (1982) *Life in the Passing Lane: An Insider's Account of Life in a Japanese Auto Factory*. London: Counterpoint.

Kant, Immanuel (1952) *Critique of Judgment*, trans. J. C. Meredith. Oxford: Clarendon Press.

Keenoy, T. (1999) 'HRM as hologram: A polemic', *Journal of Management Studies*, 36: 1–23.

Keenoy, T., Oswick, C. and Grant, D. (1997) 'Organisational discourses: Text and context', *Organization*, 4: 147–157.

Keim, J. (1993) 'Triangulation and the art of negotiation', *Journal of Systemic Therapies*, 12: 76–87.

Kelemen, M. and Hassard, J. (1997) 'Critical issues in multiple paradigm research', working paper, University of Keele.

Kelley, H. H. (1973) 'The process of causal attribution', *American Psychologist*, 28: 107–128.

Kelly, M. (2000) 'The political autonomy of contemporary art: the case of the 1993 Whitney Biennial', in S. Kemal and I. Gaskell (eds), *Politics and Aesthetics in the Arts*, 221–263. Cambridge: Cambridge University Press.

Kickert, W. (1993) 'Autopoiesis and the science of (public) administration: essence, sense and nonsense', *Organization Studies*, 14/2: 261–278.

Kieser, A. (1997) 'Rhetoric and myth in management fashion', *Organization*, 4 (1): 49–74.

Kilduff, M. (1993) 'Deconstructing organizations', *Academy of Management Review*, 18: 13–31.

Kilduff, M. and Mehra, A. (1997) 'Postmodernism and organisational research', *Academy of Management Review*, 22 (2): 453–481.

Kimberley, J., de Pouvourville, G. and Associates (1993) *The Migration of Managerial Innovation: Diagnosis Related Groups and Health Care Administration in Western Europe*. San Francisco: Jossey-Bass.

Kleinert, S. (1992) 'Deconstructing "The decorative": The impact of Euro-American artistic traditions on the reception of aboriginal art and craft', in N. Ioannou (ed.), *Craft in Society*, 115–130. South Fremantle, Western Australia: Freemantle Arts Centre Press.

Knights, D. (1997) 'Organization theory in the age of deconstruction: dualism, gender and postmodernism revisited', *Organization Studies*, 18 (1): 1–19.

Knights, D. and Morgan, G. (1994) 'Organization theory, consumption and the service sector', in J. Hassard and M. Parker (eds), *Towards a New Theory of Organizations*, 131–152. London and New York: Routledge.

Knights, D., Murray, F. and Willmott, H. (1993) 'Networking as knowledge work: A study of strategic inter-organizational development in the financial services industry', *Journal of Management Studies*, 30 (6): 975–995.

Kozel, S. (1996) 'The diabolical strategy of mimesis: Luce Irigaray's reading of Maurice Merleau-Ponty', *Hypatia*, 11 (3): 114–130.

Kritzman, L. D. (ed.) (1988) *Michel Foucault: Politics, Philosophy, Culture: Interviews And Other Writings, 1977–1984*. London and New York: Routledge.

Kroeber, A. L. (1923) *Anthropology*. New York: Charles Scribner.

Kuhn, T. (1974) *The Essential Tension: Selected Studies in Scientific Tradition and Change*. Chicago: University of Chicago Press.

Kuhn, T. S. (1962, 1970) *The Structure of Scientific Revolutions*. Chicago: The University of Chicago Press.

Kuspit, D. (1996) 'Craft in art, art as craft', *The New Art Examiner*, 23 (April): 14–53.

Kuznets, S. (1933) *Seasonal Variations in Industry and Trade*. New York: National Bureau of Economic Research.

Lacombe, D. (1996) 'Reforming Foucault: A critique of the social control thesis', *British Journal of Sociology*, 47: 332–352.

Lakatos, I. and Musgrave, A. (eds) (1970) *Criticism and the Growth of Knowledge*. Cambridge: Cambridge University Press.

Lakoff, G. and Johnson, M. (1980) *Metaphors We Live By*. Chicago: University of Chicago Press.

Landes, D. S. (1983) *Revolution in Time: Clocks and the Making of the Modern World*. Cambridge, MA: Belknap Press of Harvard University Press.

Laslett, P. (1965) *The World We Have Lost*. London: Methuen.

Latour, B. (1987) *Science in Action*. Milton Keynes: Open University Press.

Latour, B. (1988) *The Pastueurization of France*. Cambridge, MA: Harvard University Press.

Latour, B. (1991) 'Technology is society made more durable', in J. Law (ed.), *A Sociology of Monsters: Essays on Power, Technology and Domination*. London: Routledge.

Latour, B. (1992) 'Where are the missing masses?', in W. Bijker and J. Law (eds), *Shaping Technology/Building Society*. Cambridge, MA: MIT Press.

Latour, B. (1994) (trans. Porter, C.) *We Have Never Been Modern*. London: Harvester Wheatsheaf.

Latour, B. (1996) *Aramis, or the Love of Technology*. Cambridge, MA: MIT Press.

Latour, B. (1997) 'The trouble with actor-network theory', *Soziale Welt*, 47: 369–381.

Latour, B. (1999a) 'On recalling ANT', in J. Law and J. Hassard (eds), *Actor Network Theory and After*. Oxford: Blackwell.

Latour, B. (1999b) *Pandora's Hope: Essays on the Reality of Science Studies*. Cambridge, MA: Harvard University Press.

Latour, B. (2002) *'Gabriel Tarde and the End of the Social' in the Social in Question. New Bearings in the History and the Social Sciences*, 117–132, (ed.) P. Patrick Joyce. London: Routledge.

Latour, B. (2003) 'What if we talked of politics a little', *Contemporary Political Theory*, 2 (2): 143–164.

Latour, B. (2004a) *Politics of Nature: How to Bring the Sciences into Democracy*. Cambridge, MA: Harvard University Press.

Latour, B. (2004b) 'How to talk about the body? The normative dimension of science studies', special issue edited by Madeleine Akrich and Marc Berg, 'Bodies on Trial' M. Marc Berg and M. Akrich (2004) 'Introduction Bodies on Trial: Performances and Politics in Medicine and Biology', *Body and Society*, 10: 1–12 special issue of Body and Society, 10 (2/3): 205–229 (2004).

Latour, B. (2005) *Reassembling the Social*. Oxford: Oxford University Press.

Latour, B. and Johnson, J. (1988) 'Mixing humans and non-humans: sociology of a door-opener', *Social Problems*, 35, 298–310.

Latour, B. and Hermant, P. (1998) *Paris Ville Invisible*. Paris: La Decouverte-Les Empecheurs de Penser en Rond.

Latour, B. and Weibel, P. (2005) *Making Things Public: Atmospheres of Democracy*. Cambridge, MA: MIT Press.

Lauer, R. H. (1980) *Temporal Man*. New York: Praeger.

Law, J. (1987) 'Technology and heterogeneous engineering: The case of Portuguese expansion', in W. Bijker, T. Hughes and T. Pinch (eds), *The Social Construction of Technological Systems: New Directions in the Sociology of Knowledge*. Cambridge, MA: The MIT Press.

Law, J. (1991a) 'Introduction', in J. Law (ed.), *A Sociology of Monsters: Essays on Power, Technology and Domination*. London: Routledge.

Law, J. (1991b) *A Sociology of Monsters: Essays on Power Technology and Domination*. London: Routledge.

Law, J. (1994) *Organising Modernity*. Oxford: Blackwell.

Law, J. (1997) 'Heterogeneities', paper presented at the Uncertainty, Knowledge and Skill Conference, Limburg University, Belgium, November.

Law, J. (1999) 'After ANT: complexity, naming and topology', in J. Law and J. Hassard (eds), *Actor Network Theory and After*. Oxford: Blackwell.

Law, J. (2004) *After Method: Mess in Social Science Research*. London: Routledge.

Law, J. and Hassard, J. (eds) (1999) *Actor Network Theory and After*. Oxford: Blackwell.

Law, J. and Singleton, V. (2005) 'Object lessons', *Organization*, 12 (3): 331–355.

Lawrence, P. and Lorsch, J. (1967) *Organization and Environment*. Cambridge, MA: Harvard University Press.

Lawrence, T. B., Phillips, N. and Hardy, C. (1999) 'Watching whale watching: Exploring the discursive foundations of collaborative relationships', *Journal of Applied Behavioural Science*, 35: 479–502.

Lawson, H. (1985) *Reflexivity: The Post Modern Predicament*. London: Hutchinson.

Lee, N. (1998) 'Two speeds: how are real stabilities possible?', in R. Chia (ed.), *Organized Worlds: Explorations in Technology and Organization with Robert Cooper*. London: Routledge.

Lee, N. and Brown, S. (1994) 'Otherness and the actor-network: the undiscovered continent', *American Behavioural Scientist*, 37 (6): 772–790.

Lee, N. and Hassard, J. (1999) 'Organization unbound: actor-network theory, research strategy and institutional flexibility', *Organization*, 6 (3): 391–405.

Lee, N. and Stenner, P. (1996) 'Who pays? Can we pay them back?', paper presented at the Actor Network and After Workshop, Keele University, September.

Lee, T. W. (1999) *Using Qualitative Methods in Organizational Research*. Thousand Oaks: Sage.

Leibler, C. J. (1997) 'Getting comfortable with appreciative inquiry', *Global Social Innovation*, 2: 30–40.

Lengel, L. B. (1998) 'Researching the "other", transforming ourselves: Methodological considerations of feminist ethnography', *Journal of Communication Inquiry*, 22 (3): 229–253.

Levi-Strauss, C. (1950) 'Introduction', in M. Mauss (ed.), *Sociologie et Anthropologie*. Paris: Presses Universitaires de France.

Levi-Strauss, C. (1966) *The Savage Mind*. London: Weidenfeld and Nicholson.

Levi-Strauss, C. (1979) *The Raw and the Cooked*. London: Routledge and Kegan Paul.

Lewin, K. (1951) *Field Theory in Social Science: Selected Theoretical Papers*. Kurt Lewin. D. Cartwright (ed.), New York: Harper Torchbooks.

Lewis, M. (2000) 'Exploring paradox: towards a more comprehensive guide', *Academy of Management Review*, 25 (4): 760–777.

Lewis, M. W. and Grimes, A. J. (1999) 'Metatriangulation: building theory from multiple paradigms', *Academy of Management Review*, 24 (4): 672–690.

Limerick, D., Cunnington, B. and Crowther, F. (1998) *Managing The New Organization: Collaboration and Sustainability in the Post-Corporate World* (2nd ed.). Warriewood, NSW: Business and Professional Publishing.

Linell, P. (1998) 'Discourse across boundaries: On recontextualizations and the blending of voices in professional discourse', *Text*, 18: 143–157.

Linstead, S. (1993) 'Deconstruction in the study of organizations', in J. Hassard and M. Parker (eds), *Postmodernism and Organizations*, 49–70. London: Sage.

Linstead, S. (1996) 'Understanding management: Culture, critique and change', in S. Linstead, R. Grafton Small and P. Jeffcutt (eds), *Understanding Management*, 11–33. London: Sage.

Linstead, S., Grafton Small, R. and Jeffcutt, P. (eds) (1996) *Understanding Management*, 11–33. London: Sage.

Linstead, S. and Höpfl, H. (eds) (2000) *The Aesthetics of Organization*. London: Sage.

Louie, T. A., Curren, M. T. and Harich, K. R. (2000) '"I knew we could win": Hindsight bias for favourable and unfavourable team decision outcomes', *Journal of Applied Psychology*, 85: 264–272.

Lucie-Smith, E. (1981) *The Story of Craft: The Craftsman's Role in Society*. Oxford: Phaidon.

Ludema, J. D., Wilmot, T. B. and Srivastva, S. (1997) 'Organizational hope: Reaffirming the constructive task of social and organizational inquiry', *Human Relations*, 50: 1015–1052.

Luhmann, N. (1986) 'The autopoiesis of social systems', in F. Geyer and J. Van den Zouwen (eds), *Sociocybernetic Paradoxes*. London: Sage.

Luthans, F. and Davis, T. R. V. (1982) 'An ideographic approach to organizational behavior', *Academy of Management Review*, 7: 380–391.

Lynch, M. (2000) 'Against reflexivity as academic virtue and source of privileged knowledge', *Theory, Culture, Society*, 17/3: 26–54.

Lyotard, J.-F. (1984) *The Postmodern Condition: A Report on Knowledge*. Manchester: Manchester University Press.

Lyotard, J.-F. (1997) *The Postmodern Condition: A Report on Knowledge*. Manchester: Manchester University Press (first published 1984).

Macbeth, D. (2001) 'On "reflexivity" in qualitative research. Two readings, and a third', *Qualitative Inquiry*, 7: 35–68.

McCloskey, D. N. (1994) *Knowledge and Persuasion in Economics*. Cambridge: Cambridge University Press.

Macdonald, K. and Tipton, C. (1996) 'Using documents', in N. Gilbert (ed.), *Researching Social Life*, 187–200. London: Sage.

McGrath, J. E. and Rotchford, N. L. (1983) 'Time and behaviour in organizations', *Research in Organizational Behaviour*, 5: 57–101.

MacIntyre, A. (1985) *After Virtue: A Study in Moral Theory*. London: Duckworth.

McKelvey, B. (1997) 'Quasi-natural organization science', *Organization Science*, 8: 352–380.

McKelvey, B. (2003) 'From subjectivity to objectivity: a constructionist account of objectivity in organization', in R. Westwood and S. Clegg (eds), *Debating Organization: Point-Counterpoint in Organization Theory*, 142–156. Oxford: Blackwell.

McKendall, M. (1993), 'The tyranny of change: Organizational development revisited', *Journal of Business Ethics*, 12: 93–104.

McKendrick, N. (1962) 'Josiah Wedgwood and the factory discipline', *The Historical Journal*, 4: 30–35.

McKinley, W. (1995) 'Commentary: towards a reconciliation of the theory-pluralism in strategic management — incommensurability and the constructivist approach of the Erlangen School', *Advances in Strategic Management*, 12A: 249–260.

McKinley, W. and Mone, M. A. (1998) 'The re-construction of organization studies: wrestling with incommensurability', *Organization*, 5 (2): 169–189.

McKinley, W., Mone, M. A. and Moon, G. (1999) 'Determinants and development of schools in organization theory', *Academy of Management Review*, 24 (4): 634–648.

MacLachlan, G. and Reid, I. (1994) *Framing and Interpretation*. Melbourne, Australia: Melbourne University Press.

McLean, C. and Quattrone, P. (2005) 'On theorising the Object: Insights from Gabriel Tarde', paper presented at the Workshop on Gabriel Tarde, Goldsmith College, London, December.

Macnaghten, P. and Urry, J. (1998) *Contested Natures*. London: Sage.

McNay, L. (1992) *Foucault and Feminism*. Cambridge: Polity Press.

Manning, P. (1979) 'Metaphors of the field', *Administrative Science Quarterly*, 24: 660–671.

March, J. G., Sproull, L. S. and Tamuz, M. (1991) 'Learning from samples of one or fewer', *Organization Science*, 2: 1–13.

March, J. G. with R. I. Sutton (1999) 'Organizational performance as a dependent variable', in J. G. March (ed.), *The Pursuit of Organizational Intelligence*, 338–354. Malden, MA: Blackwell.

Marincola, P. (1995) 'Fabric as fine art: Thinking across the divide', *Fiberarts*, 22 (5): 34–39.

Markowitz, S. J. (1994) 'The distinction between art and craft', *Journal of Aesthetic Education*, 28 (1): 55–70.

Marsden, R. (1993) 'The politics of organizational analysis', *Organization Studies*, 14: 93–124.

Marsh, P., Rosser, E. and Harré, R. (1978) *The Rules of Disorder*. London: Routledge and Kegan Paul.

Marshall, J. (2000) 'Revisiting Simone de Beauviour: Recognizing feminist contributions to pluralism in organization studies', *Journal of Management Inquiry*, 9 (2): 166–173.

Martinko, M. J. and Thomson, N. F. (1998) 'A synthesis and extension of the Weiner and Kelley attribution models', *Basic and Applied Social Psychology*, 20: 271–284.

Marx, K. (1976) *Capital, Vol 1* (first published 1867). Harmondsworth: Penguin.

Maturana, H. (1981) 'Autopoiesis', in M. Zeleny (ed.), *Autopoiesis: A Theory of Living Organisation*. New York: North Holland.

Mauss, M. (1966) *Sociologie et Anthropologie*. Paris: Presses Universitaires de France.

Mauws, M. K. and Phillips, N. (1995) 'Understanding language games', *Organization Science*, 6 (3): 322–334.

Merton, R. K. (1975) 'Structural analysis in sociology', in P. M. Blau (ed.), *Approaches to the Study of Social Structures*, New York: Free Press.

Metcalf, B. (1993) 'Replacing the myth of modernism', *American Craft*, 53 (February–March): 40–47.

Metcalf, B. (1994) 'Toward an aesthetics of craft', *Studio Potter*, 22 (June): 14–16.

Metropolitan Health Care Services Plan (1996) Melbourne, Australia, Victorian Government Department of Human Services, October.

Metropolitan Hospitals Planning Board Reports, Phases 1 and 2 (1995) Melbourne, Australia, Victorian Government Department of Health and Community Services, February.

Meyer, A. D. (1982) 'Adapting to environmental jolts', *Administrative Science Quarterly*, 27: 515–537.

Michael, M. (1996) *Constructing Identities: The Social, the Non-Human and Change*. London: Sage.

Miles, M. and Huberman, A. M. (1994) *Qualitative Data Analysis: An Expanded Sourcebook* (2nd ed.). Thousand Oaks, CA: Sage.

Miller, C. C., Cardinal, L. B. and Glick, W. H. (1997) 'Retrospective reports in organizational research: A re-examination of recent evidence', *Academy of Management Journal*, 40: 221–246.

Miller, G. (1997) 'Building bridges: The possibility of analytic dialogue between ethnography, conversation analysis and Foucault', in D. Silverman (ed.), *Qualitative Research: Theory, Method and Practice*, 24–44. London: Sage.

Miller, P. (1996) 'The multiplying machine', *Accounting, Organizations and Society*, 21 (7/8): 615–630.

Miller, P. and Napier, C. (1993) 'Genealogies of calculation', *Accounting, Organizations and Society*, 18 (7/8): 631–647.

Miller, P. and O'Leary, T. (1993) 'The factory as laboratory', *Science in Context*, 7 (3): 25–37.

Miller, P. and Rose, N. (1993) 'Governing economic life', in M. Gane and M. Johnson (eds), *Foucault's New Domains*. London: Routledge.

Miller, W. L. and Crabtree, B. F. (1992) 'Primary care research: A multimethod typology and qualitative road map', in B. F. Crabtree and W. L. Miller (eds), *Doing Qualitative Research*, 3–30. Newbury Park: Sage.

Mills, A. (1994) 'Organization discourse and the gendering of identity', in Hassard, J. and Parker, M. (eds), *Postmodernism and Organization Theory*. London: Routledge.

Mingers, J. (1992) 'Theoretical, practical and critical, or past present and future?', in M. Alvesson and H. Willmott (eds), *Critical Management Studies*. London: Sage.

Mingers, J. (1997) 'Multiparadigm methodology', in J. Mingers and A. Gill (eds), *Multimethodology: the Theory and Practice of Combining Management Sciences*. Chichester: Wiley.

Mingers, J. (2000) 'What it is to be critical? Teaching a critical approach to management', *Management Learning*, 31 (2): 219–337.

Mohr, John W. (1998) 'Measuring meaning structures', *Annual Review of Sociology*, 24: 345–370.

Moi, T. (1985) *Sexual Textual Politics*. London: Routledge.

Mol, A. (1997) *The Body Multiple: Arteriosclerosis in Practice*. Durham, NC: Duke University Press.

Mol, A. (1999) 'Ontological politics: a word and some questions', in J. Law and J. Hassard (eds.), *Actor Network Theory and After*. Oxford: Blackwell.

Mol, A. (2002) *The Body Multiple: Ontology in Medical Practice*. Durham, North Carolina: Duke University Press.

Mol, A. and Law, J. (1994) 'Regions, networks and fluids: anaemia and social topology', *Social Studies of Science*, 26: 641–671.

Monin, N. (2004) *Management Theory: a Critical and Reflexive Reading*. Abingdon, UK: Routledge.

Monterio, E. and Hanseth, O. (1996) 'Social shaping of information infrastructure: on being specific about the technology', in W. Orlikowski, G. Walsham, M. Jones and J. DeGross (eds), *Information Technology and Changes in Organizational Work*. London: Chapman and Hall.

Moore, W. E. (1963a) *Man, Time and Society*. New York: Wiley.

Moore, W. E. (1963b) 'The temporal structure of organizations', in E. A. Tiryakian (ed.), *Sociological Theory, Values and Sociocultural Change*. New York: Free Press.

Morgan, G. (ed.) (1983) *Beyond Method*. Newbury Park, CA: Sage.

Morgan, G. (1986) *Images of Organization*. Newbury Park, CA: Sage.

Morgan, G. (1988) *Riding the Waves of Change*. San Francisco: Jossey-Bass.

Morris, M. W., Leung, K., Ames, D. and Lickel, B. (1999) 'Views from inside and outside: Integrating emic and etic insights about culture and justice judgement', *Academy of Management Review*, 24: 781–796.

Mumby, D. (1996) 'Feminist postmodernism and organization communication studies: A critical reading', *Management Communication Quarterly*, 9 (3): 259–274.

Mumford, L. (1934) *Technics and Civilisation*. New York: Harcourt, Brace and World.

Munro, R. (1998) 'Belonging on the move: market rhetoric and the future as obligatory passage', *The Sociological Review*, 46 (2): 208–243.

Munro, R. (1999a) 'After knowledge: the language of information', in S. Linstead and R. Westwood (eds), *The Language of Organization*. London: Sage.

Munro, R. (1999b) 'The cultural performance of control', *Organization Studies*, 20 (4): 619–640.

Munro, R. (1999c) 'Power and discretion; membership work in the time of technology', *Organization*, 6 (3): 429–450.

Murphy, S. (1989) 'Multiple triangulation: Applications in a program of nursing research', *Nursing Research*, 38: 294–297.

Mutch, A. (1999) Managers and information: agency and structure. Information systems — the next generation. Proceedings of 4th UKAIS Conference, April 1999, University of York, Pub McGraw Hill, 1999, 51–61.

Narayanan, V. K. and Nath, R. (1993) *Organization Theory: A Strategic Approach*. Homewood, IL: Irwin.

Naylor, G. (1990) *The Arts and Crafts Movement: A Study of its Sources, Ideals and Influence on Design Theory*. London: Tefoil.

Nelson, L. (1999) 'Bodies (and spaces) do matter: the limits of performativity', *Gender, Place and Culture*, 6 (4): 331–353.

Nelson, R. (1993) *Ornament: An Essay Concerning the Meaning of Decorative Design*. Fitzroy, Victoria: Craft Victoria.

Nettleton, S. (1997), 'Governing the risky self: How to become healthy, wealthy and wise', in A. Petersen and R. Bunton (eds), *Foucault, Health and Medicine*, 207–222. London: Routledge.

Neuman, W. L. (1994) *Social Research Methods: Qualitative and Quantitative Approaches*. Boston: Allyn and Bacon.

Newton, T. (2002) 'Creating the new ecological order? Elias and actor-network theory', *Academy of Management Review*, 27 (4): 523–540.

Nietzsche, F. (1974) 'Homer's Contest', in M. Mugge (ed.), *Complete Works*. New York: Gordon Press (originally published by T Fowlis: London, 1911).

Nilsonn, P. (1920) *Primitive Time Reckoning*. London: Oxford University Press.

Nord, W. and Jermier, J. (1992) 'Critical social sciences for managers? Promising and perverse possibilities', in M. Alvesson and H. Willmott (eds), *Critical Management Studies*, 202–222. London: Sage.

Nowotny, H. (1976) 'Time structuring and time measurement', in J. T. Fraser and N. Lawrence (eds), *The Study of Time*, Vol. 2. New York: Springer-Verlag.

Nyland, C. (1986) 'Capitalism and the history of work-time thought', *British Journal of Sociology*, 37: 513–534. Reprinted as Chapter 8 in *The Sociology of Time* (1990), J. Hassard (ed.), 130–151. London: Macmillan.

Osborne, H. (ed.) (1970) *The Oxford Companion to Art*. Oxford: Clarendon Press.

Osborne, T. (1997), 'Of health and statecraft', in A. Petersen and R. Bunton (eds), *Foucault, Health and Medicine*, 173–188. London: Routledge.

Oswick, C. and Grant, D. (1996) 'The organization of metaphors and the metaphors of organization: Where are we and where do we go from here?', in D. Grant and C. Oswick (eds), *Metaphor and Organizations*, 213–226. London: Sage.

Oswick, C., Lowe, S. and Jones, P. (1996) 'Organisational culture as personality: lessons from psychology?', in C. Oswick and D. Grant (eds), *Organisation Development: Metaphorical Explorations*, 106–120. London: Pitman.

Ott, R. (2001) *Mies, Politics and the Bauhuas Closure: Polemics and Paradigms for Architectural Education*. University of Colorado, Denver, available at: www.tulane.edu/swacasa/papers/7.html date (accessed August 19, 2003).

Palmer, I. and Dunford, R. (1996a) 'Conflicting uses of metaphors: Reconceptualizing their use in the field of organizational change', *Academy of Management Review*, 21: 691–717.

Palmer, I. and Dunford, R. (1996b) 'Interrogating reframing: Evaluating metaphor-based analyses of organizations', in S. R. Clegg and G. Palmer (eds), *The Politics of Management Knowledge*, 141–154. London: Sage.

Park, D. (1980) *The Image of Eternity: Roots of Time in the Physical World*. Amherst: University of Massachussetts Press.

Parker, I. (1990) 'Discourse: definitions and contradictions', *Philosophical Psychology*, 3: 189–204.

Parker, I. (1992) *Discourse Dynamics*. London: Routledge.

Parker, M. (1992) 'Post-modern organizations or postmodern theory?', *Organization Studies*, 13: 1–17.

Parker, M. (1995) 'Critique in the name of what? Postmodernism and critical approaches to organization', *Organization Studies*, 16/4: 553–564.

Parker, M. (ed.) (1998) *Ethics and Organizations*. London: Sage.

Parker, M. (1999) 'Capitalism, subjectivity and ethics', *Organization Studies*, 20 (1): 25–45.

Parker, M. (2001) 'Fucking management: Queer, theory and reflexivity', *Ephemera*, 1/1: 36–53.

Parker, M. (2004) *Against Management*. London: Sage.

Parkhe, A. (1993) 'Messy research, methodological predisposition and theory development in international joint ventures', *Academy of Management Review*, 18 (2): 227–268.

Paul, J. (1996) 'Between-method triangulation in organizational diagnosis', *International Journal of Organizational Diagnosis*, 4: 135–153.

Pels, D. (1995) 'The Politics of Symmetry', *Social Studies of Science*, 26 (2): 277–304.

Permanyer, L. (1999) *Barcelona Art Nouveau*. New York: Rizzoli.

Petersen, A. (1997) 'Risk, governance and the new public health', in A. Petersen and R. Bunton (eds), *Foucault, Health and Medicine*, 189–222. London: Routledge.

Petersen, A. and Bunton, R. (eds) (1997) *Foucault, Health and Medicine*, 189–222. London: Routledge.

Pevsner, Nikolaus (1991) *Pioneers of Modern Design: From William Morris to Walter Gropius*. London: Penguin.

Pfeffer, J. (1993) 'Barriers to the advance of organizational science: paradigm development as a dependent variable', *Academy of Management Review*, 18 (4): 599–620.

Pfeffer, J. (1997) 'Mortality, reproducibility, and the persistence of styles of theory', *Organization Science*, 6: 681–686.

Phillips, D. (1977) *Wittgenstein and Scientific Knowledge*. London: Macmillan.

Pier, A. S. (1999) 'Bauhaus: Walter Gropius and the influence of the Bauhaus', *Sculpture Review*, 48 (2): 13–17.

Pinder, C. and Moore, L. (1979) 'The resurrection of taxonomy to aid the development of middle range theories of organization behaviour', *Administrative Science Quarterly*, 24: 99–118.

Piore, M. J. and Sabel, C. F. (1984) *The Second Industrial Divide: Possibilities for Prosperity*. New York: Basic Books.

Platt, J. (1996) *A History of Sociological Research Methods in America, 1920–1960*. Cambridge: Cambridge University Press.

Pollert, A. (1988) 'The flexible firm: fixation or fact?', *Work, Employment and Society*, 2: 281–316.

Pollner, M. (1991) 'Left of ethnomethodology: The rise and decline of radical reflexivity', *American Sociological Review*, 56 (June): 370–380.

Powell, F. D. and Wessen, A. F. (eds) (1999a) *Health Care Systems in Transition: An International Perspective*. Thousand Oaks: Sage.

Powell, F. D. and Wessen, A. F. (1999b) 'Capitalism, subjectivity and ethics: debating labour process analysis', *Organization Studies*, 20 (1): 25–45.

Power, M. (1995) *Accounting and Science: National Inquiry and Commercial Reason*. Cambridge: Cambridge University Press.

Powers, A. (2000) 'A natural development', *Craft*, 162 (1): 26–31.

Pronovost, G. (1986) 'Time in a sociological and historical perspective', *International Social Science Journal*, 107: 5–18.

Pugh, D. and Hickson, D. (1976) *Organization Structure in its Context: The Aston Studies 1*. Farnborough: Saxon House.

Pugh, D. S. (1990) 'Introduction to the third edition', in P. S. Pugh (ed.), *Organization Theory: Selected Readings* (3rd ed.). Harmondsworth: Penguin.

Quattrone, P. and McLean, C. (2005) 'On theorising the object: insights from Gabriel Tarde', paper presented at the Workshop on Gabriel Tarde, Goldsmith College.

Radcliffe-Brown, A. R. (1952) *Structure and Function in Primitive Society*. London: Cohen and West.

Ramirez, J. A. (2000) *The Beehive Metaphor: From Gaudí to Le Corbusier*. London: Reaktion Books.

Reed, M. (1985) *Redirections in Organizational Analysis*. London: Harvester Wheatsheaf.

Reed, M. (1992) *The Sociology of Organizations: Themes, Perspectives and Prospects*. New York: Harvester Weatsheaf.

Reed, M. I. (1993) 'Organizations and modernity: Continuity and discontinuity in organization theory', in J. Hassard and M. Parker (eds), *Postmodernism and Organizations*, 163–182. London: Sage.

Reed, M. (1995) 'The Action/Structure Debate in Organizational Analysis', Conference on Structuration Theory and Organizations, Paris, France.

Reed, M. (1996) 'Organizational theorising: a historical contested terrain', in S. R. Clegg, C. Hardy and W. R. Nord (eds), *Handbook of Organization Studies*, 31–56. London: Sage.

Reed, M. (1997) 'In praise of duality and dualism: rethinking agency and structure in organizational analysis', *Organization Studies*, 18: 21–42.

Reed, M. (1998) 'Organizational analysis as discourse analysis: A critique', in D. Grant, T. Keenoy and C. Oswick (eds), *Discourse and Organization*, 192–213. London: Sage.

Reid, D. A. (1976) 'The decline of Saint Monday', *Past and Present*, 71: 76–101.

Rex, J. (1961) *Key Problems in Sociological Theory*. London: Routledge and Kegan Paul.

Richardson, L. (1994) 'Writing: A method of inquiry', in N. K. Denzin and Y. S. Lincoln (eds), *Handbook of Qualitative Research*, 516–529. Thousand Oaks: Sage.

Riley, D. (1988) *Am I that name? Feminism and the Category of Women in History*. Minneapolis: University of Minnesota Press.

Ring, P. S. (1997) 'Process facilitating reliance in trust in interorganizational networks', in Ebers, M. (ed.), *The Formation of Inter-Organizational Networks*. New York: Oxford University Press.

Ritzer, G. (1993) *The McDonaldization of Society*. Thousand Oaks, CA: Pine Forge.

Ritzer, G. (2000) *The McDonaldization of Society: New Century Edition*. Thousand Oaks, CA: Pine Forge.

Roemer, M. (1995) *Telling Stories: Postmodernism and the Invalidation of Traditional Narrative*. Lanham, Maryland: Rowman and Little.

Roper, Q. (2000) 'Art Nouveau: the importance of decoration', available online at: http://www.qdesign.co.nz/designhist (accessed 13 July 2001).

Rorty, R. (1985) 'Texts and lumps', *New Literary History*, 17: 1–15.

Rose, N. (1990) *Governing the Soul*. London and New York: Routledge.

Rose, N. (1993) 'Government, authority and expertise in advanced liberalism', *Economy and Society*, 22: 283–299.

Rose, N. (1996) 'Governing advanced liberal democracies', in A. Barry, T. Osborne and N. S. Rose (eds), *Foucault and Political Reasoning: Liberalism, Neo-Liberalism and Rationalities of Government*. London: University College London Press.

Rosenau, P. M. (1992) *Post-Modernism and the Social Sciences: Insights, Inroads and Intrusions*. Princeton, NJ: Princeton University Press.

Roth, G. (1999) 'Creating conversations for change: Lessons from learning history projects', *Academy of Management Proceedings*, Organization Development and Change: B1–B6.

Rowland, Anna (1997) *Bauhaus Source Book*. Leichardt, NSW: Quantum.

Rowlinson, M. and McArdle, L. (1993) 'Ethnography: a neglected symbol of the labour process', Paper presented at the Labour Profess Conference, Blackpool, UK.

Roy, D. (1960) 'Banana time: job satisfaction and informal interaction', *Human Organization*, 18: 156–168. (Reprinted as Chapter 9 in J. Hassard (ed.), *The Sociology of Time* (1990), 155–167, London: Macmillan).

Samuel, J. (1995) 'Triangulation as splitting in the service of ambivalence', *Current Psychology*, 14: 91–111.

Saunders, M., Lewis, P. and Thornhill, P. (2001) *Research Methods for Business Students*. London: Pitman.

Sayer, D. (1991) *Capitalism and Modernity*. London: Routledge.

Scandura, T. A. and Williams, E. A. (2000) 'Research methodology in management. Current practices, trends, and implications for future research', *Academy of Management Journal*, 43: 1248–1264.

Schaffer, S. (1989) 'Realities in the eighteenth century: nature's representatives and their cultural resources', paper presented at the Realism and Representation Conference, Rutgers University.

Schein, E. H. (1985) *Organizational Culture and Leadership*. San Francisco: Jossey-Bass Publishers.

Schein, E. H. (1988) *Process Consultation: Its Role in Organization Development, Vol. 1*. (2nd ed.). Reading, MA: Addison-Wesley.

Scherer, A. G. (1998) 'Pluralism and incommensurability in strategic management and organization theory: a problem in search of a solution', *Organization*, 5 (2): 147–169.

Scherer, A. G. and Dowling, M. J. (1995) 'Towards a reconciliation of the theory-pluralism in strategic management: Incommensurability and the constructivist approach of the Erlangen school', *Advances in Strategic Management*, 12A: 195–247.

Scherer, A. G. and Steinmann, H. (1999) 'Some remarks on the problem of incommensurability in organization studies', *Organization Studies*, 20 (3): 519–544.

Schor, N. (1994) 'This essentialism which is not one, coming to grips with Irigaray', in Whitford, M. (ed.), *Engaging With Irigaray*. New York: Columbia University Press.

Schutz, A. (1967) *The Phenomenology of the Social World*. Evanston: Northwestern University Press.

Schultz, K. L. (1990) *Mimesis on the Move: Theodor Adorno's Concept of Imitation*. Berne: Peter Lang.

Schultz, M. and Hatch, M. J. (1996) 'Living with multiple paradigms: the case of paradigm interplay in organization culture studies', *Academy of Management Review*, 1 (2): 529–557.

Schwandt, T. (1994) 'Constructivist, interpretivist approaches to human inquiry', in N. K. Denzin and Y. S. Lincoln (eds), *Handbook of Qualitative Research*, 118–137. Thousand Oaks, CA: Sage.

Seale, C. (1999) 'Quality in qualitative research', *Qualitative Inquiry*, 5: 465–478.

Serres, M. and Latour, B. (1995) *Conversations on Science, Culture, and Time* (Trans. Roxanne Lapidus), Ann Arbor: University of Michigan Press.

Shapere, D. (1971) 'The paradigm concept', *Science*, 17, 706–709.

Short, S. and Palmer, G. (2000) 'Researching health care and public policy', *Australian and New Zealand Journal of Public Health*, 24: 450–451.

Shortell, S. M., Bazzoli, G. J., Dubbs, N. L. and Kralovic, P. (2000) 'Classifying health networks and systems: Managerial and policy implications', *Health Care Management Review*, 25 (4): 9–17.

Shrivastava, P. (1987) 'Rigor and practical usefulness of research in strategic management', *Strategic Management Journal*, 8: 77–92.

Silva, L. and Backhouse, J. (1997) 'Becoming part of the furniture: the institutionalization of information systems', in A. Lee, J. Liebenau and J. DeGross (eds), *Information Systems and Qualitative Research*. London: Chapman and Hall.

Silverman, D. (1969) 'Correspondence: Organization: A rejoinder', *Sociology*, 3 (3): 420–421.

Silverman, D. (1970) *Theory of Organization*. London: Heinemann.

Silverman, D. (1997) 'Towards an aesthetics of research', in D. Silverman (ed.), *Qualitative Research: Theory, Method And Practice*, 239–253. London: Sage.

Silverman, D. (2001) *Interpreting Qualitative Data: Methods For Analysing Talk, Text and Interaction* (2nd ed.). London: Sage.

Simmel, G. (1965) *The Conflict in Modern Culture and Other Essays*. New York: Teachers' College Press.

Simmel, G. (1980) *Essays on Interpretation in Social Science*. Manchester: Manchester University Press.

Slater, H. (1997) 'Art and aesthetics', *British Journal of Aesthetics*, 37 (3): 226–231.

Smith, B. (ed.) (1979) *Documents on Art and Taste in Australia*. Melbourne: Oxford University Press.

Smith, K. (1989) 'The movement of conflict in organizations: The joint dynamics of splitting and triangulation', *Administrative Science Quarterly*, 34: 1–20.

Smith, K. and Simmons, V. (1983) 'A rumpelstiltskin organization: Metaphors on metaphors in field research', *Administrative Science Quarterly*, 28: 377–392.

Smith, V. (2001) 'Ethnographies of work and the work of ethnographers', in P. Atkinson, A. Coffey, S. Delamont, J. Lofland and L. Lofland (eds), *Handbook of Ethnography*. London: Sage.

Sommer, B. and Sommer, R. (1991) *A Practical Guide to Behavioural Research: Tools and Techniques*. New York: Oxford University Press.

Sorokin, P. A. (1943) *Sociocultural Causality, Space and Time*. Durham, NC: Duke University Press.

Sorokin, P. A. and Merton, R. K. (1937) 'Social time: a methodological and functional analysis', *American Journal of Sociology*, 42: 615–629.

Sprangers, M. (1988) *Response Shift and the Retrospective Pretest: On the Usefulness of Retrospective Pretest-Posttest Designs in Detecting Training Related Response Shifts*. Den Haag, Netherlands: Het Instituut Voor Onderzoek Van Het Onderwijs.

Sprangers, M. (1989) 'Subject bias and the retrospective pretest in retrospect', *Bulletin of the Psychonomic Society*, 27: 11–14.

Stablein, R. (1996) 'Data in organization studies', in S. R. Clegg, C. Hardy and W. R. Nord (eds), *Handbook of Organization Studies*, 509–525. London: Sage.

Stanley, L. (2000) 'From self-made women to women's made selves? Audit selves, simulation and surveillance in the rise of public woman', in Coslett, T., Lury, C. and Summerfield, P. (eds), *Feminism and Autobiography, Texts, Theories and Methods*. London: Routledge.

Star, L. (1991) 'Power, technologies and the phenomenology of conventions: of being allergic to onions', in J. Law (ed.), *A Sociology of Monsters: Essays on Power, Technology and Domination*. London: Routledge.

Starkey, K. (1988) 'Time and the Labour process: A theoretical and empirical analysis', Paper presented at the Labour Process Conference, Aston University, UK.

Strathern, M. (1991) *Partial Connections*. Savage, Maryland: Rowan and Littlefield.

Strathern, M. (1996) 'Cutting the Network', *Journal of the Royal Anthropological Institute*, 2: 517–535.

Strati, A. (1999) *Organization and Aesthetics*. London: Sage.

Strati, A. (2000a) *Theory and Method in Organization Studies*. London: Sage.

Strati, A. (2000b) 'The aesthetic approach in organization studies', in S. Linstead and H. Höpfl (eds), *The Aesthetics of Organization*, 13–34. London: Sage.

Strati, A. (2000c) 'Putting people in the picture: Art and aesthetics in photography and in understanding organizational life', *Organization Studies*, 21: 53–69.

Strauss, J. and Corbin, J. (1990) *Basics of Qualitative Research: Grounded Theory Procedures and Techniques*. Newbury Park, CA: Sage.

Strinati, D. (1993) 'The big nothing? Contemporary culture and the emergence of postmodernism', *The European Journal of Social Sciences*, 6/3: 359–375.

Suchman, L. (1987) *Plans and Situated Action: The Problems of Human Machine Communication*. Cambridge: Cambridge University Press.

Sutton, R. I. and Rafaeli, A. (1988) 'Untangling the relationship between displayed emotions and organizational sales: The case of convenience stores', *Academy of Management Journal*, 31: 461–487.

Sweeney, J. J. and Sert, J. L. (1960) *Antoni Gaudí*. London: The Architectural Press.

Taber, T. (1991) 'Triangulating job attitudes with interpretive and positivist measurement methods', *Personnel Psychology*, 44: 577–600.

Tarde, G. (1962) *The Laws of Imitation*, translated by E. C. Parsons with introduction by F. Giddings, reprint, Gloucester, MA, Peter Smith.

Tarde. G. (1999) *Monadologie et Sociologie*. Paris: Institut Synthélabo.

Taylor, F. (1911) *Principles of Scientific Management*. New York: Harper.

Taylor, J. (1993) *Rethinking the Theory of Organizational Communications: How to Read an Organization*. Norwood, New Jersey: Ablex Publishing.

Taylor, S. S. and Hansen, H. (2005) 'Finding form: looking at the field of organizational aesthetics', *Journal of Management Studies*, 42/6: 1211–1231.

Thanem, T. (2006) 'Living on the edge: Towards a monstrous organization theory', *Organization*, 13/2: 163–193.

Thomas, W. I. (1937) *The Unadjusted Girl*. Boston: Little, Brown.

Thompson, E. P. (1967) 'Time, work-discipline and industrial capitalism', *Past and Present*, 38: 56–97.

Thompson, J. D. (1967) *Organizations in Action*. New York: McGraw-Hill.

Thompson, P. and McHugh, D. (1998) *Work Organization*. London: Macmillan.

Thompson, P. and McHugh, D. (2004) *Work Organization* (2nd ed.). London: Palgrave.

Thorngate, W. (1976) 'Possible limits on a science of social behavior', in J. H. Strickland, F. E. Aboud and K. J. Gergen (eds), *Social Psychology in Transition*, 121–139. New York: Plenum.

Thrift, N. (1981) 'Owner's time and own time: the making of a capitalist time consciousness, 1300–1800', in A. Pred (ed.), *Space, Time and Geography: Essays Dedicated to Torston Hagerstrand*. Lund: CWK Gleesup.

Thrift, N. (1990) 'Owners' time and own time: the making of a capitalist time consciousness, 1300–1800', in J. Hassard (ed.), *The Sociology of Time*, 105–129. London: Macmillan.

Tinker, T. (1986) 'Metaphor or reification?', *Journal of Management Studies*, 23: 363–384.

Tsoukas, H. (1989) 'The validity of ideographic explanations', *Academy of Management Review*, 14: 551–561.

Tsoukas, H. (1991) 'The missing link: A transformational view of metaphors in organizational science', *Academy of Management Review*, 16: 566–585.

Tsoukas, H. (1994) 'Refining common sense: Types of knowledge in management studies', *Journal of Management Studies*, 31: 761–780.

Tsoukas, H. and Knudsen, C. (eds) (2003) *The Oxford Handbook of Organization Theory: Meta-Theoretical Perspectives*. Oxford: Oxford University Press.

Turner, B. S. (1997) 'From governmentality to risk: Some reflections on Foucault's contribution to medical sociology', in A. Petersen and R. Bunton (eds), *Foucault, Health and Medicine*, ix–xxi. London: Routledge.

Usher, R., Bryant, I. and Johnston, R. (1997) *Adult Education and the Postmodern Challenge: Learning Beyond the Limits*. London: Routledge.

Vaill, P. (1991) *Managing as a Performing Art*. San Francisco: Jossey-Bass.

Van de Ven, A. H. and Poole, M. S. (1995) 'Explaining development and change in organizations', *Academy of Management Review*, 20: 510–540.

Van Maanen, J. (1979) 'Reclaiming qualitative methods for organizational research: A preface', *Administrative Science Quarterly*, 24: 520–526.

Vickers, G. (1968) *Value Systems and Social Process*. New York, NY: Basic Books.

Victoria's health to 2050: Developing Melbourne's Hospital Network (1995) Melbourne, Victoria, Australia, Victorian Department of Health and Community Services, January.

Vidgen, R. and McMaster, T. (1996) 'Black boxes, non-human stakeholders and the translation of IT', in W. Orlikowski, G. Walsham, M. Jones and J. DeGross (eds), *Information Technology and Changes in Organizational Work*. London: Chapman and Hall.

Waddell, D. M., Cummings, T. G. and Worley, C. G. (2000) *Organisation Development and Change* (Pacific Rim edn.), South Melbourne, Australia, Nelson Thomson Learning.

Walsham, G. (1997) 'Actor-network theory and its research: current status and future prospects', in A. Lee, J. Liebenau and J. DeGross (eds), *Information Systems and Qualitative Research*. London: Chapman and Hall.

Weaver, G. R. and Gioia, D. A. (1994) 'Paradigms lost: incommensurability vs structurationist inquiry', *Organization Studies*, 15 (4): 565–590.

Weber, M. (1947) *The Theory of Social and Economic Organization*. Glencoe, IL: Free Press.

Webster, F. (2000) 'The politics of sex and gender: Benhabib and Butler debate subjectivity', *Hypatia*, 15 (1): 1–23.

Weedon, C. (1987) *Feminist Practice and Poststructuralist Theory* (2nd ed.). Oxford: Blackwell.

Weedon, C. (1999) *Feminism, Theory and the Politics of Difference*. Oxford: Blackwell.

Weick, K. E. (1979) *The Social Psychology of Organizing* (2nd ed.). New York: Random House.

Weick, K. E. (1995a) *Sensemaking in Organizations*. Thousand Oaks: Sage.

Weick, K. E. (1995b) 'What theory is not, theorizing is', *Administrative Science Quarterly*, 40: 385–390.

Weick, K. E. (1999) 'Theory construction as disciplined reflexivity: Tradeoffs in the 90s', *Academy of Management Review*, 24 (4): 797–806.

Weick, K. E. (2001) *Making Sense of the Organization*. Malden, MA: Blackwell.

Weick, K. E. (2002) 'Real-time reflexivity: prods to reflection', *Organization Studies*, 23/6: 893–898.

Weick, K. E. and Quinn, R. E. (1999) 'Organizational change and development', *Annual Review of Psychology*, 50: 361–386.

Weiner, B. (1985) 'An attributional theory of achievement motivation and emotion', *Psychological Review*, 92: 548–573.

Weiner, B., Frieze, I., Kukla, A., Reed, L., Rest, S. and Rosenbaum, R. M. (1971) *Perceiving the Causes of Success and Failure*. Morristown, NJ: General Learning Press.

Wessen, A. F. (1999a) 'The comparative study of health care reform', in F. D. Powell and A. F. Wessen (eds), *Health Care Systems in Transition: An International Perspective*, 3–24. Thousand Oaks: Sage.

Wessen, A. F. (1999b) 'Structural differences and health care reform', in F. D. Powell and A. F. Wessen (eds), *Health Care Systems in Transition: An International Perspective*, 369–392. Thousand Oaks: Sage.

Westwood, R. and Clegg, S. (2003) (eds) *Debating Organization: Point-Counterpoint in Organization Theory*. Oxford: Blackwell.

Wetherell, M. (2001) 'Debates in discourse research', in Wetherell, M., Taylor, S. and Yates, S. (eds), *Discourse Theory and Practice: A Reader*. London: Sage.

White, R. F. and Jaques, R. (1995) 'Operationalizing the postmodernity construct for efficient organizational change management', *Journal of Organizational Change Management*, 8 (2): 45–71.

Whitford, F. (1984) *Bauhaus*. London: Thames and Hudson Ltd.

Whitford, M. (1988) 'Luce Irigaray's critique of rationality', in M. Griffiths and M. Whitford (eds), *Feminine Perspectives in Philosophy*. London: Macmillan.

Whitford, M. (1991) *Luce Irigaray Philosophy in the Feminine*. New York: Routledge.

Whitford, M. (1994) 'Engaging with Irigaray', in *Engaging with Irigaray*. New York: Columbia University Press.

Whitley, E. and Introna, L. (1997) 'Against method-ism: exploring the limits of method', *Information Technology and People*, 10 (1): 31–45.

Wicks, A. C. and Freeman, R. E. (1998) 'Organization studies and the new pragmatism: Positivism, anti-positivism, and the search for ethics', *Organization Science*, 9: 123–140.

Wicks, R. (1995) 'Kant on fine art: Artistic sublimity shaped by beauty', *Journal of Aesthetics and Art Criticism*, 53 (Spring): 189–193.

Williams, M. (2000) *Science and Social Science*. London: Routledge.

Willmott, H. (1993) 'Breaking the paradigm mentality', *Organization Studies*, 14 (5): 681–719.

Willmott, H. (1997) 'Management and organization studies as science?', *Organization*, 4: 309–344.

Wilson, D. C. (1992) *A Strategy of Change*. London and New York: Routledge.

Winman, A. and Juslin, P. (1999) '"I was well calibrated all along": assessing accuracy in retrospect', in P. Juslin and H. Montgomery (eds), *Judgment and Decision Making: Neo-Brunswikian and Process-Tracing Approaches*, 97–120. Mahwah, NJ: Lawrence Erlbaum.

Winner, L. (1993) 'Upon opening the black box and finding it empty: social constructivism and the philosophy of technology', *Science, Technology and Human Values*, 18 (3): 362–378.

Witte, S. (1992) 'Context, text, intertext: Toward a constructivist semiotic of writing', *Written Communication*, 9: 237–308.

Wittgenstein, L. (1953) *Philosophical Investigations*. Oxford: Basil Blackwell.

Wolff, J. (1990) *Feminine Sentences: Essays on Women and Culture*. London: Polity Press.

Wolfram Cox, J. (1997) 'Manufacturing the past: Loss and absence in organizational change', *Organization Studies*, 18: 623–654.

Wolfram Cox, J. (2001) 'Remembrance of things past? Change, development and paternalism', *Journal of Organizational Change Management*, 14 (2): 168–189.

Wolfram Cox, J. and Minahan, S. (2001) 'Organizing the aesthetic: Contestation and craft', paper presented at *APROS 2001: Asia-Pacific Researchers in Organisation Studies* (December), Hong Kong.

Wolfram Cox, J. and Minahan, S. (2002) 'Crafting organization', *Culture and Organization*, 8 (3): 209–224.

Woolgar, S. (1988a) *Science: the Very Idea*. Chichester: Ellis-Horwood.

Woolgar, S. (1988b) 'Reflexivity is the ethnographer of the text', in S. Woolgar (ed.), *Knowledge and Reflexivity: New Frontiers in the Sociology of Scientific Knowledge*, 14–36. London: Sage.

Wray-Bliss, E. (2002) 'Abstract ethics, embodied ethics: the strange marriage of Foucault and positivism in Labour process theory', *Organization*, 9/1: 5–39.

Wrege, C. D. and Hodgetts, R. M. (2000) 'Frederick W. Taylor's pig iron observations: Examining fact, fiction, and lessons for the new millennium', *Academy of Management Journal*, 43: 1283–1291.

Wright, L. (1968) *Clockwork Man*. London: Elek.

Wynne, B. (1996) 'May the sheep safely graze? A reflexive view of the expert/lay knowledge divide', in Lash, S., Szerszynski, B. and Wynne, B. (eds), *Risk, Environment and Modernity: Towards a New Ecology*. London: Sage.

Yanagi, S¯oetsu. (1989) *The Unknown Craftsman: A Japanese Insight into Beauty*. London: Gillingham House.

Yardley, K. (1987) 'What do you mean "Who am I?": Exploring the implications of a self-concept measurement with subjects', in K. Yardley and T. Honess (eds), *Self and Identity: Psychosocial Perspectives*, 211–230. Chichester, United Kingdom: Wiley.

Yin, R. K. (1994) *Case Study Research: Design and Methods* (2nd ed.). Thousand Oaks, CA: Sage.

Zerbst, Rainer (1988) *Antoni Gaudí*. Cologne: Taschen.

Zuidervaart, Lambert (1991) *Adorno's Aesthetic Theory: The Redemption of Illusion*. Cambridge and London: The MIT Press.

Zuidervaart, Lambert (1997) 'Introduction', in T. Huhn and L. Zuidervaart (eds), *The Semblance of Subjectivity: Essays in Adorno's Aesthetic Theory*, 1–28. Cambridge, MA. and London: The MIT Press.

Index